Patterns, Hatches, Tactics, and Trout

Other Books by Charles R. Meck

Meeting and Fishing the Hatches
Pennsylvania Trout Streams and Their Hatches
Fishing Small Streams with a Fly Rod
Great Rivers-Great Hatches (with Greg Hoover)

Patterns, Hatches, Tactics, and Trout

Charles R. Meck

VIVID™
PUBLISHING, INC.
Williamsport, Pennsylvania

Published by
VIVID PUBLISHING, INC.
P.O. Box 1572
Williamsport, PA 17703
1-800-STREAMS

Printed in the United States of America

10 9 8 7 6 5 4 3 2 1

Library of Congress Cataloging-in-Publication Data

Meck, Charles R.
    Patterns, hatches, tactics, and trout / Charles R. Meck. — 1st ed.
        p.   cm.
Includes index.
ISBN 1-55629-050-0
    1. Trout fishing. 2. Fly fishing. 3. Fly tying. 4. Flies, Artificial. 5. Aquatic insects. I. Title.
SH687.M365   1995
799.1'755—dc20   95-12008
                                                                                CIP

Editor, Kim Leighton, Livingston, MT

Cover Photography, Jeff Edvalds, Flywater Graphics, Tacoma, WA

Cover and text design by Roger Burelle

Illustrations by Larry Seaman

Black and white photography by the author

Color photography by Dave Bowen

Dedication

This book is dedicated to my wife, Shirley, my two children, Lynne and Bryan, and granddaughter, Lauren, who have been very supportive.

Table of Contents

Acknowledgments

To complete the manuscript for *Great Rivers—Great Hatches* in 1991 I fly-fished Western rivers for seventy-two days. Rivers like Montana's Missouri and Bighorn, Oregon's Metolius, Washington's Yakima, and thirty-two others in the West were home to me for two and a half months.

In addition I visited major trout rivers in West Virginia, New York, Virginia, and Maryland. Each of the Eastern trips was with a local expert. In all I had sixteen professional guides, twenty-five local experts, and I did sixteen float trips. With each guide I learned something new—a new pattern, a new method of casting, or a new technique. I had plenty of time to test patterns like the Patriot, Green Weenie, and dozens of others. On the Bighorn I learned to use the tandem method of fly-fishing with a dry fly as a strike indicator and a wet fly behind it.

Patterns, Hatches, Tactics, and Trout evolved out of those trips with professional guides and local experts testing new patterns, tactics, and techniques.

To the guides and local experts who contributed to *Patterns, Hatches, Tactics, and Trout* I owe a debt of gratitude. Thanks for all your help and encouragement.

This book couldn't have been completed without the encouragement of a lot of friends like Craig Josephson, Bob Budd, Ken Rictor, Andre Lijoi, my son, Bryan Meck, and son-in-law, Rick Nowaczek. To all who have helped I owe a debt of gratitude and thanks.

Chapter 1

Introduction

Do you prefer using dry flies? Do you enjoy fly-fishing because you can see the action unfold on the surface? What do you do when you go fishing and no hatch appears? What do you do when few trout rise? Do you just stand around waiting for that odd trout that comes to the surface for some food? When I originally wrote *Meeting and Fishing the Hatches* in 1977, that's how I felt. I detested using anything except a dry fly, and most of the time I felt I had to match a hatch. That has all changed recently. Look at two recent incidents on the same stream.

Just this past year Pat and Paul Antolosky and I headed for a couple hours of fishing on central Pennsylvania's lower Bald Eagle. A sporadic hatch of light cahills emerged, but only three trout rose during the two hours we fly-fished. Three trout rose sporadically in a quarter-mile section where maybe a dozen or two should have surfaced. We caught only two trout that entire evening. Most of the time we stood, watched, and waited for a trout to rise.

I fished the same section the next evening with Tucker Morris. This time I tied on a tandem rig. A tandem rig consists of two flies—usually a dry fly and a wet fly. As I said, for more than 40 years I've relished seeing that dry fly riding high in full view. With the tandem rig, I assured myself that I could watch the dry fly while also covering subsurface-feeding fish with a weighted wet fly. If the floating dry fly sinks then I know I have a strike on the wet fly. In other words, the dry fly acts as a strike indicator.

Fishing in this manner you can catch trout on your strike indicator or dry fly as well as the wet fly. Two trout did strike the dry fly that evening.

On that same section of the lower Bald Eagle where Pat and Paul Antolosky and I caught two trout on dry flies the night before, I caught ten trout on the tandem rig. Does it work? You bet it does! You'll find further information on the tandem rig and how to use it in Chapter 2.

But tactics and strategies represent only a small portion of what this book contains. *Patterns, Tactics, Hatches, and Trout* also includes a great deal of information on the hatches. Did you know that entomologists now classify many *Pseudocloeon* species in the genus *Baetis*? Did you know that many of the pale evening duns once included in the Genus *Heptagenia* scientists now classify in a new genus, *Leucrocuta*? You'll find this and much more new information on some of the major hatches in Chapter 3, which also includes an up-to-date emergence chart to give you a leg up on matching the hatch.

You'll also find dozens of patterns that have produced trout when others have failed. "How in the world can you make any sense out of pattern selection?" a beginning fly-fisher once asked me. Indeed, with literally thousands of fly patterns, how can an angler who wants to succeed at fly-fishing pare the number down to a productive few? Just how many patterns do you have from which to select? In his classic book, *The Fisherman's Handbook of Trout Flies*, Donald DuBois listed almost 6,000 patterns. DuBois wrote that book in 1960, and in the intervening thirty-five years thousands of additional patterns have appeared. Today you can select from more than 10,000 patterns. How does one just starting to fly-fish narrow the enormous possibilities down to a manageable number? In Chapters 4 through 10 you'll find some topnotch patterns that have worked for me. In Chapters 4, 5, 6, and 10 you'll find discussions of and patterns for nymphs, emergers, duns, spinners, and downwings.

What about patterns that don't match mayfly, stonefly or caddis fly hatches? You'll find Chapter 7 devoted to attractor patterns, including the exciting new Patriot. If you haven't used this exciting new pattern, Chapter 7 will tell you why you should.

Aren't terrestrials important to copy, especially in midsummer? Chapter 8 includes some productive patterns for land-borne insects like ants, beetles, and grasshoppers. It also includes information on some productive caterpillar and moth patterns.

What about larger patterns like Wooly Buggers and Muddler Minnows? Chapter 9 examines several productive, large underwater patterns.

In Chapters 3 through 9 you'll find a section titled "Tandem Connection." Here you'll find ways to use two patterns at the same time. For example, in Chapter 6, on spinners and spinner patterns, you'll see that you can tie some of your smaller spinners like the Trico as the point fly a couple of feet behind a larger dry fly. If you have difficulty seeing and following a small spinner pattern, this might help.

You'll also find a lot of information on patterns that copy the hatches. In Chapter 10 you'll find patterns for nymphs, duns, spinners, and emergers. If you've fished the hatches for the past several years, you already know how successful Z-lon shucks have become. Chapter 10 includes shuck colors for all major hatches.

But Chapter 10 includes much more than just patterns for the hatches. Look also at many of the new materials available to the fly-fisher. Larva Lace can make hundreds of productive patterns; krystal flash and sparkle yarn have proved successful in many new flies; and chenille comes in new fluorescent colors and sizes. New materials and millions of new fly-fishers in the 1990s have created an overwhelming desire on the part of many anglers to limit the number of patterns to a select few. In Chapter 10 you'll find some of the new fly-tying materials and how to use them.

How do you prefer to tie your dry fly pattern? Many anglers prefer using comparaduns; others prefer parachute patterns; and still others use the more conventional high-riding Catskill-style dry fly patterns. We'll examine the advantages of each type of dry fly also in Chapter 10.

But does selecting the proper pattern really make a difference between success and failure on any given fishing day? Look what happened to me just this past year. Phil Hopersberger and I fished a local stream, the Bald Eagle, in early October. For more than two hours I carefully covered every section of one of my favorite runs on that stream. On a normal day I might catch a half dozen trout in this productive area. On that particular day I had not even one strike. I fished the water thoroughly with at least a half dozen patterns without any success. Then, with a great deal of apprehension, I tied on a new pattern, a Bead-head Pheasant Tail Nymph, that a friend, Walt Young, had encouraged me to try. On the first cast with that Bead-head I saw a swirl. On the second, another swirl. I grabbed the pattern, added a small lead shot and again cast in the same productive glide. In the next half-hour I hooked and released six heavy brown trout on that Bead-head in a section where for two hours before I caught no trout. Yes, pattern selection makes a difference. In fact, selecting the proper pattern can mean the difference between a mediocre day and a highly productive day that you'll never forget.

Will the patterns I've listed work under all circumstances? No. I'm certain you've had days where nothing works, when no pattern you try catches trout.

In fact, some streams and rivers require patterns almost unique to them. Visit a dozen famous trout streams and you'll find that on most of them, a specific pattern seems to work well. On the Waikaka River on the South Island of New Zealand, many anglers favor a pattern called Dad's Favorite. I tried the pattern and it did produce some heavy trout. On Spruce Creek in central Pennsylvania, George Harvey uses a pattern he calls the Spruce Creek Special, which has been a proven fish taker over the past few decades. When you visit a stream, talk to a guide or local angler and find out what patterns produce the most trout. But under most circumstances and on most streams, the patterns listed in this book will catch trout.

Few anglers would argue that for the majority of the day trout feed under the surface. They rise to the surface often only when a heavy hatch appears. So while I'm usually flailing away on the surface prospecting for the rare trout that will rise, most of the fish feed beneath the surface. For years I almost totally neglected subsurface patterns except during high water and the early season. As soon as water temperatures rose above 50 degrees, I resorted to dry flies. Even when no trout rose and few insects appeared I prospected on the surface with dry flies. I'd consider it a successful summer evening when no hatch appeared and few trout rose to catch just three or four trout.

After observing trout more closely during the last decade or so, I began to realize that most trout feed out of sight of the angler, beneath the surface. If this is true, then why not use a pattern that covered that situation? I still preferred the dry fly but I compromised by using a floating fly as a lead fly that also acts as a strike indicator, and a subsurface point fly that covers much of the area where trout feed. With the tandem rig I average six to seven trout on the wet fly for every trout I catch on the dry fly.

An angler once told me that he knew of only two ways you can fish a fly: "on the surface and underneath." In a way he spoke the truth. Wet and dry flies cover where a fish feeds. But there's a third possibility: fishing on and under the surface at the same time. Many nymph fishermen who frown on using any strike indicator might say that's heretical or that it won't work. But believe me, it does work, as you'll see later.

So take a journey through the following pages with an open mind. You'll read about some unconventional—almost bizarre—tactics, patterns, and recommendations. As I've often said in talks I give to fly-fishing groups, keep an open mind and keep learning new ideas. Keeping up with trends, developments, and advances in fly-fishing has an analogy with the technology age. In this time of continually growing fishing pressure, if you don't keep up with the new developments, you're going to be left behind.

A brown trout caught on the tamdem rig, on Montana's Big Horn River

Chapter 2
Different Approaches to Fly-Fishing

If you've fly-fished for several years, you probably have a preference for either wet flies or dry flies. As I stated in Chapter 1, for more than forty years I preferred following a dry fly on the surface and waiting for a trout to take the fly in full view. I had nothing but disdain for any angler who used a wet fly. But in the next few pages you'll see how my thinking has changed.

Maybe you already prefer using wet flies. If you depend on subsurface patterns, you already know that you can fish these flies several different ways. You can fish them on the bottom with weight and a short line. You can fish them near the bottom with a longer line and a strike indicator, mending almost continuously in faster water. You can fish the pattern just under the surface, imitating an emerging insect. You can cast the wet fly across or slightly upstream and let it make its swing or arc. Or you can cast the pattern upstream or across and gently twitch the line as the pattern drifts downstream.

All these methods work sometimes and you should experiment with all of them. But what about a rig that allows you to fly-fish both on the surface, or at any precise subsurface depth at the same time? What about a setup that-can catch trout on the surface and underneath at the same time? What about a tactic that allows you to watch a floating dry fly that instantaneously tells you when you've had a tandem rig strike? What about a rig that makes even a beginner an expert in just a few minutes? The tandem rig gives you all of this—and more!

7

Ask Bryan Meck if the tandem works. Here he uses a
Patriot with a Green Weenie.

Tandem Rigs

Fishing a tandem was first introduced to me on Montana's incomparable Bighorn River. Our guide for the day, Rich Montella, suggested that Bryan Meck and I try the technique. Rich rigged a size 12 attractor dry fly and added a piece of monofilament line to the bend of the hook, which he secured with an improved clinch knot. To the end of the tippet Rich attached a weighted nymph.

What an unusual setup—now I could use both a wet and dry fly at the same time. At first I resisted using any subsurface pattern. But with this tandem setup all I had to do was watch the floating pattern; in effect, the dry fly became a strike indicator. If the dry fly sank, a trout had probably hit the underwater pattern. What an easy way—especially for a dry-fly enthusiast—to detect underwater strikes! As an added bonus, trout frequently hit the strike indicator, or dry fly.

I began to wonder as I set out to use this rig on the Bighorn. Would this rig work in the East and Midwest? In four-plus decades of fly-fishing Eastern and Midwestern waters, I had never seen the tandem setup. Several days after I returned from my Montana trip I set out for central Pennsylvania's Little Juniata River armed with a couple of attractor patterns and wet flies. I tied on a Patriot dry fly, added three feet of additional tippet to the bend of the hook, and attached a Green Weenie as the dropper pattern. I began casting the rig upriver in some fairly deep pocket water. At first the tandem rig was clumsy to cast, but within a few minutes casting the two patterns became almost second nature.

I didn't have to wait long to see if the tandem setup worked. Within minutes the Patriot sank, I set the hook and landed a heavy Juniata brown. A half dozen more browns took the Green Weenie below the dry fly that morning, and I caught two trout on the Patriot dry fly.

Sure, the tandem works for me, but what do other anglers think about this system of presenting two patterns? Has it made fly-fishing easier for them?

Shortly after I returned from the trip to the Bighorn River I showed the rig to Andy Leitzinger of Collegeville, Pennsylvania. Andy now uses this technique almost exclusively. He recently made the following observation about the tandem in an article in *Bank Notes*, the Valley Forge Trout Unlimited Chapter's newsletter:

"Over the past two years, I have experimented with an established but not commonly used technique of presenting a wet and a dry fly simultaneously during a number of hatch and non-hatch conditions. Using two or more flies is a common wet-fly practice, where a second wet fly on a short leader or 'dropper' is positioned on the primary leader above the lower fly. However, the technique I am referring to utilizes a dry fly in conjunction with either a nymph or wet fly. This technique differs from fishing a dropper, first because a dry fly is used and second because the wet fly or nymph is attached to the bend of the hook of the dry fly by a second leader of eighteen to thirty inches. This arrangement has been referred to as the 'bi-cycle,' but I prefer to call it a 'tandem.' The dry fly serves the dual role as a fish getter and highly sensitive strike indicator.

"The tandem fishes well in many types of water including pocket, riffle, and pool water. Casting a tandem is not difficult; however, casting style has to be adjusted. The lower fly sometimes swings in tuck-cast fashion around the dry fly as your loop straightens out. This allows the nymph to begin sinking quickly. Occasional tangles should be expected. Surprisingly, once in the water, the nymph, weighted or not, offers little resistance to the dry fly, at least until the nymph makes contact with the stream bottom. The dry fly is allowed to float normally for long distances depending on the floatability of the dry and the weight of the nymph. For larger streams and rivers a longer second leader should be used. Shallow conditions may warrant using a shorter second leader. I normally use 5X tippet for the second section.

"The tandem increases the chances of hooking a fish by offering a choice, and turns nymph fishing into a highly visual and, in my opinion, more satisfying activity. One only has to watch the dry fly, which is more natural than a conventional strike indicator. When the strike to the nymph occurs, the dry fly will simply disappear and often a raised rod tip will result in a solidly hooked trout. The dry fly will take trout also. Double hookups are rare, but do occur. The tandem works during a variety of hatches, especially caddis and sulphur. But it also works well in overlapping hatch situations; for example, during a gray fox spinner fall that overlaps a sulphur emergence. When no hatches are occurring, the tandem serves as a highly effective prospecting tool, especially on those days when you couldn't pay a fish to come to the surface."

Andy Leitzinger is far from the only fly-fisher who has discovered the effectiveness of the tandem rig.

"It's the best system of fly-fishing I've ever seen." That's what Evan Morse, a veterinarian in Shaker Heights, Ohio, said about the tandem rig after using it successfully for less than an hour—after being nearly skunked using other patterns on some difficult water.

Evan recently called me from Wayne Harpster's cabin on central Pennsylvania's great limestone stream, Spruce Creek, and said he couldn't catch any trout. Midsummer afternoons present probably the most difficult time to catch trout. When I arrived

Within minutes of using the tandem, Evan Morse lands his first trout on the two flies.

at the stream I showed Evan how to tie and cast the tandem rig, a process that took only a few minutes. Next, he cast to a nearby riffle so that I could show him how to detect a strike at the Green

Weenie wet fly he had tied on. I told him if the dry fly sank, he should set the hook. Within an hour Evan landed five heavy trout on the rig. Before using the tandem rig that day Evan had caught only two trout in an entire morning of fly-fishing.

You can make a successful fly-fisher out of almost anyone using the tandem rig. Recently I met Greg Smith and his son, Ryan of Yorklyn, Delaware, again on Wayne Harpster's Spruce Creek section. Other than a couple of hatchery trout, seven-year-old Ryan had never caught a trout in a wild setting before. Ten minutes after tying on the tandem rig, Ryan caught his first trout, an eighteen-inch rainbow.

Gordon Brick releases a heavy rainbow caught on the tandem on the Salt River just 25 miles East of Phoenix, Arizona.

Eric Steinfeldt and Bill Ray live and work in northern New Jersey and had planned a trip to the Bitterroot River in Montana. Eric was new to fly-fishing and this trip to central Pennsylvania was his inaugural fly-fishing experience. Bill asked me to join them on Spring Creek. As soon as we arrived at the stream I showed both how to rig the two-pattern tandem. We chose a size 12 Yellow Drake for the lead fly and the Bead-head Pheasant Tail Nymph for the point fly. We tied a three-foot piece of 4X tippet between the two patterns and Eric and Bill began casting. On about the fourth cast Bill hooked a heavy rainbow on the Bead-head. Within a half hour Eric, who again had never fly-fished before, landed a seventeen-inch brown trout on the Bead-head. Before we ended that afternoon of fly-fishing, the two anglers had more than twenty strikes on the rig, and Eric lost a heavy brown that hit the Yellow Drake dry fly. All of this action occurred on a late-June afternoon, on a heavily fished trout stream, with no special regulations.

Bob Budd fly-fishes every chance he gets, and he's one of the finest fly casters I know. Recently Bob invited me to a member-guest weekend outing at the famous Spruce Creek Rod and Gun Club in central Pennsylvania. The club, which owns two productive stretches of Spruce Creek, recently celebrated its ninetieth anniversary. For two days every year about thirty members and guests join in the fun and frivolity of angling and shooting.

Friday evening Bob and I fished the lower section of the club water with tandem rigs to see how they worked on this highly productive stretch of water. On the second cast, my dry fly sank and I set the hook on a nineteen-inch brown. Just two more casts later, a second heavy trout took the wet fly. In an evening of fishing the tandem rig with the Green Weenie as the subsurface pattern, I caught fifteen hefty trout. During the entire evening, I saw only two rises and not a single mayfly.

The next morning Bob and I again fished Spruce Creek, this time several miles upstream. I sat and watched several other bait fishermen fish a riffle-and-pool section. When they left I rigged up a tandem rig, a Patriot and a Bead-head Pheasant Tail Nymph. In a half hour I picked up five heavy trout in the pool just vacated by the bait fishermen. As I caught these trout, several other anglers gathered to watch. By the fifth trout one of the fishermen came over and asked if I'd show them how to catch these trout. I handed each of the anglers a Bead-head and a Patriot and demonstrated how to rig them. I then explained how to cast and fish the tandem flies. During the demonstration, on the second drift in a short glide, the Patriot sank, I set the hook, and landed a seventeen-inch brown trout. The proof is in the pudding!

Don Bastian lands a 20-inch brown trout in late fall taken on the tandem.

I recently traveled to Honey Creek near Lewistown, Pennsylvania, to fish the green and brown drake hatches. Only a few drakes appeared and hardly any trout rose for them. I tied on a tandem-rigged Patriot and Bead-head Pheasant Tail Nymph and began casting. Nearby, Terry Yocum and Andy Arnold watched as I caught six trout on the Bead-head from one pool. Both anglers, now more than curious, approached me. I showed them the rig and how easy it was to fish, and I gave each a Patriot and a Bead-head. Andy Arnold of Belltown waded to shore and tied on a tandem rig. Within minutes he had completed rigging the two patterns and began casting. You'll find, as he did, that it takes a little practice to cast the two flies, but on the tenth cast, the Patriot sank and Andy set the hook. He let out a triumphant whoop as he landed a twelve-inch brown trout on the Bead-head. After that episode, Terry and Andy went away saying they'd use the tandem for the rest of their fishing days.

In the next few pages you'll read about the tandem rig and some other different approaches to catching trout. I've been using the tandem rig throughout the United States for more than five years with highly productive results. Angler friends like Bryan Meck, Craig Josephson, Ken Rictor, Andre Lijoi, and many others have also reported similar success with the rig. If you don't like using wet flies, you've got to test this highly productive method of catching trout.

Many purists frown upon using this two-fly setup, and I've had several anglers glare at the rig and walk away. I'll never forget the first time I showed the tandem rig to George Harvey, dean of American fly-fishers. George watched the dry fly sink when a trout hit the submerged fly and walked away mumbling. Fly-fishing is nothing if not a sport of many choices. So while it's well within the right of dry-fly purists to eschew the tandem, it works. Try it yourself, according to your own philosophy of fly-fishing.

If you've fly-fished for any period of time you probably know that you can connect the lead and point flies in several different ways. You can connect the lead (dry) fly through the eye with your tippet. You can also connect the second tippet leading to your point

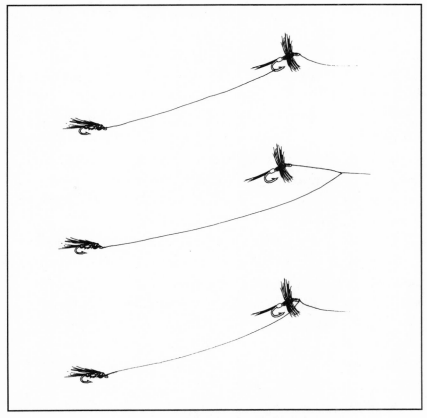

TANDEM CONSTRUCTION

1. Connect the point (nymph or wet) fly to the lead (dry) fly at the bend of the hook. This method works the best and is the easiest to cast.

2. Tie a dry fly on a short dropper and the point or wet fly on the leader. The dropper can also serve as a strike indicator. This works well from a boat, but not when casting.

3. Connect the second tippet leading to the point (nymph or wet) fly through the same eye of the lead fly. The weight of the two lines often upsets the dry fly and makes it ride unnaturally on the water.

(nymph or wet) fly through the same eye of the lead fly (#3 above). Other anglers prefer to tie a dry fly on a short dropper and the point or wet fly on the leader (#2 above). The dropper can also serve as a strike indicator. But neither of these two methods of connecting

16

the two patterns on the line works as well as connecting the point fly (wet) at the bend of the hook of the lead fly (dry). With the first method, both leaders passing through the eye of the dry fly, the weight of the two lines often upsets the dry fly and makes it ride unnaturally on the water with its tail extending skyward. The second method, using a dry fly on a short dropper, works well from a boat,but not when casting.

One of more than a dozen trout Craig Josephson
caught on the tandem. He found that ten wraps
of .010 lead sinks the pattern quickly.

Why does the tandem rig work so well? First, when trout strike the wet fly they don't feel the tension from the dry fly as much as they do with a strike indicator. Since the dry fly sinks quickly you can readily detect when a trout strikes the underwater pattern. Second, with a size 12 pattern like the Patriot and its white calf-tail wings you can easily follow the rig, detect any takes, and strike quickly. Third, while the dry fly floats drag-free on the surface, the wet fly drifts drag-free near the bottom. I try to rig the length of the wet fly so that it sinks and drifts just off the bottom. This strategy presents the fly to trout rather than getting it hung up on every rock in the stream.

"Won't the dry fly sink?" is one of the first questions anglers ask. If you use a fairly large dry fly and if you don't add too much weight to the wet fly, the strike indicator dry fly will float. For example, a size 12 or 14 Patriot will float with a Green Weenie tied on a size 10 Mustad 71980 hook with ten wraps of .015 lead added to the shank of the hook.

In most cases—and this is precisely what makes this rig exceptionally valuable to beginners—rather than trying to detect a strike indicator that might be a foot or two underwater, the angler can easily follow the dry fly on the surface.

Anglers who first use the tandem method ask how they can vary the depth of their wet fly. You do that in two ways. You can change the length of the tippet between the two patterns. The shorter the distance, the shallower your wet fly will drift. The greater the distance between the two patterns, the deeper the subsurface fly will drift. Adding weight to the subsurface pattern also helps. If you plan to use weighted flies, add weight to the pattern when you tie it. The alternative, pinching lead shot on the tippet in front of the subsurface fly, will cause the leader connecting the two patterns to tangle quickly.

It's important to get that sinking pattern down quickly. I add five or ten wraps of .010 lead wire to my Bead-head Pheasant Tail Nymphs. If you're fishing shallow and slow water, use an unweighted Bead-head. If you're fishing fast and deep water, use one with 10 wraps of lead wire. I most often opt for the heaviest pattern.

I add weight to most of my wet-fly patterns. I color-code the patterns or mark the compartments on my fly box so I know just how much weight each pattern contains. I use different colored tying thread for the Green Weenie so I know how many wraps of lead each has. I've used these patterns with as many as 20 wraps of .015 lead and they did not sink the dry fly.

In the fall and winter when I use the tandem rig I often fish with five or six feet between the two flies. You'll be surprised how relatively easy it is to cast the two patterns.

Depth can be critical. Just recently I fished a productive riffle with a Yellow Drake as the lead fly and a Bead-head Pheasant Tail Nymph as my dropper. On my way up the riffle I picked up five trout on the Bead-head tied four feet behind the lead fly. After I fished the run I added two more feet between the two patterns, making them six feet apart. I waded downstream and fished the same area I had just fished and picked up three additional trout at the deeper depth. Remember, if you fish a section of river that should produce trout, fish that same area again but vary the depth of your point fly. If you previously fished it with two or three feet between patterns, move them four or five feet apart.

If you continually find the dry fly sinking you can do one of a number of things. First, use a larger dry fly. I often resort to a size 12 Patriot or a long-shank size 12 Yellow Drake to float even fairly heavy wet flies. You can also use a wet fly with less weight, or shorten the tippet between the two flies. All three methods should help keep the "strike attractor" afloat.

Does the tandem rig work with patterns like the Bead-head Pheasant Tail Nymph and the Patriot on Western waters? You bet it does! Arizona has some great trout fishing in the White Mountains just 200 miles northeast of Phoenix. Recently, Craig Josephson of Johnstown, Pennsylvania, and I fly-fished with Josh David of nearby Lakeside on the North Fork of the White River. In one short riffle I picked up three trout on the Bead-head, while in another riffle, just upstream, Craig picked up three trout on the Patriot dry fly.

Ken Rictor of Chambersburg recently returned from a trip to

Montana's Ruby River, where at first nothing seemed to work for him. The trout seemed to shut off completely. Then he tied on a Patriot dry fly with a Bead-head Pheasant Tail Nymph. In the next hour Ken picked up six heavy brown trout on the Bead-head.

Many anglers in the East look forward to the green drake hatch in late May and early June. This huge mayfly emerges on many streams in unbelievable numbers. In hordes, fly-fishers follow the hatch from stream to stream. Often during this hatch I've seen trout feeding on the smaller sulphur, sulphur emerger, or sulphur nymph, totally ignoring the green drake. I often tie on a huge Green Drake pattern, then attach a Bead-head Pheasant Tail Nymph to the huge dry fly. This way you can fish the Drake pattern and catch trout on the Bead-head, and the huge dry fly provides a good strike indicator.

Casting the two patterns might seem a bit difficult at first. Make certain you use a relatively short leader—about eight feet long, and a short tippet—about one foot and not longer than two feet. Also, don't go too fine on your tippet, which should be the same diameter for the dry fly and the wet fly. For most cases use a 4X tippet. The finer the tippet, the more it tangles.

Practice casting the tandem rig and after a few minutes you won't even notice that you're casting two patterns at once. Even with the weighted dropper fly and even if you extend the distance between the two patterns to five or six feet you'll find them fairly easy to cast. Just practice before you attempt casting the two flies. Make certain you have a leader less than ten feet long; pull out plenty of fly line before you begin; and use a nine-foot fly rod requiring at least a five-weight line. If you follow these simple rules you should have no difficulty.

If you don't think you're reaching trout then go deeper. I've cast many tandem rigs where I had six feet between the two patterns and had no difficulty.

So why should you try this method of fly-fishing? First, you can reach trout and detect strikes over a larger section of water than you can fishing the regular nymph method.

Second, with the dry fly as a strike indicator you'll find that you'll occasionally catch trout on that floating pattern. Often during the summer I catch one out of six trout on the "strike indicator." On a recent trip to the Little Juniata River in central Pennsylvania I experimented with several wet flies and used a Patriot as a strike indicator. In an hour of fishing I picked up none on a Red Weenie and Pink Weenie, but I did pick up ten trout on the dry fly strike indicator.

Third, you'll be able to detect even the most subtle strikes with the dry-fly indicator.

Fourth, trout seem to hold onto the subsurface pattern longer than they do when you use a dedicated strike indicator, because, again, they don't feel the resistance of the dry fly as much as a strike indicator.

The fifth advantage to using this method is for anglers who have difficulty seeing subtle strikes on a nymph. I can remember fly-fishing with a friend on a Western river who kept missing trout on a Bead-head pattern because he had poor eyesight and couldn't see many of those subtle strikes. We attached a piece of poly yarn three feet above his wet fly and he began to catch trout.

If you use this method of fishing you'll find other advantages like being able to fish nymphs near the bottom of algae-laden streams. From June through September the bottoms of many fertile limestone streams are covered with moss and algae. Nymph fishing on or near the bottom under these conditions tests the will of even the best nymph fisherman. By using the tandem you can keep the subsurface pattern just off the bottom and in full view of bottom-feeding trout. Imagine a nymph fished on the bottom among the rocks and debris, often out of sight of many trout. Now picture that same pattern drifting just above the bottom, above the rocks and debris, and in full view of bottom-feeding trout. The advantages of the latter are clear. And what about when you see trout suspended in three or four feet of water in a deep pool? They won't take a dry fly, and a wet fly sinks beneath them. Consider what happened in just such a situation recently.

Austin Morrow of Aurora, Ohio, and I tested a smaller version of the Green Weenie on a small, private limestone stream suitably named Sinking Run, in central Pennsylvania. A spring flows out of a limestone cave and carves a picturesque arch over the chilled stream. Settlers appropriately named the area Arch Spring. The stream flows no farther than 300 yards before going underground again. That 300-yard section, however, holds some streambred brown trout up to twenty inches long. Austin complained that the Green Weenie didn't seem to work on the stream the two times he fished it. Sinking Run in midsummer has a high nutrient content and plenty of algae. Every time Austin sank the Weenie to the bottom it collected green algae. I tied this same small Weenie a short eighteen inches behind a Patriot so that the Weenie would drift above the algae-covered rocks. On the second cast a beautiful Sinking Run brown hit the Weenie and sank the Patriot. On the fourth or fifth try another trout hit the Green Weenie.

Now Austin wanted to test the pattern and he selected the Arch Spring pool, the most unique fly-fishing you'd ever experience, for the test. In this section of Sinking Run you're actually fly-fishing under a huge limestone dome. While the early-July afternoon temperature soared above 90 degrees, the air temperature near the spring remained a cool 70. Shortly after we arrived at the arch, Austin spotted a brown trout suspended in the pool, a trout we estimated to be eighteen or twenty inches long. The trout stayed about three or four feet below the surface, cruising in search of food.

Austin cast a couple dry flies with no success. Then he tied on a small Green Weenie three feet behind the dry fly. The Patriot floated on the surface and the Weenie sank three feet below the surface and stayed there. On the fifth cast the dry fly and Weenie landed two feet upstream from the trout, in very slow water. This time the brown came over, opened its mouth, and struck the Weenie. With all the action in full view of both of us, Austin struck early and missed the heavy trout.

The very next day Austin set out for that same big trout. He figured he'd try a Bead-head Pheasant Tail Nymph this time since the Green Weenie might be too fresh in the trout's memory. As Austin and I entered the Arch Spring we again saw the trout suspended in about three feet of water and cruising back and forth in the ten-foot-deep limestone pool. On about the tenth cast the trout moved past the Bead-head, then turned, headed back to the nymph, and struck it. Austin set the hook on the lunker brown and the heavy trout broke off.

So both the Green Weenie and the Bead-head Pheasant Tail Nymph worked on this large streambred brown trout. But why did he fool this wizened trout on two occasions in two days? Because Austin skillfully suspended the wet fly at the fish's depth.

With all its advantages, however, you'll also find some disadvantages to using the tandem method. First, the subsurface pattern often doesn't go deep enough. On many occasions in high water I've had to remove the dry fly and add weight to the wet fly to fish it on the bottom. Second, you will get your leader tangled more often using the two flies. Catch a trout on the dry fly and you'll have to remove the fly carefully and then make certain you don't hook it with the trailing wet fly. Third, where do you store used tandem rigs? It's difficult to place the two connected patterns so they don't tangle. Fourth, it'll take you longer to get your rig ready than if you use only a wet fly or a dry fly. One solution is to take your fly rod apart, with tandem rig attached, and keep the rig ready for the next day of fly-fishing. Fifth, some trout attempting to strike the dry fly will see or feel the leader attaching the two patterns and refuse it. You'll see many splashes and rises to the dry fly, but when you set the hook they're gone. On Michigan's Père Marquette, I missed five trout in a row on the Patriot dry fly before removing the point fly and fishing just with the floating pattern. In the next hour I caught ten trout on that attractor pattern. Finally, you'll find casting the two patterns more difficult than just one. If you plan to use the tandem rig, you'll have to practice a few minutes.

CLINCH KNOT

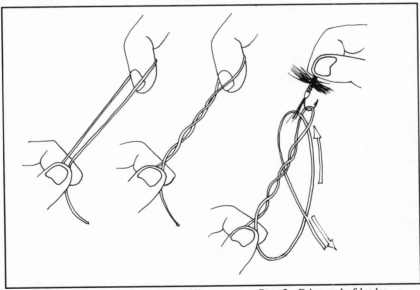

Step 1. Make a loop in end of leader.

Step 2. Put middle finger in loop, twirl finger five times.

Step 3. Bring end of leader through loop and back through second loop, put open end over bend of hook, pull tight.

I had difficulty tying a clinch knot at the bend of the hook of the dry fly until Craig Josephson showed me his extremely simple method of tying that knot. Craig makes a loop in the end of the leader that he uses to tie at the bend of the hook of the dry fly, puts his middle finger in the loop, and twirls his finger five times, twisting the loop. He then brings the end of the leader through the loop and back through the second loop, completing the clinch knot. Craig then pulls the knot tight, puts the open loop over the bend of the hook of the dry fly, and pulls it tight. This method makes it extremely easy to tie the clinch knot to the back of the dry fly—so easy, in fact, that I'm surprised I haven't seen it before.

Meanwhile, the tandem rig doesn't work well on small streams. To cast the two flies suitably you need lots of space—just the luxury you don't have on many small streams. I've tested it several times on small streams and continued to get hung up on the branches overhanging the stream. But wait! Just recently Chuck Catchall and I fly-fished a small, open stream in western Pennsylvania. We used a Patriot dry fly all morning with only limited success. Chuck decided to tie a size 16 Bead-head Pheasant Tail Nymph a foot behind the Patriot on a tandem rig. In a deep pool that I had just fished, Chuck quickly proceeded to catch three trout on the tandem rig. If you find a small stream that has a fairly open canopy, try the tandem rig.

Other Tandem Choices

Up to this point you might think there's only one way to fish the tandem rig—with a dry fly as the lead fly and a weighted wet fly as the point fly. But that's only part of the story. Why not attach two dry flies? How about using two wet flies with this method? Let's look at some of the possibilities.

How many times have I prepared for a sulphur dun hatch near dark and trout fed on an unexpectedly heavy sulphur spinner fall? I often found myself continuing to fish the dun pattern because

I couldn't change patterns in the dark. As a result, I often swore I'd carry two fly rods during sulphur hatches, one with a dun pattern tied on and on the other with a spinner pattern. That way I'd be prepared for either. But a far simpler solution lies in the tandem rig. Prepare for this hatch by tying a spinner pattern on a tippet a couple feet behind the dun pattern.

Do you have difficulty locating your size 24 Trico pattern during that spinner fall? Why not tie the Trico on a short tippet behind a larger size 14 or 16 Patriot? This way you can easily see the attractor pattern and the smaller Trico just behind it. Besides, trout might take the larger pattern just because it's different.

How about using two wet flies? Why not tie on a Sulphur Nymph and an Sulphur Emerger during a hatch? Tie the nymph on as the point fly and the emerger as the lead fly. The emerger will stay closer to the surface and the nymph nearer the bottom.

As you begin using the tandem rig you'll realize that the possibilities are many. You can use a rig with two wet flies, with a dry fly at the lead and a wet fly at the point, or with two dry flies. If you use two dry flies, use a smaller one as your point fly and a larger one as the lead.

Telltale

Larry Madison, Jack Conyngham, and Bill Sutton make an annual trip to Wayne Harpster's Spruce Creek cabin in central Pennsylvania, and recently I joined them during a trico hatch. I watched Larry attach a three-inch piece of poly to his leader about three feet up from his olive shrimp pattern and cast the pattern into a deep pool. The red poly stayed on top as a strike indicator and the shrimp pattern sank near the bottom. The line traveled only two feet before the poly sank, Larry set the hook, and landed a heavy rainbow. Before he finished fishing in that small pool Larry picked up seven trout. I was amazed at the effectiveness of his strike indicator. It sat high on the water for visibility and readily sank when a trout struck.

Larry uses the poly in red or yellow, and both show up well. If you don't like tossing a dry fly and a wet fly in the tandem rig, try this simple method of detecting a strike.

Tandem Combinations

Lead Fly (L)	Point Fly (P)	Examples
Dry Fly	Dry Fly	Patriot (L) Trico (P)
Dry Fly	Dry Fly	Sulphur Dun (L) and Sulphur Spinner (P)
Wet Fly	Wet Fly	Sulphur Emerger (L) and Sulphur Nymph (P)
Dry Fly	Wet Fly	Patriot (L) and Green Weenie (P)

Suggested tandem-rig fly combinations.

Leaders and Fly Rods for the Tandem Setup

Tucker Morris recently went fly-fishing with me, and after he saw how effective the tandem rig worked, he tried one with a three-weight fly rod with a twelve-foot leader. If you plan to use this rig regularly, use a rod made for a five-weight or heavier line, and a leader no longer than nine or ten feet, one like the following:

> .017—17 inches
> .015—15 inches
> .013—13 inches
> .011—11 inches
> .009—11 inches
> .007—16 inches
> .007—30 inches (tippet between the two patterns)
> Total—112 inches (nine feet, four inches)

Patterns to Fish Deep

Over the past five years I've found three wet flies that work

best in tandem with a dry fly when there's no hatch. The Green
Weenie and Bead-head Pheasant Tail Nymph, and Bead-head
Wooly Bugger with a Flashabou tail have proved valuable in all parts
of the country. If one doesn't work, I try the other. On those few
occasions when all three failed me I quit fishing early, convinced
that if these wet flies won't produce nothing will.

Before you quit, however, make certain you've varied your
retrieve and the placement of your wet fly. On Arizona waters like
the Little Colorado, trout hit the Bead-head Pheasant Tail Nymph
only when I fished it on the bottom. And on the same river, trout
hit the Bead-head Wooly Bugger more often when I twitched it as
the pattern made its arc or swing.

Especially try Wooly Buggers near the bottom if you've had
little success and you know the river holds trout.

Patterns to Fish Shallow

It's a whole other story when you see trout feed on emergers
or nymphs. I can remember a late-September afternoon when I saw
thousands of slate drakes on the surface. On many streams you'll
see this mayfly crawl onto a rock and emerge there, safely away from
feeding trout. On this particular trip, I noted that many of these
dark mayflies were emerging right in the water. I added an
Isonychia Emerger as a point fly to the Patriot and proceeded to
catch dozens of trout on the Emerger.

I attempted to fish the *Isonychia* Emerger not on the bottom
but near the top. When I use most caddis and mayfly emergers in
wet-dry tandem I usually start with less than three feet of tippet
between the two. On faster water, this keeps the emerger just a few
inches under the surface.

Patterns like the Isonychia Emerger, Baetis Emerger, and
Sulphur Emerger often work best just a few inches under the
surface. Make the tippet between the two patterns shorter if you're

going too deep.

Don't forget the downwings. Craig Josephson uses a fluttering Green Caddis as the lead fly. Just add an emerging Green Caddis Pupa as the point fly during a hatch and watch the action. Trout often select the emerging pupa over the dry fly.

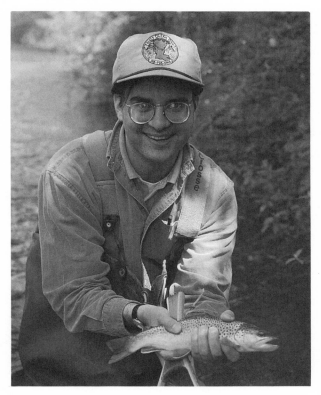

Andrew Goldman lands his first trout caught on the Bead-Head Pheasant Tail Nymph.   Bryan Meck

But the tandem setup won't always work, so be prepared to use the subsurface patterns singly. Let me explain. Dick Cheney, secretary of defense under President Bush, is an accomplished fly-fisher who hails from Wyoming. Recently Dick came to Pennsylvania State University to give the graduation address. Dick wanted to fly-fish after his talk, so Penn State officials asked me to take him fishing. On May 14, Dick, Sean O'Keefe, Andrew Goldman, Bryan Meck, and I fished Joe McMullen's stretch on Spruce Creek in central Pennsylvania. This section of Spruce Creek holds plenty of twenty-inch-plus trout, and hundreds of fly-fishers flock here each year to catch and release these lunkers. When I checked the water temperature that morning, I knew the 50-degree reading did not bode well for us.

On about the tenth cast, Dick Cheney landed an eighteen-inch brown on a tandem rig—a Patriot dry fly and a Bead-head Pheasant Tail Nymph. For the next hour we didn't have a strike. In retrospect, after an hour of non-productive fishing, we should have just fished the Bead-head on the bottom. In the next three hours with the tandem, Dick and I caught only a couple more trout.

Michigan's Père Marquette trout took Dave Tongue's Patriot attractor readily.

That's not the only case where the tandem has proved an inappropriate choice. Craig Josephson and I fished the Little Colorado River near Greer, Arizona. The river on the X Diamond

Ranch averages thirty feet wide and bushes and branches overhang almost every productive pool. Under these circumstances Craig and I resorted to Bead-head Wooly Buggers fished singly. Later in the afternoon Craig and I moved downriver to a section of the Little Colorado dammed by a family of ambitious beavers. Here the water pooled and widened to forty feet, and I could cast the tandem rig comfortably.

I don't recommend the tandem rig in high-water conditions so often associated with early season in the East and Midwest and with snowmelt in the West. Instead, fish a weighted nymph or wet fly alone as deep as possible.

And then there are times when the tandem rig just plain doesn't work. Dave Tongue of Grand Rapids, Michigan, captains a boat he calls "Tongue Tide II." Dave runs his boat out of Ludington at the mouth of the Père Marquette, and just about every weekend during the summer you'll find Dave and some of his friends fishing for coho or king salmon, lake trout, or steelhead on Lake Michigan. On a recent trip on the lake, fishing was so slow that all of us agreed to head back to shore.

Attractor patterns work well on Michigan's Père Marquette when no hatches appear.

I convinced Dave that we should go fly-fishing on the Père Marquette that evening, and Dave agreed to accompany me. We arrived just above the M-37 bridge and headed upriver. Just below the bridge, and for seven miles downriver, you'll find a fly-fishing-only section. Dave and I, however, opted to test the tandem rig on the unregulated water above.

I used a Patriot dry fly and a Green Weenie. For the first half-hour few trout hit the rig. Those that did splashed at the Patriot. Just a few hundred feet below me Dave tried to cast a Patriot and a Bead-head Pheasant Tail Nymph. Finally, after about the fifth time he tangled the rig, I suggested he cut off the wet fly and just use the Patriot. Meanwhile I tied on a Pheasant Tail Nymph as my wet fly. Within ten minutes I caught two trout on the Bead-head, and Dave had three on the Patriot. I, too, cut off the Bead-head and just used the Patriot and began catching more trout. It seemed that the Père Marquette trout were intent on taking that attractor dry fly and almost refusing the wet fly.

Fishing the Hatches with the Tandem

Earlier, I quoted Andy Leitzinger using the word "bi-cycle" in his discussion of the tandem rig. I often use that term when I use the tandem and both patterns copy emerging insects.

I've said several times before that I'm a dry-fly fisher first and foremost. I've preferred using dry flies for more than forty years. But let's face it, you'll often see trout chasing nymphs and emergers rather than taking duns off the surface. With hatches like the sulphur and pale morning dun, trout often prefer the emerger over the dun. Here's an example.

Paul Antolosky is the consummate dry-fly purist. He's one of the most accomplished fly casters and fly-fishers I know. Paul would never consider using a tandem rig, would he? Recently Paul and I fly-fished for a day on central Pennsylvania's Elk Creek. We leapfrogged upstream as Paul used a dry fly and I used the tandem rig with a Patriot and a Bead-head. At the end of the day Paul asked me if I could tie him some Bead-heads for a trip he planned the next week to the Missouri River in Montana.

One evening on the Missouri, Paul ran into a respectable hatch of pale morning duns. The trout, however, refused his dry-fly imitation. Paul tied on a size 16 Bead-head Pheasant Tail Nymph about a foot behind his Pale Morning Dun pattern and began casting to rising trout. In a short time Paul caught more than a dozen fish on that Bead-head while ten other anglers around him caught none.

That's just part of the story. How many times have emergers and hatches confused you? If you're uncertain whether trout are taking duns or emergers, try the bi-cycle. Tie a size 16 Sulphur as your dry fly and a size 14 or 16 Sulphur Emerger as your wet fly. Place the emerger just a couple of feet behind the dry fly so it sinks just beneath the surface. If you don't have any success with either pattern, change from an emerger to a weighted nymph. Bryan Meck and I often find the white fly hatch (*Ephoron*) on waters across the United States baffling. Just ask the anglers who regularly fish this hatch and they too will tell you how trout often refuse the dry fly. Recently, Bryan and I fly-fished on the Yellow Breeches in south-central Pennsylvania during the late-August white fly hatch.

Bryan and I tried an experiment that evening. We tied a size 14 floating White Fly onto the tippet, then a pale grayish-tan nymph behind it in tandem or the bi-cycle. Guess what? At dusk, most trout took the nymph and refused the dry fly. Bryan and I averaged four trout on the nymph for every one that took the dry fly.

Give the tandem rig a thorough try with some of the patterns listed in Chapters 3 through 10.

Chapter 3
The Hatches

Several years ago I asked a local fly-
fisher to alert me when he first saw the white fly appearing on the
Little Juniata River. He fished the river nightly and lived only a
couple hundred yards away. The white fly (*Ephoron* species) begins
appearing on the river any time after August 10, and once it starts,
you'll find white flies emerging nightly for the next two weeks. One
night in early August, I received a call from the angler. He said he
had seen a dozen or more white flies two nights before and that the
hatch should now be heavy. I agreed to meet him on the river that
evening.

I canceled an appointment I had for that evening to hit the
hatch and arrived by 7:00 p.m. For the next hour and a half I
watched and waited, but no white flies appeared. Sure, I saw a few
cream cahills emerge, but not in any numbers. The angler friend
who said he had seen white flies the night before pointed to the
cream cahills and called them white flies. When I told him that
white flies seldom rise that high above the surface, he said he hadn't
known that. I also mentioned that white flies move up and down
river usually only a foot or two off the surface.

Recently I experienced a similar incident. I stopped by the
Little Juniata River one late-August evening to see if the white fly
had begun its annual emergence. While I stood by the stream
looking for the first signs of male spinners just above the water,
another angler walked by. As he passed several trees along the
stream, he shook each one vigorously. When I asked him what he
was doing he replied that he was checking for white flies. I told

him that white flies die a couple of hours after emerging and they don't last from one day to the next. Besides that, with their atrophied legs, they can't rest on trees. If this angler would have known more about the white fly hatch, he could have reacted more perceptively.

By learning a little about some of the more important hatches, you'll become a better fly-fisher. Here's another example.

I had just witnessed a heavy slate drake hatch on Penns Creek in early June. Rising trout eagerly took the size 12 darkbodied Slate Drake imitation. For the next couple of days I hit the same hatch in the evening and had the same great success. Finally, by mid-June the large gray-bodied drakes appeared in more meager numbers and few trout rose.

I remembered this heavy hatch and waited for September so I could fish it again. Fish it again, you say? Yes, this slate drake produces two generations a year on many streams and rivers. If you see a good hatch in June, you'll see another one in September. The fall hatch usually appears earlier in the day, and fly-fishers match it with a size 14 pattern.

I returned in mid-September in the afternoon and again hit the hatch. This time a cool, drizzly day kept many drakes from taking flight and trout fed on stragglers all afternoon and evening.

Many other mayflies appear more than once a year. Little blue-winged olive duns, speckle-winged duns, and tricos have more than one generation a year.

The more you know about the caddis flies, mayflies, and stoneflies, the better you'll fish them. How do you find information on the hatches and the patterns to match them? Much of the information comes from research papers, books, and plain old observation. Greg Hoover and I included recent scientific studies of the trico and slate drake in our book, *Great Rivers—Great Hatches*.

It's important to tie patterns to match the hatches because many of the most productive flies you'll use will be those imitating one of the hatch phases. Do trout really key in on mayflies, caddis flies, and stoneflies? Decades ago, Paul Needham conducted one of the best studies of food selection by trout. In his book, *Trout Streams*, Needham lists the percentages of foods consumed by the brook, brown, and rainbow trout as shown in Figure 1.

Species	*Mayflies*	*Caddis flies*	*Stoneflies*	*Terrestrials*	*Other*
Brook Trout (1)	17.6	30.0	1.5	37.	13.6
Brown Trout (2)	79.3	9.5	.7	5.	4.8
Rainbow Trout(2)	37.1	18.7	3.3	35.	5.9

(1) Stomachs checked in May, June, and July
(2) Stomachs checked each month for a year
Figure 1. Percent of mayflies, caddis flies, stoneflies, and terrestrials

Why place so much emphasis on the hatches in a book called *Patterns, Hatches, Tactics, and Trout*? If you examine Figure 1 carefully, you'll see why it's important to include chapters on emergers, duns, spinners, nymphs, downwings (caddis flies and stoneflies), and terrestrials. The study shows that brown trout prefer mayflies by a wide margin, rainbow trout much less, and brook trout even less. These preferences probably stem from the location of these species. You'll find brook trout often confined to smaller streams often void of heavy mayfly hatches, so they have to depend on terrestrials for food.

Why include an entire chapter on terrestrials? Because land-borne insects make up an important part of the diet of brook and rainbow trout.

Also, because of the importance as a source of food from aquatic insects, in the next few chapters you'll read about spinners, duns, nymphs, and emergers. Before you do, however, it's important to know what each phase of an aquatic insect's life means to fly-fishing. You'll find patterns for nymphs, emergers, duns, and spinners in Chapter 10.

The lifecycle of a mayfly begins with the female mayfly spinner, or mature mayfly (scientists call the spinner an "imago"), mating with the male spinner. This usually occurs over fast stretches of a stream and most often in the evening. The male appears over the stream first, waiting for the female spinner. After mating, the female deposits her fertilized eggs by one of three methods: (1) flying just above the surface, (2) sitting or dipping on the surface, or (3) diving underwater. After they complete the egg laying, many females fall with wings outstretched or spent onto the water.

Nymphs hatch from the fertilized eggs in a couple of weeks. With fall mayflies, eggs often don't hatch until the following spring. The white fly (*Ephoron* species) and trico don't hatch from the fertilized eggs until the following May. The nymph spends approximately a year (there are many exceptions like the green drake, slate drake and little blue-winged olive dun) in slow, medium, or fast stretches on rocky or muddy bottoms (many species are specific in their habitat). After almost a year of growing and shedding their outer coverings many times (instars), the nymphs are ready to emerge.

After several false dashes, the nymph reaches the surface. Here it sheds its nymphal skin dorsally (a few do this on the bottom of the stream) and becomes a dun (often called a "subimago"). The process of changing from a water-based larva to an air-breathing adult takes some time. Anglers call a nymph, once it moves toward the surface, and in the process of changing to adult an "emerger". More trout feed on emergers than on any other stage of the cycle because of the vulnerability of the insect at that time.

Many of the duns, including the quill gordon (*Epeorus*

Life Cycle and Pattern Chart for the Little Blue-Winged Olive Dun
(Baetis tricaudatus) Hook size 18 to 20 - adult and mature nymph.

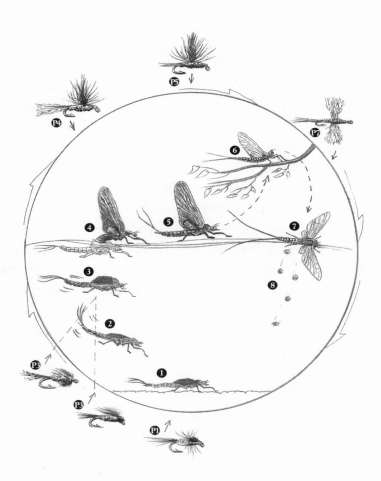

1. Nymph grows by shedding exoskeleton (instars), free-swimming and feed on bottom . Often goes through more than twenty instars (molts). Lives approximately six months under water before emerging. Next brood will live under water from October until August (nine months). Next brood will live under water from August to May (nine months). And the fourth brood will live under water as a nymph from May to October (six months). **2.** Nymph begin to emerge (may take several attempts). **3.** Nymphal skin splits often just under the surface. **4.** Cool wet weather delays take off, rests on water for a short time. Dun emerges out of nymphal shuck, may not readily escape. **5.** Dun is free of shuck, then suceeds in becoming airborne and heads for trees or bushes on shore. **6.** After several hours or a few days, dun molts, becomes a spinner with clear wings. Male and female spinners mate over water. Male dies usually away from water. **7.** Female deposits eggs and dies, usually spent on the water. Some baetis spinners dive under water to lay eggs. **8.** Nymphs hatch from eggs (ten to thirty days).
Patterns: P-1. Baetis Nymph **P-3.** Baetis Emerger **P-3.** Baetis Emerger **P-4.** Little Blue-winged Olive Dun (with Z-lon shuck) **P-5.** Little Blue-winged Olive Dun **P-7.** Rusty Spinner

Life Cycle and Pattern Chart for the Grannom Caddis Fly

(Brachycentrus fuliginosus) Hook size 14 - adult and mature larva.

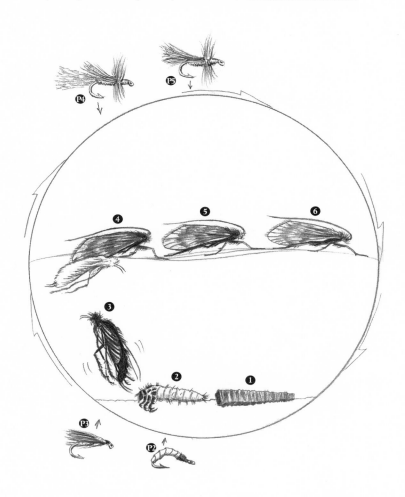

1. Four sided log cabin case for grannom larva, lives in protective case. Generally cases are alike for each member of a species. Larva grows larger through instars (molting or shedding outer skin), usually five. 2. Caddis Larva is unprotected (no hard outer covering).
3. Emerging Pupa often lasts for about three weeks. 4. When the pupa emerges it sheds its case and becomes an adult. Often you'll see thousands of these tannish cases in the stream during and shortly after a heavy caddis emergence. 5. Caddis Adult mates on vegetation, sometimes on ground but never in air. 6. Female dips abdomen on surface to lay eggs.
Patterns: P-2. Caddis Larva P-3. Emerging Caddis Pupa P-4. Grannom (with shuck)
P-5. Grannom

Life Cycle and Pattern Chart for the Brown Drake

(Ephemera simulans) *Hook size 12 or 14 long shank - adult and mature nymph.*

1. Nymph grows by shedding exoskeleton as many as twenty times (instars), burrows in fine to medium gravel. 2. Nymph emerges near the end of May or early June in the east and the Midwest and in late June in the west. 3. Duns often emerge in large numbers usually near dusk. Anglers often see thousands of nymphal shucks drifting in the water at the height of the hatch. 4. Large duns like the brown drake (15mm) may rest on surface for some time before taking flight. Duns rest in vegetation for a day or two and change to spinners with glassy color wings. Dun and spinner activity often occur for less than a week annually. Swarms of males often meet high above trees. Females enter swarm and are mated.
5. Females move towards surface of water often in large numbers. Females die spent on surface. 6. Nymphs develop from eggs in two to three weeks.
Patterns: **P-1 & P-2.** Brown Drake Nymph **P-3.** Brown Drake (with Z-lon shuck)
P-4. Brown Drake **P-5.** Brown Drake Spinner

pleuralis), yellow drake (*Ephemera varia*), and green drake (*Ephemera guttulata*), have difficulty leaving the water and ride the surface for some distance before taking flight. If you hit a mayfly hatch when the temperature and weather conditions are right, you'll find trout feeding on the dun. On cold, overcast, drizzly days mayflies often can't escape and you're in for some great matching-the-hatch activity. Trout key in on mayflies that struggle to escape. These duns are especially important to imitate with dry-fly patterns. Even during midsummer on cool, overcast days, you'll find blue-winged olives and blue quills appearing but unable to escape from the surface.

When the dun finally becomes airborne, it usually heads for the nearest tree or a bush close to the stream. Duns emerging early in the season sometimes rest on sun-warmed rocks or debris next to the water to protect themselves from early-season frosts.

Although a few genera (*Tricorythodes*, *Caenis*, and *Ephoron*) change from dun to spinner in an hour or less, and a few never change (*Ephoron* female), in most genera the transformation requires one or two days. With a final molt, the dun shucks its outer covering and reappears over the water as a more brightly colored mayfly with clear, glassy wings. These spinners then meet and mate to complete the lifecycle.

Thus, trout can actively feed on four stages of the mayfly: the nymph, emerger, dun, and spinner. I stated earlier how important it is to copy the emerger. Trout discriminate little and take either male or female nymph and dun. With the fourth phase, the spinner or imago, the female is devoured more often than the male. In many species, the female dies spent on the water after completing her egg-laying task. The male, conversely, often leaves the stream area after mating and frequently dies over land.

If you plan to fish the hatches, it's important to understand the relationship of aquatic insects to the total fauna. Mayflies, caddis flies, and stoneflies are members of the Class Insecta. Class Insecta belongs to the Phylum Arthropoda, and all phyla are components of the Animal Kingdom. If we look at the brown drake (*Ephemera simulans*) as an example, you'll see more clearly just how mayflies fit into the Animal Kingdom:

Kingdom: Animal (all animals from one-celled to humans)

Phylum: Arthropoda (animals that have outer skeleton called exoskeletons)

Class: Insecta (insects)

Order: Ephemeroptera (all mayflies)

Family: Ephemeridae (nymphs usually are burrowers; in adults longitudinal vein M2 is bent sharply toward Cu at its base)

Genus: *Ephemera* (forewing darkened or heavily spotted)

Species: *simulans* (differentiated by the coloration of various body parts and the shape of the penis—the brown drake)

The basic unit in the classification system is species. A species is sometimes divided into subspecies. When this occurs, the subspecies is listed as *Drunella grandis grandis*, with the last name referring to the subspecies. Usually only members of the same species can mate and have offspring. Often several species (sometimes only one) belong to the same genus. In our sample genus, *Ephemera*, we also have *Ephemera varia* (yellow drake), *Ephemera guttulata* (green drake), and others. The genus of a mayfly is much easier to determine than is the species and more difficult to ascertain than family.

The next rung up the ladder is the family. The family of a mayfly is easier to determine than is the genus. In our example, the genus *Ephemera* belongs to the Family Ephemeridae, or the true burrowers. In addition to *Ephemera*, other genera, such as *Hexa-*

genia and *Litobrancha*, belong to the Family Ephemeridae.

Ephemeridae is one of at least seventeen families of the Order Ephemeroptera (mayflies) found in the United States. Below are some of the more common families and genera, along with some of the characteristics of each. Under each genus, I have listed the most common species.

You'll find many recent changes in mayfly classification. For example, entomologists have now bunched many previous *Isonychia* species under *Isonychia bicolor*. Many of the blue duns so familiar to anglers and classified in the Genus *Pseudocloeon*, have now been grouped with *Baetis*. You'll find many more changes in the classification in the next few pages.

A. Family Ephemeridae

Most members of this family inhabit slow to moderate stretches of streams, rivers, lakes, and ponds. Most nymphs burrow in mud, silt, and fine to coarse gravel. Duns usually appear, and spinners fall at dusk or later from late May until early September. This family contains many of the largest mayflies in North America.

1. Genus *Ephemera*

This genus contains moderate to large (10-25 mm) gravel-burrowing nymphs. Many burrow in rather coarse gravel often in moderate stretches of a river or stream. Most species emerge and fall (as spinners) at dusk, and many continue well past dark. Wings on duns and spinners are heavily spotted, and all adults have three tails, unlike members of the genus *Hexagenia*, which have no spotting and only two tails. Sternites (underside of abdomen) vary in color from pale cream for *Ephemera guttulata* to tannish yellow for *E. simulans*. This latter species, called a brown drake by anglers, inhabits rivers and streams from Connecticut to Idaho. This genus contains the well-known drake hatches (green, yellow, and brown) and anglers find them an extremely important genus to meet and fish. Most emerge from late May until early July. Duns range in size from 14 to 30 mm. Following are some Ephemera species that you might encounter:

>Ephemera compar (West)
>Ephemera simulans (East, Midwest & W)
>Ephemera guttulata (E)
>Ephemera varia (E & M)

2. Genus Hexagenia

These are large mayflies (14-30 mm). The nymph usually inhabits slow stretches of rivers and lakes or ponds where it burrows in silt. The dun emergence and spinner fall often occur at dusk or later and continue well past that time. Wings of the duns are heavily barred, and the veins of the spinners' wings are often dark reddish brown. In all species, the middle tail is reduced to a barely visible vestige, and only two tails are prominent. Hexagenia recurvata is now placed in a new genus, Litobrancha. Hatches often occur after dark. This genus includes the Michigan caddis (H. limbata) and the giant slate drake (H. atrocaudata). The latter species appears in mid to late August. Others appear from late May through July. Following are some of the Hexagenia (and Litobrancha) species that might appear:

>Hexagenia atrocaudata (E & M)
>Hexagenia munda (E & M)
>Hexagenia limbata (E, M & W)
>Litobrancha recurvata (E & M)

B. Family Polymitarcidae

This resurrected family includes mayflies with nonfunctional legs. Until recently these species were included in the true burrowers in the Family Ephemeridae.

1. Genus *Ephoron*

These medium-sized (6-12 mm) burrowers frequent large and medium-sized streams. Duns of these species emerge most abundantly in July, August, or September, in the evening. The female never molts, but emerges, mates, and lays her eggs as a subimago—all in the same evening. Legs of both sexes (front legs of the male are an exception) are atrophied (nonfunctional) in the adult stage. The number of tails differs with the sex of the individual: the female has three and the male two. Tails in the male (spinner) are longer and better developed than in the female (dun). Often you'll see the pellicle of the dun still clinging to the tail of the male spinner.

Most adults are white, sometimes with a gray cast, and the male has some tannish brown. Anglers call these mayflies "white flies." The White Wulff is an effective imitation during the *Ephoron* hatch. Although these mayflies aren't as common as many other species, they appear late in the season when few other true hatches occur and are, therefore, important to fish. Hatches are often found on some of the larger rivers like the Potomac in Maryland, the Susquehanna in Pennsylvania, the Housatonic in Connecticut, and the White in Vermont. Hatches do appear on some small streams. Members of these species die a few hours after they emerge. They do not live from one day to the next. Nymphs emerge from fertilized eggs the following May. In the West, the lower Yellowstone River above Billings, and the North Platte in Wyoming, hold late-summer hatches. Following are the common *Ephoron* species:

> *Ephoron album* (M&W)
> *Ephoron leukon* (E&M)

C. Family Potamanthidae

Until recently, the *Anthopotamanthus* species also were

included in the Family Ephemeridae. However, *Anthopotamanthus* nymphs are not true burrowers, and adults can be distinguished from the true burrowers by the branching of the wing veins in these species. Only one genus is presently in this family, genus *Anthopotamanthus*.

These moderate-sized (9-16 mm) nymphs are crawlers rather than burrowers, although they inhabit the same areas of a stream as the true burrowers (Ephemeridae). Duns emerge and spinners fall at dusk or shortly thereafter, and all have white, cream, or creamish yellow bodies and wings, sometimes with tan shading on the abdomen. Many species emerge in late June.

Fishermen commonly call mayflies of this genus golden or cream drakes. Wing venation and body shading is important in separating species. Many of these species inhabit warmer waters more common for bass than trout. Following are some of the *Anthopotamanthus* species that might produce fishable hatches:

> *Anthopotamanthus distinctus (E)*
> *Anthopotamanthus rufous (E & M)*
> *Anthopotamanthus verticus (E & M)*

D. Family Caenidae

Members of this family are often found in quiet water, where the nymphs move about freely in debris, trash, or silt. These diminutive mayflies rarely exceed 6 mm. Dun emergence and spinner fall occur at evening, in the dark, before morning appears, or in the early morning hours. Most species appear after June. Members of this family are separated from other families by the size of the ocelli (simple eyes located between the compound eyes).

1. Genus *Caenis*

These tiny mayflies are rarely longer than 4 mm and inhabit lakes, ponds, and slow stretches of streams. Adults are white, cream, or buff-colored, and usually appear at or shortly before dark. Duns change to spinners shortly after they emerge, and these imagos meet at dark, or in the early morning hours, to mate. Spinners are strongly attracted to light, and thousands can be seen near lighted areas at night. Following are *Caenis* species that you may encounter:

> *Caenis anceps (E & M)*
> *Caenis simulans (E,M & W)*

I have seen *Caenis anceps* emerge by the thousands in late July and August on Spruce Creek. But to imitate this mayfly, one would have to choose a size 26 hook, which is almost impossible to use effectively.

E. Family Tricorythidae

Until recently, members of this family were included in Caenidae; however, *Tricorythodes* adults have claspers with three distinct segments (parts), compared to one in *Brachycercus* and *Caenis*.

1. Genus *Tricorythodes*

We find these tiny (3-5 mm) but important species on small streams like Falling Springs in south-central Pennsylvania and Mossy Creek in Virginia, and on large ones like the Beaverkill in New York, the Au Sable in Michigan, Namekagon in Wisconsin, the South Platte in Colorado, the McKenzie in Oregon, and the Bighorn in Montana. Possibly the heaviest hatch in the United States occurs on the Missouri River in Montana. Male duns often emerge at dark and females near or shortly after dawn, depending on the temperature. Duns molt to spinners and mate within a couple of hours. Male and female spinners often fall spent to the water, so it's important to have imitations of both sexes on hand. All species have three tails. Most tricos can be copied on a size 24 hook or a size 20 short-shank hook. Some species have two generations each year, and you'll often find these species emerging from mid-July through late September. Nymphs emerge from second-generation eggs in May of the following year. Some *Tricorythodes* species that seem to be common and can produce fishable hatches follow:

> *Tricorythodes atratus (E & M)*
> *Tricorythodes minutus (E & W)*
> *Tricorythodes stygiatus (E & W)*

The pale morning dun appears throughout the West from late May into August.

F. Family Ephemerellidae

Until a few years ago this family contained only one genus, *Ephemerella*. This one genus has since been split into *Ephemerella, Dannella, Drunella, Attenella, Eurylophella, Serratella,* and *Timpanoga*. The family is still separated from other families by the few cross veins adults have in their fore wings. The three tails present on all members are often extremely weak on subimagos or duns. You'll find female spinners often carrying egg sacs after mating. For the fly-fishermen *Ephemerella* and *Drunella* contain the most important members of the genus.

1. Genus *Ephemerella*

Members of this genus range in size from 5 to 14 mm. The genus contains many of the more common members of the family. Most of the sulphurs, pale morning duns, and hendricksons belong to this genus. Many female spinners carry egg sacs at the tip of their abdomen after they've mated. Some of the more common species follow:

> *Ephemerella dorothea (E&W)*
> *Ephemerella inermis (W)*
> *Ephemerella infrequens (W)*
> *Ephemerella invaria (E&M)*
> *Ephemerella needhami (E&M)*
> *Ephemerella rotunda (E&M)*
> *Ephemerella septentrionalis (E)*
> *Ephemerella subvaria (E&M)*

2. Genus *Drunella*

Body length of the members of this genus usually ranges from 6 to 15 mm. Fly-fishermen call many species in this group "blue-winged olives." Important mayflies in the East, Midwest, and West are found in this genus. *D. cornuta, D. cornutella, and D. lata* produce major hatches on many Eastern and some Midwestern waters. *D. flavilinea* appears on many Western waters from late May through June. Duns often emerge in late morning. Spinners usually mate in the evening and females carry dark-olive egg sacs. *D. grandis* and its subspecies and *D. doddsi* produce the famous green drake hatches in the West. The Henry's Fork in Idaho hosts an unbelievable hatch of green drakes. Some of the more common Drunella follow:

> *Drunella coloradensis (W)*
> *Drunella cornuta (E&M)*
> *Drunella cornutella (E)*
> *Drunella doddsi (W)*
> *Drunella flavilinea (W)*
> *Drunella grandis flavitincta, ingens, and grandis (W)*
> *Drunella lata (E&M)*
> *Drunella longicornus (E)*
> *Drunella walkeri (E & M)*

3. Genus *Eurylophella*

These moderate-sized mayflies range from 6 to 11 mm in length. Anglers call some of the members of the genus "chocolate duns." Species of this genus are usually found in the East and Midwest. Often imitated with size 16 or 18 hooks, these mayflies frequently appear at midday. *E. bicolor,* although relatively undiscovered, creates great matching-the-hatch opportunities in early June. Here are some common members:

> *Eurylophella bicolor (E&M)*
> *Eurylophella funeralis (E&M)*
> *Eurylophella aestiva (E&M)*

4. Genus *Dannella*

Entomologists have placed only two species in this genus and only one, *D. simplex,* is important to fishermen. Members are small with body lengths near 6 mm. *D. simplex* has been overlooked in angling literature but can produce explosive hatches in mid-June. It can be copied with a size 18 Blue-winged Olive Dun.

> *Dannella simplex (E & M)*

5. Genus *Serratella*

Members of this genus are usually small, ranging from 4 to 9 mm. *S. deficiens* is small, dark, and important to imitate in early June. A size 18 or 20 Dark Blue Quill matches the hatch adequately. Two of the more common members follow:

Serratella deficiens (E & M)

Serratella tibialis (W)

6. Genus *Caudatella*

Members of this species are found in the West and range in size from 5 to 11 mm. The most important members are three subspecies of

C. heterocaudata.

7. Genus *Timpanoga*

This genus holds one Western species, *T. hecuba*, with two subspecies, *pacifica and hecuba. T. hecuba* is a fairly large (size 10 to 12) mayfly.

G. Family Leptophlebiidae

These small to moderate-size (6-14) mm) nymphs prefer lakes or ponds, or slow-to-moderate stretches of streams. Subimagos of most species appear dark brown or dark grayish brown, and most imagos are dark brown or reddish brown. Fishermen call the male imagos of many species of this family "Jenny Spinners." Many males have an abdomen of white or amber, with the last few segments dark brown.

1. Genus *Leptophlebia*

Many duns of these species appear around noon or shortly thereafter. Both dun and spinner have three tails; however, the middle tail of the male is almost always only one-third to two-thirds as long as the outer ones. Dark brown or black imitations (Early Brown Spinner and Black Quill) work well when a hatch or fall of this genus occurs. You'll find good hatches of *L. cupida* on small streams with some fast water. Male spinners are active in late April in the afternoon. Four of the more common Leptophlebia species follow:

> *Leptophlebia cupida (E & M)*
> *Leptophlebia johnsoni (E)*
> *Leptophlebia gravastella (W)*
> *Leptophlebia nebulosa (E, M & W)*

2. Genus *Paraleptophlebia*

These small to moderate-size (5-9 mm) nymphs can tolerate much more current than *Leptophlebia,* and are, therefore, common on trout streams and abundant on many smaller streams. Fly-fishermen match the dun effectively with the Blue Quill or Dark Blue Quill and the female spinner with the Dark Brown Spinner. The dark-grayish-brown duns often appear during the morning or early afternoon. Male spinners have a characteristic undulating mating flight and are active from morning until early evening. Fishermen sometimes confuse these spinners with the smaller *Tricorythodes.*

The genus *Paraleptophlebia* contains many species that, on occasion, can produce fishable hatches. Among some of the more common examples of these species are the following:

> *Paraleptophlebia adoptiva (E & M)*
> *Paraleptophlebia bicornuta (W)*
> *Paraleptophlebia debilis (E, M, & W)*
> *Paraleptophlebia guttata (E & M)*
> *Paraleptophlebia heteronea (W)*
> *Paraleptophlebia memorialis (W)*
> *Paraleptophlebia mollis (E & M)*

Paraleptophlebia packi (W)

Paraleptophlebia strigula (E)

Paraleptophlebia vaciva (W)

H. Family Baetidae

Nymphs are free-swimming, highly streamlined, and range in size from 3 mm in species like *Acentrella* to 10 mm in *Callibaetis*. Nymphs vary in their habitat from ponds and slow-water stretches, where we find species like *Callibaetis*, to fast water, where several species of *Baetis* live.

1. Genus *Acentrella*

These are small mayflies, but sometimes extremely important to match. They used to be part of the now-nonexistent genus *Pseudocloeon*. Species of *Acentrella* often produce two or three broods a year. Duns emerge on Eastern and Midwestern waters on many cold May afternoons and evenings. They also appear in late September and early October in the afternoon. Fishermen can match many of these species with a Blue Dun (size 20-24) and a Rusty Spinner for the spinner. Rivers of the West, like the Missouri in Montana, and the Green in Utah, hold tremendous hatches. *Acentrella carolina* (E)

A male Baetis dun found on streams and rivers across the United States in spring and again in fall.

A female Baetis spinner. You'll find plenty of Baetis tricaudatus on streams across the United States in spring and again in fall.

2. Genus *Baetis*

These small (3-7 mm) nymphs often inhabit shallow areas of streams. Many duns of this genus rest for protracted periods before taking flight. Therefore, even though they're extremely small, many of these species are important for the fly-fisherman to imitate. Furthermore, many of these species, including *Baetis hageni* (previously *parvus*), a common Western species, emerge on midsummer afternoons, a period often void of other mayfly species. Many of those mayflies, which entomologists had previously included in the genus *Pseudocloeon*, are now part of *Baetis*.

Duns usually have dark gray, dark brown, or tan bodies, often with an olive cast, contrasted to the rusty brown or dark brown bodies of the imagos. The Blue Dun, Blue Upright, or Blue-Winged Olive Dun are used to match the subimago. Many male spinners resemble some of the *Paraleptophlebia* species, and have abdomens with the middle segments almost colorless (hyaline). *Baetis* species are difficult to differentiate. The venation of the hind wing and the presence of projections on that wing are important

A male Baetis spinner.

factors to consider in determining species. Here are eight common species:

> *Baetis bicaudatus (W)*
> *Baetis brunneicolor (M)*
> *Baetis tricaudatus (vagans) (all)*
> *Baetis flavistriga (levitans) (E&M)*
> *Baetis hageni (parvus) (W)*
> *Baetis flavistriga (phoebus) (M)*
> *Baetis dubium (E & M)*
> *Baetis punctiventrus (M)*

Note that the former *Baetis phoebus* and *Baetis levitans* have been reclassified as *Baetis flavistriga. Baetis parvus* is now listed as *Baetis hageni.*

3. Genus *Callibaetis*

The free-swimming nymphs of this genus dwell in still water of ponds and lakes, or sluggish areas of streams. Many species develop from egg to adult in five to six weeks, and consequently appear throughout the summer. You'll find these mayflies in such diverse places as Sunrise Lake in northeastern Arizona and

Nunnally Lake in central Washington. Duns begin appearing late in May, in late morning. Adult females live a week or more after mating. When the eggs are finally deposited in still water, the young hatch almost immediately.

Adults range in size from 5 to 10 mm. The female spinner has wings washed heavily with gray flecks, and all species have two tails. Anglers often match the hatch with a size 16 Adams pattern. Mayflies previously placed in C. *nigritus* and C. *coloradensis* have now been placed in C. *americanus*. If you find an alkaline lake or pond in the East or Midwest, C. *skokianus* can appear in abundance. Following are four *Callibaetis* species you might encounter:

> *Callibaetis americanus (M & W)*
> *Callibaetis ferrugineus (E & M)*
> *Callibaetis fluctuans (E & M)*
> *Callibaetis skokianus (E & M)*

I. Family Siphlonuridae

Members of this family, until recently, were included in the Family Baetidae. It is now Siphonuridae because all members have four segments on the hind tarsi (Baetidae members have three).

1. Genus *Siphlonurus*

These moderate-size (9-14 mm) mayflies are often called "gray drakes." Emergences of different species occur throughout the season. *Siphlonurus quebecensis* appears near the end of May in the East and Midwest, S. *alternatus* emerges around the end of June in the same areas, and S. *occidentalis* appears on Western waters from mid-July into August. Species often emerge sporadically in the afternoon. Spinners create frenzied feeding on many Michigan rivers on June evenings. The legs, wings, tails, and bodies of many species are dark gray, with the bodies ribbed slightly lighter. Some of the more common *Siphlonurus* species follow:

Siphlonurus alternatus (E & M)
Siphlonurus occidentalis (M & W)
Siphlonurus quebecensis (E & M)
Siphlonurus rapidus (E & M)

2. Genus *Ameletus*

Duns and spinners of these moderate-size mayflies are usually grayish brown, brown, or yellowish brown. Some species of this genus are locally important in the West, but I have noted only one species that appeared in fishable numbers there. That species, *Ameletus cooki*, can be important to imitate. In the East, *Ameletus ludens* emerges in mid-April. I have never seen a male member of this species so I agree with Needham in *Biology of Mayflies* that it is parthenogenic (the eggs hatch without fertilization from the male). This could be an important species to match in mid-April. A. *ludens* looks a lot like a slate drake. Two important species follow:

Ameletus cooki (W)
Ameletus ludens (E & M).

Craig Josephson lands a heavy brown trout on a size 14 Slate Drake dry fly during an afternoon hatch.

J. Family Isomyehiidae

This new family has rather diverse genera. In adults the forelegs are shorter than the second pair and longitudinal veins are reduced or similar to *Siphlonurus*. The Genus *Isonychia* is extremely important to fly-fishermen.

1. Genus *Isonychia*

Recent studies suggest that some of these species may have more than one brood a year. This might indicate why slate drakes appear all summer and again in late September and early October. The brood that emerges in June appears as a size 12 insect while the brood emerging in September is a size 14. Studies also suggest that those emerging in the fall do not crawl as far onto rocks as the spring emergers do. This habit might indicate that the fall slate drakes are more readily available to trout as food when they emerge.

A male slate drake. These appear in late May and June and again in September and October.

These large, streamlined nymphs prefer rapid water. When emerging, the nymphs often swim to shallow rapids, crawl onto an exposed rock, break their nymphal skin, and escape to a nearby tree. On some streams, however, many duns emerge in the surface film, making them extremely important to copy. *I. bicolor* has two generations a year. *Isonychia matilda, saderli,* and *harperi* genera have now been classified with *I. bicolor.*

Adults usually have dark forelegs and creamish hind legs. All have two tails. Duns often have slate-colored bodies, while spinners are dark maroon or dark rusty brown. The Slate Drake effectively imitates many species of this genus. Two common *Isonychia* species follow:

> *Isonychia bicolor (E&M)*
> *Isonychia velma (W)*

K. Family Heptageniidae

Nymphs of this rock-clinging family often dwell in moderate and fast water. All individuals have two tails.

1. Genus *Stenonema*

Many species of this genus spend much of their nymphal life attached to rocks in moderate and fast water. Adults vary in size from 8 to 16 mm, and most have cream, yellow, or tan bodies. Legs of duns and spinners are cream or yellow with characteristic darker banding. Males and females of the same species often vary considerably in color, sometimes necessitating two patterns. Few *Stenonema* species are found in the West. Many entomologists now place *S. fuscum,* or the gray fox, with *S. vicarium,* the March brown. Anglers call many of these species light cahills and cream cahills. Members can be important in late summer and early fall.

Species previously listed in the interpunctatum group of this genus are now included in a new genus, *Stenacron.* Six important members of *Stenonema* follow:

Stenonema fuscum (E & M)
Stenonema ithaca (E)
Stenonema luteum (E & M)
Stenonema pulchellum (E & M)
Stenonema vicarium (E & M)
Stenonema modestum (E)

2. Genus *Stenacron*

This Genus holds many of the "light cahills." Most species range from 8 to 13 mm long. Most appear from late May through June and July in early evening. Body colors range from yellow to orange. Here are three of the more common *Stenacron* species:

Stenacron interpunctatum canadense (E & M)
Stenacron interpunctatum heterotarsale (E & M)
Stenacron interpunctatum interpunctatum (E & M)

3. Genus *Heptagenia*

Duns of this genus often escape rapidly from the surface when emerging and, therefore, many duns are of questionable value to the angler. Spinners sometimes take on more importance because they characteristically rest on the surface while depositing eggs. Duns and spinners usually have bodies of cream, pale yellow, or tan, often with an olive cast. Some Western species like *Heptagenia solitaria* are more important than their Eastern counterparts because of their size and type of emergence. Fishermen imitate many species of this genus with the Pale Evening Dun or Gray Fox. Entomologists have recently placed some *Heptagenia* species in *Leucrota* and *Nixie*. Some of the more common *Heptagenia* species include these three:

Heptagenia pulla (E & M)
Heptagenia solitaria (W)
Heptagenia elegantula (W)

4. Genus *Leucrocuta*

This genus includes members previously included in *Heptagenia*, which are now included in this genus and in *Nixie*. The naturals are usually cream colored and range in size from 6 to 12 mm. Most species can be copied by a Pale Evening Dun. Members of *Leucrocuta* usually appear from late May through the summer. Some of the more common species follow:

> *Leucrocuta aphrodite (E)*
> *Leucrocuta hebe (E & M)*
> *Leucrocuta juno (E)*
> *Leucrocuta marginalis (E & M)*
> *Leucrocuta minerva (E)*

5. Genus *Epeorus*

These nymphs often inhabit fast, shallow sections of pure, cool water. Duns emerge near the bottom of the stream or river, and wet flies work well during the emergence of these species. These species are most important in fast-flowing trout streams of the East and West. Some species have cream to pink bodies while others have tan to gray bodies. Some common *Epeorus* species include these six:

> *Epeorus albertae (W)*
> *Epeorus longimanus (W)*
> *Epeorus deceptivus (W)*
> *Epeorus grandis (W)*
> *Epeorus pleuralis (E)*
> *Epeorus vitreus (E & M)*

6. Genus *Rhithrogena*

Nymphs of these species usually cling to gravel in a fairly fast current. Adults are often dark tan, dark gray, or dark brown. Hatches often occur during late morning and early afternoon. The species can be locally important, especially on Western waters. The fore wings of spinners are anastomosed (netlike) in the stigmatic area. Spinners are usually dark brown or gray. Some common *Rhithrogena* species include these four:

> *Rhithrogena morrisoni (W)*
> *Rhithrogena futilis (W)*
> *Rhithrogena hageni (W)*
> *Rhithrogena undulata (M & W)*

7. Genus *Cinygma*

Cinygma dimicki, which outwardly resembles *Stenonema fuscum,* is important on some Western streams.

8. Genus *Cinygmula*

Species of this genus are often in moderate to small streams that are relatively cool. The wings of most members have a decided gray or yellow cast. The wings of the spinners are not anastomosed, in contrast to *Cinygma* and *Rhithrogena.* Two common *Cinygmula* species follow:

> *Cinygmula ramaleyi (W)*
> *Cinygmula reticulata (W)*

L. Family Metretopodidae.

Nymphs of this family are streamlined and fairly large, ranging from 9 to 16 mm. *Siphloplecton* adults have heavily spotted fore wings. Not until Greg Hoover identified *S. basale* on Clarks Creek did I realize that this species emerged in heavy enough numbers to create a fishable hatch. Anglers often confuse this mid-to-late-April hatch with the hendrickson or march brown. Called the great speckled olive dun, *S. basale* produces fishable hatches in April. There's only one common species:

> *Siphloplecton basale (E&M)*

M. Family Baetiscidae

These two-tailed adults are noted for their humpbacked appearance. Most are 8 to 12 mm long. The Genus *Baetisca* produces hatches on some of the more acidic streams in the Northeast and Midwest. Nymphs often crawl onto rocks to emerge, similar to *Isonychia*. One of the most common species is *Baetisca laurentina* (E&M).

The number of tails a mayfly species has is helpful in identifying it. All mayflies have two or three tails, and although there are a few exceptions like *Ephoron*, all species of a genus have the same number of tails. Here is a list of mayfly genera according to the number of tails each has:

Two Tails			
Baetis	Cinygmula	Heptagenia	
Callibaetis	Hexagenia	Siphlonurus	
Cinygma	Epeorus	Isonychia	Stenacron
	Ephoron (male)	Litobrancha	Stenonema

Three Tails			
Caenis	Leptophlebia	Attenella	
Ephemera	Paraleptophlebia	Eurylophella	
Ephemerella	Anthopotamanthus	Serratella	
Ephoron (female)	Tricorythodes	Dannella	
	Drunella		

Tails are extremely fragile, so make certain when examining mayflies that none of them have broken.

Caddis flies

Up to this point we have mentioned little about the caddis flies. This order, Trichoptera, might be able to withstand a greater degree of pollution than some other orders of aquatic insects, especially mayflies. You'll find caddis flies emerging from March through November, and on many streams and rivers you'll find a surge of caddis activity from late April until mid May. In the Far

West you'll find Black Caddis, or as some call it, the "Mother's Day Caddis," on rivers from early to late May. The Bitterroot River in Montana, the Yakima River in central Washington, and many others hold this downwing in mid-May. Usually the early mayfly hatches in the East and Midwest like the blue quill, quill gordon, and hendrickson have ended by early May.

Unlike the mayfly, the caddis goes through a complete metamorphosis. It has a pupal stage, which lasts a couple of weeks. After the male and female mate, the female dives underwater and deposits the eggs. Some species drop the fertilized eggs in flight like many mayflies, while others actually swim underwater to place them. The eggs develop in a few weeks, and the newly hatched larvae build cases to protect their fragile bodies.

Unlike the mayfly nymph, which has a hard outer covering called an exoskeleton, the caddis larva has a thin integument covering the greater part of the body. Only the legs and head of the larva are heavily protected (sclerotized), because these parts usually extend from the case.

To construct a covering, the larva uses sand, pebbles, stones, sticks, or any number of things found in a stream. Each genus is usually specific in selecting building materials. In some genera, however, the larva moves about freely and has no case. An example of the latter is the green caddis (*Rhyacophila lobifera*). Imitations of this larva usually work well.

Most species, however, do build cases. The grannom (*Brachycentrus fuliginosus*) and related species builds its case of sticks, usually in backwater areas of streams. Another important caddis, the dark blue sedge (*Psilotreta frontalis*), found most often in fast water, builds its case of sand and pebbles. Anglers and ento-mologists call genera like *Hydropsyche* and *Chimarra* "net spinners" because they build small fibrous nets to collect food.

As the larva feeds and grows, it adds to its case. About two weeks before it emerges as an adult, it goes into a pupal stage. In this stage, the case (sometimes called a cocoon) is almost completely closed except for a small hole that allows some water to enter. During this stage the adult develops. After about two weeks, the pupa, encased in a protective membrane, swims to the surface. For a split second in this emerging stage the pupa is defenseless. Trout seem to recognize the extreme vulnerability of the pupa and chase this stage much more than the adult. At the surface, it breaks the covering membrane and flies to the shore. You can usually tell that a hatch has just occurred when you see these transparent pupal cases floating in the water.

Adults usually live longer than mayfly adults, perhaps a week or more. Since adults that have just emerged are capable of mating; no change occurs from dun to spinner as it does in mayflies. At the time of emergence and during the egg-laying process, trout seize emerging adults eagerly. The wings of the adult are folded back over the body in a tent-like fashion, so the wings of your imitations, whether wet or dry, should be shaped similarly. Wet fly patterns imitating the emerging caddis perform exceptionally well during a hatch. You'll find pattern descriptions for the caddis flies in Chapter 10. In the following pages you'll find some of the more important families, genera, and species of caddis flies.

A. Family Brachycentridae
Genus *Brachycentrus*
This genus contains the famous hatches, called grannoms and American sedges, so common on many waters across the United States. Some of the heaviest hatches occur in late April and May. Others appear in the West in July and August. Body colors range from dark brown to cream to black. The grannom hatch on Penns Creek in the East (*B. solomoni*) is blizzard-like, and *B. occidentalis* creates great hatches in the West in early May.

Some of the more important species include these five:

Brachycentrus fuliginosus (E&M)

Brachycentrus solomoni (E&M)

Brachycentrus numerosus (E&M)

Brachycentrus americanus (E&M)

Brachycentrus occidentalis (M&W)

B. Family Rhyacophilidae

These are fairly large larvae ranging from 10 to 25 mm. The main genus of this family is *Rhyacophila*.

1. Genus *Rhyacophila*

This genus includes many important free-swimming caddis. These larvae build no case or shelter until they go into the pupal stage. Here they often build a case of stones. To offset their lack of a shelter, these caddis flies have strong legs and a large anal hook. The most common body color of the larvae is green. Fly-fishers commonly call the adults of this genus, green caddis flies. Six common species follow:

Rhyacophila lobifera (E&M)

Rhyacophila grandis (W)

Rhyacophila basalis (W)

Rhyacophila fuscula (E&M)

Rhyacophila angelita (W)

Rhyacophila coloradensis (W)

C. Family Hydropsychidae

1. Genus *Hydropsyche*

Unlike most other emerging caddis pupae, members of this genus take an inordinate amount of time to escape from their pupal shuck when emerging. Anglers often refer to these adults as spotted sedges. A common Eastern species, *Hydropsyche slossanae*, has now been placed in the Genus *Symphitopsyche*. Here are four common

Hydropsyche species:

> *Hydropsyche alternans (E)*
> *Hydropsyche simulans (E&M)*
> *Hydropsyche betteni (E&M)*
> *Hydropsyche occidentalis (W)*

2. Genus *Symphitopsyche*

The common spotted sedge belongs to this new genus. Members range from 8 to 15 mm. Adults appear often in late May and early June. Adults often have tan or cream body colors. One common species is *Symphitopsyche slossanae* (E&M).

3. Genus *Cheumatopsyche*

You'll find these small sedges common across the United States. One species, *Cheumatopsyche gracilis*, is found in all three regions.

D. Family Philopotamidae

Members of this family spin fingernets. The larvae range in size from 9 to 12 mm. One genus, *Chimarra*, is important.

1. Genus *Chimarra*

This genus contains some important early-season emergers like the little black caddis (*Chimarra aterrima*). Larvae most often are found in riffled areas. Some look bright orange and can be matched with Larva Lace bodies. Two important species follow:

> *Chimarra aterrima (E&M)*
> *Chimarra obscura (E&M)*

E. Family Limnephilidae

This large family contains many genera, which range in size from 6 to 30 mm. The famous caddis of the West Coast, the October Caddis, is a member. Members construct true tube cases of plant material or rock particles.

1. Genus *Dicosmoecus*

Members of this genus produce really great hatches in the West. Oregon's McKenzie River and Washington's Yakima River are only two of dozens of important rivers where you'll find these caddis flies emerging in September and October. Adults can be as large as 30 mm. Three common species follow:

Dicosmoecus gilvipes (W)
Dicosmoecus jucundus (W)
Dicosmoecus atripes (W)

2. Genus Pycnopsyche

Members make their cases out of sticks and leaf material. Their size ranges from 15 to 25 mm. Many emerge in late summer and early fall. Body colors range from ginger to brown. Anglers call *P. scrabnipennis* the giant red sedge, and two important species follow:

Pycnopsyche scrabnipennis (E&M)
Pycnopsyche lepida (E&M)

F. Family Odontoceridae

This family builds cylindrical stone-fragment cases. When the adults emerge in May and June, they often do so in unbelievable numbers, so several of these species are important to copy. *P. frontalis*, called the dark blue sedge, appears in early June and *P. labida*, called by locals the green egg sac caddis emerges in heavy numbers in early and mid May in the Northeast. Here are two common species:

Psilotreta frontalis (E)
Psilotreta labida (E)

Eastern and Midwestern Hatches

Scientific and Common Name C = Caddis fly S = Stonefly	Emergence Date (dates are extremely variable)	Time of Day Largest Hatches Emerge (Duns) or Flights Take Place (Spinners)	Hook Size
Baetis tricaudatus **Dun: Little Blue Dun** **Spinner: Rusty Spinner**	April 1	10:00 a.m.-6:00 p.m.	18 or 20
Strophopteryx fasciata (S) **Early Brown Stonefly**	April 10	Afternoon	14
Paraleptophlebia adoptiva **Dun: Dark Blue Quill** **Spinner: Dark Brown Spinner**	April 15	11:00 a.m.-4:00 p.m. Heaviest: 2:00-4:00 p.m. Spinner: 4:00-7:00 p.m.	18
Epeorus pleuralis **Dun: Quill Gordon** **Spinner: Red Quill Spinner**	April 18	1:00-3:00 p.m. Spinner: 11:30 a.m.-2:00 p.m.	14
Ameletus ludens **Dun: Slate Drake** **Spinner: Quill Gordon Spinner**	April 18	Afternoon	14
Chimarra atterima **Little Black Caddis**	April 20	11:00 a.m.-6:00 p.m.	16
Ephemerella subvaria **Male dun: Red Quill** **Female dun: Hendrickson** **Spinner: Red Quill**	April 20	2:00-4:00 p.m. Spinner: 3:00-8:00 p.m	12-16

Leptophlebia cupida	**April 27**	2:00-4:00 p.m.	*12 or 14*
Dun: Black Quill		*Spinner: 1:00-6:00 p.m.*	
Spinner: Early Brown Spinner			

Brachycentrus	**April 27**	3:00-7:00 p.m.	*14*
fuliginosus **(C)**			
Grannom			

Isoperla signata(S)	**May 8**	*Afternoon*	*12 or 14*
Light Stonefly			

Ephemerella rotunda	**May 8**	2:00-8:00 p.m.	*14 or 16*
Dun: Sulphur		*Spinner: 6:00-8:00 p.m.*	
Spinner: Sulphur Spinner			

Rhyacophila	**May 10**	4:00-9:00 p.m.;	*14*
lobifera **(C)**		*later (around dusk)*	
Green Caddis		*in June and July*	

Stenonema fuscum	**May 15**	*Dun emerges*	*12*
Dun: Gray Fox		*sporadically throughout;*	
Spinner: Ginger Quill Spinner		*chance of heaviest*	
Quill Spinner		*hatches 4:00-8:30 p.m.*	
		Spinner: 7:00-8:00 p.m.	

Ephemerella	**May 18**	8:00 p.m.	*14 or 16*
septentrionalis			
Dun: Pale Evening Dun			
Spinner: Pale Evening Dun			

Leucrocuta	**May18**	8:00 p.m.	*16*
aphrodite			
Dun: Pale Evening Dun			
Spinner: Pale Evening Dun			

Ephemerella invaria	**May 20**	3:00-8:00 p.m.	*16 or 18*
Dun: Pale Evening Dun		*Spinner: 7:00-8:30 p.m.*	
Spinner: Pale Evening Spinner			

Stenonema vicarium	**May 20**	10:00 a.m.-7:00 p.m.	*12*
Dun: American March Brown		*Spinner: 8:00 p.m.*	
Spinner: Great Red Spinner			

Hydropsyche *symphitopsyche* (C) **Spotted Sedge**	*May 23*	1:00-6:00 p.m.	14 *or* 16
Eurylophella *bicolor* **Dun: Chocolate Dun** **Spinner: Chocolate Spinner**	*May 25*	*Late morning and* *early afternoon*	16
Stenonema ithaca **Dun: Light Cahill** **Spinner: Light Cahill**	*May 25*	*Evening*	12 *or* 14
Isonychia bicolor **Dun: Slate Drake** **Spinner: White-gloved Howdy**	*May 25*	*Evening*	12
Epeorus vitreus **Male Dun: Light Cahill** **Female Dun: Pink Cahill** **Spinner: Salmon Spinner**	*May 25*	*Evening*	14
Stenacron *interpunctatum* **Dun: Light Cahill** **Spinner: Light Cahill**	*May 25*	*Evening*	14
Stenacron *canadense* **Dun: Light Cahill** **Spinner: Light Cahill**	*May 25*	*Sporadic during day* *but mainly 6:00-8:30 p.m.* *Spinner: 7:00-9:00 p.m.*	12 *or* 14
Litobrancha *recurvata* **Dun: Dark Green Drake** **Spinner: Brown Drake**	*May 25*	1:00-8:00 p.m. *Spinner: 7:00 p.m.*	8 *or* 10
Ephemera simulans **Dun: Brown Drake** **Spinner: Brown Drake**	*May 25*	8:00 p.m.	10 *or* 12

Ephemera guttulata	May 25	8:00 p.m.	*8 or 10*
Dun: Green Drake			
Spinner: Coffin Fly			

Drunella cornuta	May 26	*Sporadic during day*	*14*
Dun: Blue-Winged Olive Dun		*spurt at 11:00-12:00 noon*	
Spinner: Dark Olive Spinner		*Spinner: 7:00-9:00 p.m.*	

Serratella deficiens	May 26	*Afternoon and*	*20*
Dun: Dark Blue Quill		*evening*	
Spinner: Blue Quill Spinner			

Ephemerella	May 30	*Afternoon (early*	*14 or 16*
needhami		*and morning (late)*	
Dun: Chocolate Dun		*Spinner: afternoon and evening*	
Spinner: Chocolate Spinner			

Ephemerella	June 1	8:00 p.m.	*16 or 18*
dorothea			
Dun: Pale Evening Dun			
Spinner: Pale Evening Dun			

Paraleptophlebia mollis	June 3	*10:00 a.m.-4:00 p.m.*	*18*
Dun: Dark Blue Quill			
Male spinner: Jenny Spinner			
Female spinner: Dark Brown Spinner			

Paraleptophlebia	June 5	*Early morning to*	*18 or 20*
strigula (M)		*midafternoon*	
Dun: Dark Blue Quill			
Male spinner: Jenny Spinner			
Female spinner: Dark Brown Spinner			

Drunella	June5	*Sporadic during*	*14 or 16*
attenuata		*day often with a*	
Dun: Blue-Winged Olive Dun		*heavy burst at 11:00 a.m.*	
Spinner: Dark Olive Spinner		*Spinner: evening*	

Psilotreta	June 8	8:00 p.m.	*12*
frontalis (C)			
Dark Blue Sedge			

Drunella	*June 15*	Morning and after-	16
cornutella		noon	
Dun: Blue-Winged Olive		*Spinner: evening*	
Spinner: Dark Olive Spinner			

Leptophlebia	*June 9*	11:00 a.m.	14 or 16
johnsoni		*Spinner: evening*	
Dun: Iron Blue Dun			
Male spinner: Jenny Spinner			
Female spinner: Blue Quill Spinner Cahill			

Dannella simplex	*June 15*	Morning (sometimes	20
Dun: Blue-Winged Olive Dun		into afternoon	
Spinner: Dark Olive Spinner		*Spinner: evening*	

Stenacron	*June 15*	Evening	14
heterotarsale			
Dun: Light Cahill			
Spinner: Light Cahill			

Leucrocuta marginalis	*June 15*	8:00 p.m.	12
Dun: Light Cahill			
Spinner: Olive Cahill Spinner			

Stenonema pulchellum	*June 15*	Sporadic, around	12
Dun: Cream Cahill		midday to evening	
Spinner: Cream Cahill Spinner		*Spinner: evening*	

Ephemeravaria	*June 22*	8:00-9:15 p.m.	10 or 12
Dun: Yellow Drake			
Spinner: Yellow Drake			

Leucrocuta hebe	*June 22*	8:00 p.m.	16
Dun: Pale Evening Dun			
Spinner: Pale Evening Dun			

Paraleptophlebia	*June 25*	Sporadic during day	18
guttata		*Spinner: morning and afternoon*	
Dun: Dark Blue Quill			
Male spinner: Jenny Spinner			
Female spinner: Dark Brown Spinner			

Anthopotamanthus	*June 28*	9:00 p.m.	12
distinctus			

Dun: Golden Drake
Spinner: Golden Spinner

Tricorythodes	*July 15*	7:00-9:00 a.m.	24
stygiatus		*Spinner: 8:00-11:00 a.m.*	

Dun: Pale Olive Dun
Female spinner: Reverse Jenny Spinner
Male spinner: Dark Brown Spinner

Tricorythodes	*July 23*	7:00-9:00 a.m.	24
attratus		*Spinner: 8:00 a.m.*	

Dun: Pale Olive Dun
Male spinner: Dark Brown Spinner
Female spinner: Reverse Jenny Spinner

Ephoron leukon	*August 15*	7:00 p.m.	12-16

Dun: White Mayfly
Spinner: White Mayfly

Hexagenia	*August 15*	8:00 p.m.	6 or 8
atrocaudata		*Spinner: 6:00-7:00 p.m.*	

Dun: Big Slate Drake
Spinner: Dark Rusty Spinner

Baetis tricaudatus	*September 1*	10:00 a.m.-6:00 p.m.	18
		Spinner: early afternoon and evening	

Dun: Little Blue Dun
Spinner: Rusty Spinner

Isonychia bicolor	*September 10*	Afternoon	12

Dun: Slate Drake
Spinner: White-gloved Howdy

Acentrella carolina	*September 15*	Afternoon and	22
Dun: Blue Dun		evening	

Spinner: Rusty Spinner

Western Hatches

Rhithrogena morrisoni	*February 25*	Afternoon	14
Dun: Western March Brown **Spinner: Dark Tan Spinner**			

Baetis tricaudatus **Dun: Little Blue Dun** **Spinner: Light Rusty Spinner**	*April through* *October*	Morning and afternoon *Spinner: early morning and evening*	*16 or 20*

Baetis intermedius **Dun: Little Blue Dun** **Spinner: Dark Rusty Spinner**	*April through* *October*	Morning and afternoon *Spinner: early morning and evening*	*18 or 20*

Ephemera simulans **Dun: Brown Drake** **Spinner: Brown Drake**	*May 25*	Evening	*10 or 12*

Ephemerella inermis **Dun: Pale Morning Dun** **Spinner: Pale Morning Spinner**	*May 25*	Morning, afternoon and evening *Spinner: Morning and evening*	*16 or 18*

Pteronarcys californica (S) **Salmon Fly**	*May through July*	Emergence often occurs in the morning; egg laying can occur almost any time of the day or evening	6

Brachycentrus species (C) *Dark Gray Caddis;* **Dark Brown Caddis** **Black Caddis-Grannom**	*April through* *October*	Egg laying can occur almost any time of day—sometimes in the morning on colder streams, but often in the evening on many streams	12-16

Rhyacophila species (C) **Green Caddis**	*May through* *October*	Variable	12-16

Baetis bicaudatus **Dun: Pale Olive Dun** **Spinner: Light Rusty Spinner**	*June through* *October*	Morning and afternoon *Morning evening*	20

Acroneuria pacifica (S)	*June and July*	*Variable*	6
Willow Fly			

Callibaetis	*June through*	*Late Morning*	14
americanus	*September*		
Dun: Speckle-winged Dun			
Spinner: Speckle-winged Spinner			

Paraleptophlebia	*June 1*	*Morning and afternoon*	16
heteronea			
Dun: Blue Quill			
Spinner: Dark Brown Spinner			

Cinygmula ramaleyi	*Late May and*	*Late morning*	16 or 18
Dun: Dark Red Quill	*early June*	*Spinner: midday*	
Spinner: Red Quill Spinner			

Drunella	*June 5*	*Late morning*	10 or 12
grandis		*and afternoon*	
Dun: Western Green Drake		*Spinner: evening*	
Spinner: Great Red Spinner			

Serratella	*June 5*	*Midday*	16 or 18
tibialis		*Spinner: evening*	
Dun: Red Quill			
Spinner: White-gloved Howdy			

Hexagenia limbata	*June 12*	*Dusk and later*	8
Dun: Michigan Caddis			
Spinner: Michigan Spinner			

Epeorus longimanus	*June 12*	*Late morning and afternoon*	16
Dun: Quill Gordon		*Spinner: afternoon*	
Spinner: Red Quill Spinner			

Drunella doddsi	*June 15*	*Late morning and*	10
Dun: Western Green Drake		*afternoon*	
Spinner: Great Red Spinner			

Drunella *flavilinea* **Dun: Blue-Winged Olive Dun** **Spinner: Dark Olive Spinner**	*June 15*	Morning and evening *(heaviest hatch seems to appear in* *the evening)*	*14 or 16*
Heptagenia *elegantula* **Dun: Pale Evening Dun** **Spinner: Pale Evening Spinner**	*June 20*	*Late afternoon* *and evening* *Spinner: evening*	*14*
Baetis hageni **Dun: Dark Brown Dun** **Spinner: Dark Brown Spinner**	*June 20*	*Late morning, afternoon,* *and early evening* *Spinner: earlymorning and evening*	*20*
Ephemerella *infrequens* **Dun: Pale Morning Dun** **Spinner: Rusty Spinner**	*July 1*	*Late morning and* *afternoon* *Spinner: morning and evening*	*18*
Paraleptophlebia *memorialis* **Dun: Dark Blue Quill** **Spinner: Dark Brown Spinner**	*July 1*	*Morning and afternoon*	*18*
Rhithrogena futilis **Dun: Quill Gordon** **Spinner: Quill Gordon**	*July 1*	*Late morning and* *afternoon*	*12*
Cinygmula *reticulata* **Dun: Pale Brown Dun** **Spinner: Dark Rusty Spinner**	*July 5*	*Late morning* *and afternoon* *Spinner: early morning*	*14*
Paraleptophlebia *vaciva* **Dun: Dark Blue Quill** **Spinner: Dark Brown Spinner**	*July 5*	*Morning and* *afternoon*	*18*
Heptagenia *solitaria* **Dun: Gray Fox** **Spinner: Ginger Quill Spinner**	*July 5*	*Late afternoon* *and evening* *Spinner: late morning and evening*	*12 or 16*

Epeorus albertae	July 5	Evening	12
Dun: Pink Lady 17			
Spinner: Salmon Spinner			17

Paraleptophlebia debilis	July 5	Morning and afternoon	18
Dun: Dark Blue Quill			
Spinner: Dark Brown Spinner			

Siphlonurus occidentalis	July 5	*Late morning and afternoon; heaviest appear around 3:00 p.m.*	10 or 12
Dun: Gray Drake			
Spinner: Brown Quill Spinner		*Spinner: morning and evening; evening seems to be heavier*	

Cinygma dimicki	July 5	Evening	12
Dun: Light Cahill			
Spinner: Light Cahill			

Ephemerella hecuba	July 5	Evening	10
Dun: Great Red Quill			
Spinner: Great Brown Spinner			

Rhithrogena hageni	July 10	*Late morning and afternoon*	12 or 14
Dun: Pale Brown Dun			
Spinner: Dark Tan Spinner		*Spinner: morning and evening*	

Ameletus cooki	July 10	*Late morning and afternoon*	14
Dun: Dark Brown Dun			
Spinner: Dark Brown Spinner		*Spinner: early afternoon*	

Rhithrogena undulata	July 10	*Morning and afternoon* *Spinner: afternoon and evening*	12
Dun: Quill Gordon			
Spinner: Red Quill or Dark Red Quill			

Tricorythodes minutus	July 15	Morning	24
Dun: Pale Olive Dun			
Male spinner: Reverse Jenny Spinner			
Female spinner: Dark Brown Spinner			

Drunella	**August 1**	Midday	12
coloradensis		Spinner: evening	
Dun: Dark Olive Dun			
Spinner: Dark Brown Spinner			

Ephoron album	**August 15**	Evening	12
Dun: White Mayfly			
Spinner: White Mayfly			

Paraleptophlebia	**September 10**	Morning and	18
bicornuta		afternoon	
Dun: Dark Blue Quill			
Spinner: Dark Brown Spinner			

Isonychia bicolor

Chapter 4
Patterns for Fishing Underneath

When I wrote *Meeting and Fishing the Hatches* in 1976, I reported that I preferred using dry flies and watching the action unfold on top. For more than four decades I almost shunned wet flies for action on the surface. Sure, I used heavy nymphs, wet flies, streamers, and bucktails early in the season and under high-water conditions. But as soon as water temperatures rose into the mid-fifties and the water dropped, I quickly opted for

Craig Josephson releases an Eastern brown trout taken on a size 12 Bead-head Pheasant Tail Nymph.

floating patterns. Something changed for me about ten years ago. I began using wet flies like the Bead-heads and midge pupae when I saw no action on top. Guess what? My catch increased twofold and threefold with these sinking patterns—even more in late fall. Sure, I still prefer fishing a great hatch with a dry fly, but if I see no action, I'll quickly resort to underwater patterns.

I can vividly remember that trip to the Little Colorado River with Craig Josephson. Not once during six hours of fly-fishing did we use a dry fly. Every one of the thirty trout Craig and I caught that day took a subsurface pattern. Contrast that to a few years ago and you would have seen me using a floating pattern and catching probably less than ten trout on it.

We'll look here in this chapter at some dynamite patterns that you should definitely include in your arsenal of weapons to catch trout. The Bead-head Pheasant Tail Nymph merits my first choice when there's no hatch to match. You'll find standard nymph patterns to match the hatches in Chapter 10.

How to Fish the Patterns

In Chapter 2, I said you can fish a pattern on top, near the surface, underneath, and on the bottom. How you achieve the fly location varies with your preferences as an angler. Some anglers prefer fishing on or near the bottom with no strike indicators. Others use strike indicators almost all the time. Still others fish wet flies across and downstream, fishing them above the bottom, and still others fish just under the surface, or on top. The more adaptable you are as a fly-fisher the better results you'll obtain. All of the patterns discussed in this chapter work well on or near the bottom. I recommend you use one of the tandem methods I talked about in Chapter 2.

If you use the Bead-head Pheasant Tail Nymph as the point fly, try twitching it when you're ready to cast again. I can't count the number of times trout have hit this dynamite pattern just before I lifted it out of the water to cast again. Bryan Meck has also had this experience, and before each new cast he now purposely twitches or lifts the Bead-head slowly from the water in anticipation of a last-minute strike.

Tandem Connection

All patterns listed in this chapter make excellent point flies. In fact, the Bead-head Pheasant Tail Nymph along with the Green Weenie (discussed in Chapter 9) constitute my top two choices when no hatch appears. Tie both weighted patterns behind a size 12 or 14 Patriot or a long-shank size 12 Yellow Drake. Or if you prefer using just one pattern, tie a piece of fiber that I discussed in Chapter 2 as a strike indicator. Tie a three-inch piece of this floating fiber a couple feet above the wet fly. If you want the wet fly to go deeper, increase the distance between the indicator and the fly; shallower, decrease the distance.

If you expect to see a sulphur or pale morning dun hatch the day you're fishing, then you might want to try the Sulphur Emerger with a Sulphur dry fly. Conversely, most of the other emerger patterns work well when hatches they copy appear. Don't fish the emerger patterns quite as deep as the Bead-heads and the Green Weenie. Trout usually take emergers just under the surface.

We'll examine a series of underwater patterns that merit your careful consideration. All have produced under a variety of otherwise frustrating circumstances for me. As I almost continuously noted over the past two years, the Bead-head Pheasant Nymph has been my top fish catcher. If I see no hatch, I most often start with this pattern. In lakes and slow sections of rivers when I think I see trout rising to midges, I often start with an Emerging Pupa or a Stillborn Pupa. Both have produced from rivers like the Green in Utah, the Cache la Poudre in Colorado, the Little Colorado in Eagar, Arizona, and on many of Washington's high-desert lakes. On Eastern, Midwestern and many Western rivers I often rely on an Olive Shrimp.

Tucker Morris lands a Spruce Creek brown trout on a size 16 Bead-head Pheasant Tail Nymph.

The Bead-head Pheasant Tail Nymph

For weeks Walt Young and Steve Sywensky had boasted about a Bead-head pattern they used successfully on central Pennsylvania streams. Both tie flies professionally and Steve runs Flyfisher's Paradise, a shop near my home. Both said they picked up hundreds of streambred brown trout using the pattern on the often frustrating Spring Creek. Finally I had enough and asked Walt for a copy of his pattern.

Two months passed before I felt the need to test the pattern. In early October, Phil Hopersberger and I fished a section of the Bald Eagle below Milesburg, again in central Pennsylvania. For two hours neither of us had a strike on any of a number of wet and dry fly patterns we tried. Then, in a fit of frustration, I changed patterns—I switched to one of those Bead-heads that Walt Young handed me two months earlier, and I'll never be the same fly-fisherman again. That day the Bead-head changed my approach to fly-fishing forever.

On the second cast I saw a swirl. On the fifth cast I saw another swirl. I missed both trout so I added some weight just above the Bead-head so it would sink a bit deeper. After a few more casts a heavy streambred brown struck, and this time I hooked the fish. On the same stretch where I had just had two barren hours with several potentially productive patterns, I now caught a half dozen trout on the Bead-head. That pattern—that day—that experience—changed my thinking on fly-fishing for the rest of my life.

A weighted Bead-head Pheasant Tail Nymph really produces when used with a dry fly like the Patriot. On four trips to central Pennsylvania's lower Bald Eagle in October, I landed two sixteen-inch, two nineteen-inch and one twenty-three-inch brown trout on the Bead-head. That's on a heavily fished public stream where too many anglers have the philosophy of catch and kill.

If you use a Patriot and Bead-head, practice casting both patterns. After a few minutes you won't even notice that you're casting two patterns. Even with the weighted dropper fly and even if you extend the distance between the two patterns to five or six feet, you'll find them easy to cast. Just practice before you attempt casting the two flies; make certain you have a leader less than ten feet long; pull out plenty of fly line before you begin casting; and use a nine-foot fly rod requiring at least a five-weight line. If you follow these simple rules you should have no difficulty.

If you prefer to use only a Bead-head, or you prefer a more conventional strike indicator, then omit the dry fly. If you eliminate all strike indicators, fish the nymph on a sinking-tip fly line with a six-foot 4X wet fly leader. Vary the depth at which you fish the pattern. Try it from just under the surface down to the bottom. Usually a Bead-head just under the surface works better from April to October and one on or near the bottom works well from November through March when you'll usually find water temperatures under 50 degrees. On some of the patterns I add weight to the body. I code the patterns with different colors of tying thread so I know exactly how many wraps of .015 wire I've used.

I fished the Bead-head on the bottom without a dry fly just this past year on the Little Colorado River in Arizona. Craig Josephson and I fished with two Bead-head Wooly Buggers with Flashabou tails for two hours, and we caught maybe fifteen trout between us. What happened? We both lost the big Bead-head patterns on the bottom of this rocky river.

We switched for a while to Green Weenies and caught a couple more trout. I then changed patterns again and tied on a Bead-head Pheasant Tail Nymph. Within seconds I hooked a twenty-inch rainbow on the pattern. I yelled to Craig to come down to see the fish, but by the time he arrived I had already released it. I described where I caught the huge trout by tossing the pattern across and upriver a few feet. As I described the take on the previous cast, I had another strike, set the hook, and landed another trout close to twenty inches long. Two twenty-inch trout in two casts on that Bead-head! Wow! It really does produce on Western rivers.

Up to this point, all my stories about this fantastic pattern refer to a size 12 Bead-head, but don't overlook smaller sizes. Just this past year I gave a half dozen size 16 Bead-heads to Paul Antolosky to try on his trip to Montana's Missouri River near Craig. I mentioned in Chapter 2 that Paul prefers dry-fly fishing almost to the exclusion of wet flies. But Paul agreed to test the Bead-heads for me. You'll recall from that earlier chapter how well he did during a hatch of pale morning duns using a size 16 Bead-head Pheasant Tail Nymph.

The Bead-head has also produced a good number of strikes on Michigan's Père Marquette River. When all other wet fly patterns failed me, the Bead-head Pheasant Tail Nymph caught trout.

East, Midwest, and West—the Bead-head proved a top notch
fish catcher in all regions of the United States.

Bead-head Pheasant Tail Nymph
> HOOK: Tiemco 2457, #12-#16.
> THREAD: Dark brown.
> THORAX: Copper bead.
> TAIL: Five or six fibers from a ringneck pheasant tail.
> BODY: Continue winding the pheasant tail fibers used to tie
> in the tail up to the bead and tie in.
> HACKLE: Ten pheasant tail fibers.

Tying Notes: Take the hook and bend back the barb. Take a brass bead and place the larger hole on top and on the rim of a tube of fly-tying wax. Placing the bead on the wax makes it much easier to handle. (Otherwise you'll find it difficult to get the point of the hook through the hole in the bead.) Place the point of the hook through the large hole in the bead and move the bead up to the eye. If you want additional weight you can add five or ten wraps of .015 lead wire. Take the tail fibers and tie on the bend of the hook. Don't cut the butt sections off, but wind all of them up to the bead. Place a coat of head cement on the body to prevent the fibers from splitting. Add ten pheasant tail fibers on the right side as hackle and ten on the left. Distribute the fibers equally around the fly.

Caddis Larva

Jake Peppers lives in Townsend, Tennessee, and on almost any
day of the year you'll find him fly-fishing a stream or river near his
home. Jake lives near the Smoky Mountain National Forest and only
two hours away from a famous piece of trout water, the Hiwassee
River. Jake's caught plenty of big rainbows on these Tennessee
streams, and the Caddis Larva ranks as one of Jake's most popular
patterns on all these Volunteer State waters. Jake says he hasn't taken
it off his line in five straight months of fly-fishing. The white Caddis
Larva consistently out-produces any other pattern he uses.

Jake has found the pattern effective on large and small
streams. He's used it effectively on streams so small he had to feed
line under bushes. The first time Jake fished the Hiwassee River

Chapter 4 - Patterns for Fishing Underneath

**Bead-head Pheasant
Tail Nymph,
page 86**

**Caddis Larva,
page 87**

**Tony's Sulphur Nymph,
page 89**

**Gold Ribbed Hare's Ear
page 90**

**Bead-head
Peacock Nymph
page 91**

**Stonefly Nymph
page 92**

**Pteronarcys Nymph
page 96**

**Don's Damselfly Nymph
page 97**

**Damselfly Nymph
page 98**

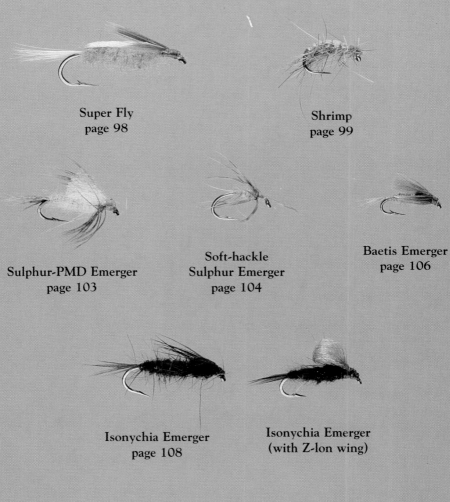

Super Fly
page 98

Shrimp
page 99

Sulphur-PMD Emerger
page 103

Soft-hackle
Sulphur Emerger
page 104

Baetis Emerger
page 106

Isonychia Emerger
page 108

Isonychia Emerger
(with Z-lon wing)

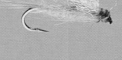

Hendrickson Emerger
page 109

White Fly Emerger
page 113

Emerging Green
Caddis Pupa
page 117

Gary LaFontaine's Emergent Pupa
page 117

Dry Emerger
page 117

Black Midge Pupa*
page 120

Stillborn Midge
page 122

*Enlarged to show detail.

Chapter 5 - Patterns for Fishing on Top -
Matching the Hatches

Black Caddis
page 157

**Charlie Meck's
Black Caddis**
page 158

Tan Caddis
page 159

Green Caddis
page 160

Simple Salmon
page 162

Patriot Downwing
page 163

Cream Caddis
page 164

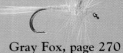

Gray Fox, page 270

Gray Fox
(parachute)

Green Drake
page 280

Western Green Drake
page 312

Light Cahill, page 275

Light Cahill
(parachute)

Sulphur
page 270

Pale Morning Dun
page 306

Chapter 5 - Patterns for Fishing on Top - Matching the Hatches (cont'd.)

Blue Winged Olive Dun
page 279

Blue Quill
page 264

Hendrickson
(with shuck)
page 267

Western March Brown
page 298

Dark Brown
Sparkle Dun
page 145

Dark Gray Midge*
page 147

*Enlarged to show detail.

Chapter 6 - Patterns That Copy Mayflies That Return to the Water

Patriot Spinner
page 168

Sulphur Spinner/Dun
page 168

Light Cahill Spinner
page 171

Sulphur/Pale Morning Spinner
page 173

Trico Cluster
page 177

Chapter 6 - Patterns That Copy Mayflies
That Return to the Water (cont'd.)

Quill Gordon Spinner
page 180

Rusty Spinner*
page 181

Sunken Trico Spinner*
page 186

*Enlarged to show detail.

Sunken Sulphur/Pale Morning Spinner
page 186

Sunken Dark Brown Spinner
page 186

Chapter 7 - Topwater Patterns When
There's No Hatch to Match

Patriot
page 197

Wulff Royal Coachman
page 200

Adams
page 202

Humpy
page 203

Trout Fin
page 204

Chapter 8 - Patterns That Copy
Land-Based Insects

Green Inchworm
page 210

Winged Ant*
page 211

* Enlarged to show detail.

Deer-Hair Ant
page 212

Poly Ant
page 212

Black Ant
page 212

LeTort Cricket
page 215

Gypsy Moth Caterpillar
page 217

White Moth
page 222

Chapter 9 - Larger Underwater Patterns

Green Weenie
page 228

San Juan Red Worm
page 229

Wooly Bugger
page 231

Fish Fly Larva
page 231

Bead-head Wooly Bugger
page 234

Muddler Minnow
page 235

Peacock Lady
page 237

Lady Ghost
page 239

tailwater he caught five heavy trout on the pattern.

Jake adds a little weight to the pattern and fishes it up and across stream. When the fly drifts below him, he uses the Leisenring lift and gets plenty of strikes that way.

Using the latex makes an effective, lifelike caddis larva body. If your stream holds a good number of caddis hatches, you've got to try this effective pattern. Just look at a stick caddis. Remove the larva from its shell and you'll see how adequately the Caddis Larva copies the natural.

Caddis Larva
> HOOK: Tiemco, 2457, sizes 12 to 20
> THREAD: Black
> BODY: Cream latex cut in a 1/2-inch strip and wrapped around the hook. After tying off the latex at the eye, use a black permanent marking pen and darken the front 1/6 of the latex.

Sulphur Nymph
It's been more than twenty-five years since I fished my first sulphur hatch on the Little Juniata River in central Pennsylvania. That early-May afternoon brought on an unexpected four-hour hatch of mayflies the likes of which I had never experienced before and probably never will again. But even with the heavy hatch and many struggling sulphurs on the surface, few trout rose. I can still remember my dismay when so few trout surfaced to this bountiful supply of surface food. After an hour of fishing dry flies I gave up in disgust and tied on a weighted Sulphur Nymph. I cast the pattern upriver, fished it near or on the bottom, then lifted it toward the surface when it drifted below me. That method of lifting the nymph up off the bottom and moving it toward the surface copied sulphur naturals emerging. For more than two hours that afternoon I caught trout on that pat-

tern. Dozens of trout took the nymph when few struck at the dry fly.

Even though I detested using wet flies at the expense of floating patterns, I learned an important lesson that afternoon: During a hatch—or for that matter at any time—if you don't see any action on the surface, try something underneath.

But that hatch appeared almost thirty years ago. And with the tandem method, or, as I called it in *Great Rivers—Great Hatches*, the "bi-cycle," you can use a dry fly with the Sulphur Nymph. I call it "bi-cycle" because with the tandem setup you can fish the dun on top and the nymph or emerger underneath. Whether trout feed on the top, just under the surface, or near the bottom, you'll be able to reach them with the bi-cycle.

The same fly—the Sulphur Nymph—performs well on Western waters during a pale morning dun hatch. Washington's Yakima River holds a respectable pale morning dun hatch. Craig Shuman and Jack Mitchell drifted Dave Engerbretson and me down the river for five straight days. On the Yakima the pale morning dun begins hatching in late May. I noticed several stillborns near the surface and grabbed one. I looked at the dark brown body and speculated that the same pattern I used for the sulphur hatch in the East and Midwest would work here. I tied a Sulphur dry and Sulphur Nymph on the tandem rig and began casting. For the next hour or two I landed a half dozen native Yakima rainbows on that rig. Five hit the nymph and one took the dry fly.

Tony Kibelbek practices dentistry in central Pennsylvania, and when he's not working you'll find Tony fly-tying or fly-fishing all over the United States. An accomplished angler and fly-tier, over the years Tony has nevertheless experienced many frustrating moments during the sulphur hatch with an ordinary Sulphur Nymph pattern. Because of these barren fishing trips Tony has developed his own Sulphur Nymph pattern. This pattern has proved a top fish catcher for Tony. He uses the pattern before and during the sulphur hatch. He often uses the nymph on the tandem rig with a Sulphur dry fly. If you get plenty of refusals with an ordinary Sulphur Nymph, try this productive new nymph imitation.

Tony's Sulphur Nymph
>   HOOK: Mustad 9671, sizes 14 to 18
>   THREAD: Pale olive thread
>   TAIL-BODY: Brown pheasant tail fibers tied near bend.
>   Usually 10-12 fibers over top of a body of dubbed amber
>   poly.
>   HACKLE: Lemon or beige wood duck fibers tied pointing
>   forward.

Tying Notes: Tie in the pheasant tail at the bend of the hook. Cut off a few of the tails so you have only four or five remaining. Don't cut off the butts of these tails—they'll become the dark back of the nymph. Dub in the poly body, then cover the back with the pheasant tail butts. Tie off at the eye and cut off the excess pheasant tails. Tie in the wood duck fibers and extend them out over the eye. Pull half to the right and the other half to the left side and secure with several turns of the thread.

Gold-Ribbed Hare's Ear

When you talk about effective nymph patterns, be sure to include the Gold-Ribbed Hare's Ear. I'm certain it's productive because it copies so many natural nymphs. Just look at how this nymph performs during a sulphur hatch. Look at the pattern and look at the natural and you see a striking resemblance. Examine a gray fox nymph and again you'll see a striking resemblance between that natural and the Gold Ribbed Hare's Ear. In a size 18 or 20 the Hare's Ear even works well during one of the many *Baetis* hatches. You'll find great *Baetis* hatches below many tailwaters, but the mother of all *Baetis* hatches appears on the San Juan in New Mexico. For about seven months of the year you'll see little blue-winged olives emerging. Trout feed on these emerging nymphs so much that they really key in on them. Some of the best hatches of these important little mayflies occur in March and April and again in September, October and November on the San Juan River. A size 18 Hare's Ear works well when these nymphs appear.

Add a bead head to the Hare's Ear and you might even find it more productive.

Gold Ribbed Hare's Ear
>HOOK: Mustad 9671, size 12 to 20
>THREAD: Brown
>TAIL: Light brown
>BODY: Medium grayish brown rabbit hair from the face
>   dubbed and ribbed with fine gold wire
>WING: Brown mottled turkey
>HACKLE: Dark grouse

Peacock Nymph
>For more than forty years George Harvey and Ralph Dougherty have fly-fished fabled Spruce Creek. They're two of the best fly-fishers I've had the pleasure to know. One day while the two fished together George kept landing one trout after another while Ralph didn't do nearly as well. That morning George caught more than twenty trout on his secret pattern. Finally, Ralph had enough and asked George what pattern caught so many trout. George showed him a nymph with a tail of gray hackle fibers, a body of peacock with a back of dark gray, a body ribbed with fine gold wire, and dark gray hackle for legs. George appropriately calls it a Peacock Nymph and it has become one of his all-time favorite wet fly patterns.

I recently tied the same pattern but added a bead head. I tested the pattern on Fishing Creek in central Pennsylvania. I tied a size 12 Patriot as the lead fly and fished it in a fast, deep riffle, and in two hours of mid-July morning fishing the Bead-head Peacock, I picked up a half dozen trout.

Peacock Nymph

> HOOK: Mustad 9671, size 12 to 16
> THREAD: Dark gray
> TAIL: Dark gray hackle fibers
> BODY: Peacock with the butts of the dark gray hackle fibers
> pulled over top and tied off near the eye. Rib the body
> with a fine piece of gold wire.
> HACKLE: Tie a dozen dark gray hackle fibers under the
> throat.

Tying Notes: I often add a bead head to this pattern and find it extremely effective.

Stonefly Nymph

Greg Hoover works for Penn State University as an entomolo-gist, and he's currently working on a study of the mayflies of Pennsyl-vania. Greg also fly-fishes frequently and ties some of the finest flies I've ever seen. If you've ever watched Greg tie, you probably have seen him tying his specialty, the woven Stonefly Nymph.

Back in 1980, Greg fished the Stonefly Nymph on Loyalsock Creek on opening day. In the middle of dozens of other anglers he caught the state record brook trout that day on—you guessed it—the Stonefly Nymph. That record has since been surpassed, but Greg still does well with this underwater pattern.

Does the nymph work on Midwestern waters? As co-author of *Great Rivers—Great Hatches*, Greg covered Michigan rivers as part of his assignment. He spent a week fly-fishing the AuSable and Père Marquette rivers. Greg floated the Père Marquette near Baldwin with John Kestner of Johnson's Père Marquette Lodge and caught dozens of trout on that Stonefly Nymph, one of the top flies he used the entire week.

Clayton Peters first developed this woven stonefly nymph

many years ago after studying large stoneflies and their larva on Penns Creek in central Pennsylvania. To get a broad, flat imitation to match the natural, Greg Hoover places lead wire on each side of the shank. He then places some Super Glue to hold it in place and wraps the tying thread to secure the weight. Weaving the body might prove difficult the first couple of times.

With a dark brown back and a pale yellow body, the woven Stonefly Nymph ably copies many nymph naturals like those in the *Perla* and *Acroneuria* genera. Just look at some of the stonefly nymphs on your favorite streams the next time you fish. Check the belly and the back of that nymph and you'll see two distinct colors. You'll often find a pale belly or abdomen and a much darker back. You get this configuration with the woven Stonefly Nymph.

Stonefly Nymph

> HOOK: Mustad 366A, size 8 and 10
> THREAD: Yellow
> TAILS: Two stripped brown hackle or goose fibers
> BODY: Brown and creamy yellow embroidery floss
> WINGS: Turkey quill feather
> THORAX: Yellow rabbit fur
> HACKLE: Rear (two gold-dyed duck quill fibers); front (one
> pale dun and one ginger hackle)

(Tying notes from Pennsylvania Angler *magazine)*

1. Hook sizes range from #8 to #12, 3X or 4X long. The underbody may be of lead wire wound around shank and flattened with pliers, or a strip of thin aluminum 3/32-inch wide, cemented and bound to top of shank; or two strips of .015 lead on either side secured with Super Glue.

2. For tails, bind two stripped brown hackle ribs at rear of

underbody with yellow nymph thread. Cut an 8-inch length each of dark brown and creamy yellow six-strand cotton embroidery floss and bind along shank with brown floss nearest tier. Then whip-finish thread about midway on shank. Cut and remove thread.

3. Below the hook make a simple overhand knot, beginning with the dark floss behind the light.

4. At the point where the dark floss crosses the light, open a small loop and slip it over the eye of hook with dark above and light underneath.

5. Slide the loop to the rear of the underbody and pull strands tight. Yellow floss will now be on near side.

6. Repeat steps 3 and 4, always beginning the overhand knot with brown strand behind yellow.

7. Continue the knotting sequence until abdomen is completed. Again bind thread to hook and tie off the floss with three turns. Trim away ends of floss.

8. For rear legs, tie two gold-dyed duck quill fibers underneath forward end of abdomen. For the wing case, cut a section of brightly marked turkey quill feather slightly wider than the abdomen. Cut a V-shaped notch in tip end of turkey quill and bind over underbody opposite base of rear legs, with notch overlapping several front segments of abdomen. Pull long end of wing case upright, out of the way. Tie in a pale dun and a ginger hackle midway in thorax area. Then apply a blended dubbing of fox and yellow-dyed rabbit fur to the tying thread.

9. Wind dubbing to form rear half of thorax and half-hitch thread in front of hackles. Wind hackles individually, two turns each, over thorax and tie off in front of dubbing. Apply a little more dubbing to thread and finished thorax to eye. Trim hackles above and below thorax. Pull wing case over thorax and bind down behind eye. For antennae, separate the two edge fibers of turkey quill extending beyond eye and trim excess. Whip-finish thread at eye and lacquer.

For durability apply a thin coat of vinyl cement to wing case and antennae.

Pteronarcys Nymph

Jay Kapolka builds some of the finest fly rods I've ever seen. He's an accountant by trade but in his spare time you'll find Jay tying excellent flies, building rods, or fly-fishing. Recently Jay and I spent two weeks on some of Oregon's best rivers like the Metolius, McKenzie, Williamson, and Deschutes. We had two weeks to fly-fish on some of Oregon's best rivers so I could write about them in *Great Rivers—Great Hatches.* Jay and I had just spent a frustrating day on the Metolius River in central Oregon near the end of May. Few hatches appeared that day and few trout rose. That's unusual on this productive stream, since it hosts hatches almost daily in late May. We both went away from the river extremely disappointed; in fact, I went away so frustrated that I didn't care if I ever returned.

Jay Kapolka catches a rainbow on a Pteronarcys Nymph on Oregon's Deschutes River.

The next day, May 25, Jay and I headed for the Deschutes River less than forty miles from the Metolius. Our guide, Craig Lacy of Bend, Oregon, greeted us near Madras. As we boarded the McKenzie boat, Craig handed Jay and me a couple Pteronarcys Nymphs. He seined several large black nymphs from the bottom and showed us how closely the Pteronarcys Nymph copied the natural.

"Maybe they'll emerge today," Craig said as he showed us several huge, dark nymphs he had just found on the bottom. It's about that time of year when the hatch appears."

We drifted through several sets of rapids and anchored near an island to eat lunch. The morning had come and gone without much distinction. Jay and I both had a couple of Deschutes rainbows to show for several tedious hours of casting. As we sat in the boat eating salsa and sandwiches, Craig showed us a couple of salmon fly adults that had just emerged motionless on grasses along the banks. Soon we saw more adults climbing the vegetation near the shoreline, and a major stonefly hatch began. We abruptly ended our noontime break and tied on the Pteronarcys Nymphs Craig had given us earlier.

While we tied on the huge nymph pattern, Craig showed us the high-stick nymphing technique. He said we should cast the black nymph upriver on a short line, hold the tip of the fly rod high, and follow the pattern downriver. In the next two hours, more than a dozen heavy Deschutes rainbows took that huge nymph. Several hundred yards downriver, Jay Kapolka had the same success with the Pteronarcys Nymph. That day of fishing on the Deschutes with the Pteronarcys Nymph changed my thinking about and my disdain for nymphs forever.

As more and more nymphs swam toward the shore, trout actively fed on them. So it's only natural that a black pattern copying these stonefly nymphs would catch trout. I didn't have to wait long. On maybe the fifth cast I felt a trout hit the nymph, and I set the hook on a fifteen-inch rainbow. Two more drifts, and I landed another rainbow about the same size. Only a couple more drifts and another trout hit. The action on the Pteronarcys Nymph continued for more than two hours. What a day of fishing!

Three weeks later completed my assignment to fly-fish Idaho and Montana rivers for the manuscript *Great Rivers—Great Hatches*. Nick Nicklas guided Jerry Meck and me on the Madison River. The salmon fly hatch on the Madison appears near the end of June or early July, about a month later than the same hatch on the Deschutes River.

"It's about time for the salmon fly to appear and the nymphs have become active," said Nick as he handed me a Pteronarcys Nymph. I again used the high-stick nymphing technique in this extremely high snow-fed water. It didn't take long for the first rainbow to hit the nymph. Meanwhile, downriver Nick hooked onto a heavy 'bow. The action continued for a couple of hours before we quit.

If you plan to fly-fish Western rivers from late May through early July, carry the Pteronarcys Nymph with you. So many rivers of the West hold this hatch and because the nymph lives underwater for three years, a Pteronarcys Nymph works almost any time of the year.

Pteronarcys Nymph
> HOOK: Mustad 94831, #4 or #6
> THREAD: Black
> TAILS: Black goose quill fibers
> BODY: Orange and black grindle chenille
> WINGS: Black goose quill

Damselfly Nymph
> By early June on many Western waters you'll find damselflies emerging. Especially on the lakes of central Washington, the Damselfly Nymph takes on importance as a productive pattern.

Recently, Craig Shuman of Federal, Washington, George Cook, and I met on Isaak Ranch for a late-spring fishing trip. George guides anglers on the three highly productive lakes on the ranch. He casts a fly like nobody I've ever watched before and he ties patterns that really catch trout in those lakes. A Damselfly Nymph has long been one of George's favorite patterns for the Kamloops rainbows on the ranch. George calls it the "Super-Fly." He says it also works well in black and burgundy.

On our first trip to the ranch, Craig and I landed several heavy trout on his highly effective pattern. You'll also find the damselfly on Eastern and Midwestern lakes and on slow sections of streams. So have a supply of these handy if you plan to fish these types of waters.

Don Baylor lives in Stroudsburg, Pennsylvania. Don gives talks on fly-fishing, he's a skilled entomologist, and he's an expert fly-fisher. Every chance he gets you'll find him fly-fishing in Alaska or on some Western river. In fact, Don spends at least two weeks every year fishing some of the great waters in the Yellowstone Park area, often several days on Slough Creek in the northeastern section of the park. As its name suggests, Slough Creek holds many still pools that look like small ponds. Don has developed a dynamite Damselfly Nymph that he uses just for these slow sections. This nymph has consistently produced heavy trout for Don on Slough Creek.

Don's Damselfly Nymph
> HOOK: Mustad 3906B, size 14
> THREAD: Olive
> TAILS: Tannish olive raffia extended out over the bend
> BODY: Olive rabbit
> WINGS: Tannish olive raffia
> HACKLE: Barred pale olive mallard for a throat

Tying Notes: Take a piece of thirty-pound monofilament and tie it on just behind the eye. Burn the two ends to form eyes. Take a four-inch piece of tannish olive raffia, make a knot near one end and place that end extending back over the bend of the hook. Dub the body, then bring the front end of the raffia up over the eyes and tie off just behind them. Cut the excess raffia, leaving a quarter-inch behind where you tied it off. Add the hackle.

Damselfly Nymph

> HOOK: Mustad 79580, size 12
> THREAD: Olive
> TAILS: Dark olive marabou herl tips
> BODY: Dark olive marabou
> WINGS: Pheasant tail
> HACKLE: Pheasant tail

Super-Fly

> HOOK: Mustad 79580, sizes 8 to 12
> THREAD: Olive
> TAILS: Olive hackle fibers
> BODY: Olive caddis emerger dubbing (before dubbing tie in
>   a piece of white Z-lon for the body shell)
> HACKLE: Dark grouse along both sides

Tying Notes: After dubbing the body and tying in the grouse fibers on both sides for the legs, pull the Z-lon over top of body and tie in at the eye.

Shrimp

What a terrible week we picked to fly-fish on the Bighorn River in southeastern Montana! Nothing went right. For three days of intense fishing Mike Manfredo and I landed only a dozen trout, and I promised Mike I'd never return to this river. Mike kept apologizing and said the river deserved a better opinion.

On our fourth day, we drifted the same thirteen miles we had the three days before. I searched and searched again for a new pattern to test on this fourth float, something that might change our luck. Mike suggested that we try an olive shrimp pattern, and fish it just off the bottom.

As we entered the chilly waters that early October morning

the nearby mountains held the light layer of snow that had fallen the night before. A fine, cold drizzle fell as we left the Afterbay put-in area. What else could happen on this lousy week of fishing? But wait! Not far downriver I picked up a heavy brown on the shrimp pattern. Mike followed suit shortly, landing an even heavier trout. By the time we had exited at the Bighorn access Mike and I had landed ten heavy trout on our shrimp patterns, and they had saved our late-season visit to the Bighorn.

But the pattern works on other streams as well. Just recently I watched well-known outdoor photographer Larry Madison catch at least a dozen trout on his olive shrimp pattern. While Bill Sutton, Jack Conyngham, and I watched, Larry caught one trout after another on that pattern, with a strike indicator attached about three feet above the pattern.

Shrimp

> HOOK: Tiemco 2457, sizes 12 through 18
> THREAD: Olive
> TAILS: Olive hackle fibers
> BODY: Olive rabbit (place a strip of clear plastic over top
>   and rib with olive monocord)

Tying Notes: Take a piece of clear plastic about 3/8 inch wide and two inches long and tie in at the bend of the hook. After you dub the body with a dubbing loop, pull the plastic up over top of the body and secure with the olive thread or gold wire.

Emerger Patterns

If you skipped the previous chapter on the hatches, you might want to review the life cycle of a mayfly. Until a few years ago fly-fishers thought they had one of several choices to match what happened during a hatch or spinner fall. They copied nymphs on or near the bottom, and emerged duns and returning spinners on the surface with dry flies. A few decades ago, anglers began copying spinners coming back to the water, using spent-wing imitations made of poly and other synthetic materials. More recently fly-fishers have realized the vulnerability of mayflies, caddis flies, and some other aquatic insects when they prepare to emerge. As the nymph, larva, or pupa moves toward the surface and transforms into a winged adult, it becomes extremely defenseless. For a moment during the change trout can grab most aquatic emergers without much effort. If trout wait until the nymph has transformed into a dun, they've often lost their window of opportunity. Many duns and most winged caddis flies escape rapidly from the surface and often trout give up chasing this phase.

The change from nymph to dun usually occurs at or near the surface. (With some mayflies like the quill gordon the change takes place near the bottom of the stream.) This process can take a split second or several seconds. The change from nymph to dun, often called the emerger by anglers, puts the mayfly in jeopardy and makes it easy prey for trout. Since the transformation takes place near or just under the surface, anglers often confuse rises to the emerger as a rise to a dun because of the splash associated with the rise.

Caddis flies, too, are most vulnerable when the pupa emerges to the surface. After the adult fully emerges from the pupa, it escapes rapidly from the surface. But the process of transformation from the pupa to the adult also makes the caddis vulnerable to attack from feeding trout. You can find information on caddis fly adults in Chapter 5.

Tandem Connection

If you've fly-fished enough hatches, you already know how frustrating fishing some of them can be. For example, when the sulphur appears you can cast flawlessly over risers and come up empty. If you tie a weighted Sulphur Emerger a couple of feet behind your Sulphur dry, you're now covering the emerger phase. During some hatches, when I use the tandem rig, I'll average six trout on the emerger for every trout caught on the dry fly. If the emerger fails, tie on a Sulphur Nymph and fish it even deeper.

I remember early hatches like the hendrickson when I've seen literally thousands of duns on the surface and not one trout rising to them. Maybe—just maybe—in those cold waters of spring you'll find trout taking nymphs near the bottom. If you see nothing rising during a hatch, switch to something underneath or use the tandem rig. Tie the nymph behind a Hendrickson dry fly and get it deep. If you can't get deep enough with the rig, use only the nymph and fish it on the bottom.

Tying the Emerger Patterns

I like to tie my emerger patterns with angora, muskrat or fox fur. Use white or gray poly, short gray turkey fibers, or crinkled Z-lon to imitate the wing emerging from the wing pad. Add a few hackle at the throat. On many of my emerger patterns like the Hendrickson, Isonychia or White Fly, just before the final whip finish, I make a small loop of crinkled Z-lon, shape it about 1/8" inch long and extend it back over the wing pad.

I add weight to most of my emerger patterns. If you connect the emerger two or three feet behind a dry fly on the tandem rig, or if you use a strike indicator, the emerger will not sink very deeply. By adding about ten to fifteen turns of .015 lead to the body when tying the pattern you'll find that the emerger gets just a few inches beneath the surface.

For downwing emergers, I usually add weight to the body, then dub with ultra-translucent nymph dubbing and add four or five turns of brown and black speckled woodcock or grouse.

Soft-hackle Emergers

Many fly-fishers prefer using an emerger pattern with a poly body or hen hackle tied on a dry-fly hook. This suggests the dun's initial exit from the nymphal shuck. Using this pattern for the sulphur and trico hatches has made anglers like Bob Duffus of State College, Pennsylvania, much more successful. He greases the pattern so it floats on the surface, and he finds it successful during a hatch.

If you have no luck with any of the regular emerger patterns, you might want to tie some soft-hackle emergers. For the Sulphur soft hackle, Bob uses dark brown Z-lon for the shuck, pale orange poly for the body, and cream hen hackle for the legs. When he ties the Trico soft-hackle emerger he uses a brown Z-lon shuck, black beaver for the body, and a pale gray hen hackle.

Sulphur-PMD Emerger

On many Eastern and Midwestern waters, sulphurs appear for more than a month. But for many anglers the hatch often proves frustrating. Often you think you see trout rising to the sulphur dun, but in reality they're chasing nymphs and feeding on emergers just under the surface. It's imperative to concoct an effective emerger pattern to cope with this important hatch.

Andy Leitzinger of Collegeville, Pennsylvania, boasts about the success he's had with his Sulphur Emerger pattern. He tells how the pattern increased his catch fourfold before and during the sulphur hatch. Andy ties his emerger on what we reverently refer to as a bicycle, two phases of the life cycle of a mayfly, the dun (dry fly) and the emerger (wet fly). Andy ties a size 14 Sulphur dry onto a 4X tippet. He then ties a two- to three-foot 4X tippet onto the bend of the dry fly, securing it with an improved clinch knot. Andy then ties a weighted Sulphur Emerger pattern to the second tippet.

Andy and I arrived at central Pennsylvania's Little Juniata River in late May with plenty of new Sulphur Emergers in hand. By

8:15 p.m. the hatch appeared on the surface in full strength. Trout made splashing rises in the riffle and at the head of the pool in front of us, and each time the Sulphur "strike indicator" sank we set the hook and landed a brown trout. Within a half-hour the hatch had ended and darkness enveloped the entire river. Each of us caught about four trout on the emerger pattern for every trout we caught on the floating Sulphur. Finally we had succeeded during the often baffling sulphur hatch. We caught more trout than normal because we changed our tactics for fishing this sometimes puzzling hatch.

But does the emerger pattern work over a great number of waters? Ask Craig Shuman and Jack Mitchell how well the emerger performs on Washington's Yakima River during a pale morning dun hatch. Craig and Jack have guided thousands of anglers down the Yakima over the past five years, and they'll tell you that heavy rainbows take the Sulphur Emerger when these pale morning duns appear. Ask Dave Blackburn, who guides on northwestern Montana's Kootenai River, whether the pattern works when the hatch appears in July. He'll tell you how the Kootenai rainbows react to a full-fledged pale morning dun hatch and how well the emerger pattern produces.

I mentioned earlier that you might want to try a Soft-hackle Sulphur during the hatch. If trout refuse your emerger, try a Sulphur dry fly. If they refuse your dry fly, purposely sink the pattern. If they reject that tactic, try a Soft-hackle Sulphur Emerger.

Sulphur-PMD Emerger
>HOOK: Mustad 9671, sizes 14 and 16
>THREAD: Pale tan
>TAILS: Grouse or woodcock fibers (dark brown, barred)
>BODY: Light tan angora
>WING CASE: White poly yarn

Tying Notes: Tie in a throat of grouse fibers about two-thirds up the shank of the hook. Tie in a piece of white poly yarn, then finish dubbing to a point just behind the eye of the hook. Bring the poly yarn up over the thorax and tie in at the eye. Make the yarn look like a bubble.

Soft-hackle Sulphur Emerger
> HOOK: Mustad 94840, sizes 14 and 16
> THREAD: Yellow
> TAILS: Dark brown Z-lon
> BODY: Pale orange poly
> HACKLE: Cream hen hackle

Baetis Emerger

A couple years ago I tied flies and autographed books at the Rocky Mountain Sporting Goods store in Fort Collins, Colorado. Ray Smith, a local fly-tier and fly-fisher, asked if I wanted to see a new technique for tying a Baetis Emerger. I've always contended that Western fly-tiers are among the most innovative, so I eagerly agreed to watch.

The Baetis Emerger works well on Colorado's Cache la Poudre River.

If you've fly-fished for any time at all, you know how important *Baetis* hatches are. You'll find ample hatches of these little blue-winged olives from Oregon's Metolius River to New York's Beaverkill. If you're fortunate enough to fly-fish the San Juan in northern New Mexico, you'll find this hatch appearing almost every month of the year. This particular species (*Baetis tricaudatus*) appears on streams and rivers throughout the country in March and April and again in September and October—in other words, the species produces two broods per year.

The method Ray Smith used made tying an emerger easy, effective, and quick. But would it catch trout? I often contend that many patterns catch fly-fishers, not trout: They look great to the tiers but not to the fish. I didn't have to wait long to find out if the Baetis Emerger would produce. The next morning Mike Manfredo, also of Fort Collins, and I headed out for two hours of fishing on the Cache la Poudre River before my plane left for Pennsylvania. Mike and I both used Baetis Emergers that Ray had showed us how to tie the day before. In those two short hours of fishing on the Poudre, Mike and I caught two dozen trout on those new emergers—on a morning when we saw few trout rise.

But how would this new pattern work back East, on Pennsylvania waters? Two days after I returned from Colorado, I tested the pattern on central Pennsylvania's Little Juniata River. I tied a half dozen Baetis Emergers for that late-September trip. By noon several little blue-winged naturals appeared on the surface and trout began to feed on this diminutive late-season bonanza. I tied the Baetis Emerger behind a Patriot dry fly, using the technique that I've mentioned before. I cast the tandem flies upriver and the action began. For two hours trout took that emerger. On a rare occasion a brown came to the surface and took the strike indicator, the Patriot.

Almost every good trout river you'll fish across the United States holds good populations of little blue-winged olives. That's why you must carry a good imitation of the Baetis Emerger with you. The Baetis Emerger should prove effective on many of those otherwise frustrating trips.

Baetis Emerger

> HOOK: #16 and #18, Mustad 3906B
> THREAD: Olive
> TAILS: Olive dun hackle fibers
> BODY: Olive gray muskrat fur
> WING CASE: Olive gray hackle
> HACKLE: Olive gray hackle

Tying Notes: To get a full body, I often use a dubbing loop for my emerger patterns. Double your tying thread, wax it, and distribute the muskrat fur in the loop. Twist the loop with hackle pliers about thirty times. Wrap the dubbed material around the shank. Tie in a dozen long hackle fibers just behind the thorax. Dub additional fur in front of the fibers. Bring the fibers over the top of the thorax and tie off at the eye of the hook. Don't cut off the tips of the hackle fibers. Divide the hackle tips and place half on the right side and the other half on the left side. Let the tips flare back toward the bend of the hook. These hackle tips become the legs of the emerger. Optional: just before you whip finish add a small loop of crinkled Z-lon and place it back over the top of the wing pad.

Isonychia Emerger

After experiencing how well the Baetis Emerger performed on waters in the East and West, I experimented with several additional emerger patterns like the Isonychia Emerger. Anglers call these fairly large mayflies slate drakes. They appear as two separate broods in June and July and again in September and October, so they're important to copy. Would the technique for tying the Baetis Emerger work for this *Isonychia* hatch?

I tied a half dozen Isonychia Emergers, using the same methods Ray Smith taught me a few days earlier and headed out to central Pennsylvania's Penns Creek, which provides myriad hatches throughout the year. When you mention this topnotch limestone stream, anglers immediately think of green drakes. Fish Penns Creek when the green drake appears in late May or early June and you'll find hundreds of fly-fishers eager to match the hatch. But Penns Creek holds many more great hatches than just the green drake. For example, in early June and again in September you'll find plenty of emerging slate drakes.

An Isonychia Emerger pattern works well when the large, dark gray mayfly emerges in early fall.

By early afternoon on that late-September afternoon, slate drakes appeared on the surface. Normally these nymphs climb out onto an exposed rock to emerge and the dun escapes rapidly. But a cold, light drizzle slowed their takeoff on this early-fall day, and trout fed eagerly on sluggish duns and emergers. I tied on a Slate Drake dry fly on the 4X tippet, using the same tandem technique I explained earlier. Then I tied a thirty-inch piece of 4X tippet onto the bend of the hook of the Slate Drake and secured the tippet with an improved clinch knot. I then tied onto the end of this extended tippet a weighted Isonychia Emerger. During a hatch, whether trout are actively feeding on duns or emergers, top or bottom, you're covered.

On the second drift the Slate Drake sank, I set the hook, and landed a 12-inch brown. Several more casts into the riffle and another trout took the emerger. In several hours of fishing that afternoon I caught a dozen trout on that deadly emerger pattern. In addition, I caught four trout on the strike indicator, the Slate Drake dry fly.

Once you try this simple new method for tying emergers you, too, will agree how effective it is. Try the same tying method for your favorite hatches.

Isonychia Emerger
> HOOK: #12 or #14, Mustad 3906B
> THREAD: Black
> TAILS: Black hackle tips
> BODY: Black angora, use a dubbing loop
> WING CASE: Black hackle
> HACKLE: Black hackle

Tying Notes: I weight each pattern with thirty turns of .015 lead wire, tie on three black hackle tips for the tail, dub in a black angora body two-thirds of the way up the shank, then tie in about thirty long hackle barbules. I take these fibers or barbules from the biggest, most webbed hackles at the back of the neck—usually those that you never use. I tie the fibers in by their butts, with the tips pointing back over the body of the emerger. I cut off the butts, dub the front third of the body or the thorax with more black angora, then pull the hackle fibers over the top of the thorax and tie them in just behind the eye. Next, divide the tips of the barbules equally, tying one half on one side of the wing case and the other half on the other side. These barbules copy the legs of the emerger. If the legs appear too long, cut off the excess. Dub a bit more angora on the thorax than you did on the rear two-thirds of the body. This enlarged thorax gives the impression of a dun emerging from the nymphal shuck.

Again, you can add crinkled Z-lon to copy the wings emerging.

Hendrickson Emerger

If the Sulphur Emerger works so well during the hatch why wouldn't the Hendrickson Emerger work equally well? Believe me, it does!

I have yet to find a description of the Hendrickson that really copies the natural. The nymph has dark ginger legs and tail and a black body with one or two dark brown spots on its back. Have you ever seen a nymph that dark used to copy the natural? I tied up a half dozen black emerger patterns and headed for Fishing Creek in central Pennsylvania.

Fishing Creek flows with cool limestone water all summer. Expect temperatures in the low sixties throughout the summer months. On some days around mid-April you can witness little blue-wings, quill gordons, blue quills, and hendricksons appearing at the same time. As I entered the water, I had already seen several trout rising for blue quills.

Soon a burst of hendricksons appeared on the surface and I tied on the Hendrickson Emerger. I tied it on a thirty-inch tippet and connected it to the bend of the hook of a Patriot dry fly. Within minutes, the dry fly sank and I set the hook on a sixteen-inch native rainbow. Several more casts and another trout, this time a brookie, took the emerger pattern. Before the hatch ended I had released four trout on that wet fly. That doesn't seem like many, but the hatch ended a half-hour after it had begun. Besides, these trout had been pounded for days and days by scores of fly-fishers.

Hendrickson Emerger

> HOOK: Mustad 3906B, size 12 or 14
> THREAD: Black
> TAILS: Dark ginger hackle fibers

BODY: Black or very dark brown angora, use a dubbing loop
WINGS: Pale gray poly yarn tied in, then some angora
    dubbed and the poly yarn tied in just behind the eye. Make
    certain you make a loop in the yarn.
THORAX: Black angora, dubbed
HACKLE: Dark ginger hackle fibers

The White Fly Emerger

Rod Walinchus raced Bryan Meck and me down a steep, rutted dirt road to the river. Halfway down that treacherous route we made a sharp turn to the left. We had only a couple of hours to fish the "miracle mile" section of Wyoming's North Platte River on this late-July evening, and Rod wanted to make certain we saw it at its best. As we arrived at the river Rod pointed to a section and told us that in another month white flies would appear there. White flies on the North Platte River?

Nick Nicklas drove Jerry Meck from Gardiner, Montana, to Reed Point, just outside Yellowstone Park, and told Jerry that this section of the Yellowstone River held some white flies in late August and September. White flies on the Yellowstone?

Yes, you'll find some good white fly hatches across the United States. But if you ever fish this hatch, you'll need to use some different techniques and patterns. Let me explain.

Ten years have passed since my first encounter with a new hatch on central Pennsylvania's Little Juniata River. For decades man mistreated this river. In the 1950s and 1960s it flowed brown from the tannic acid poured into it upriver. Add to its woes raw sewage from several communities and you can see how man mistreated this natural resource.

Then the authorities decided to do something with the river, and by the late 1960s, upriver communities had added sewage-treatment facilities and the paper mill ceased pouring in its tannic acid. Almost overnight the river cleared and hatches began appearing. Each year since, the river boasts at least one new, vibrant hatch, and ten years ago it added white flies (*Ephoron*) to its list. I can still remember that first encounter with this unusual hatch. I stood there in awe that evening watching these low-flying mayflies moving up-stream, then downstream. Trout jumped completely out of the water trying to catch some of them. Thank God for the White Wulff pattern! That's the only pattern in a size 14 I had that came close to matching the hatch. I went away from that first encounter vowing that this frustrating hatch wouldn't get the best of me. The hatch lasts for more than two weeks on most rivers and streams where it occurs, so I had ample time to experiment with new patterns.

The white fly hatch confuses many anglers because it's com-pletely different from most other mayflies. First, mayflies that appear in an evening live only for an hour or so, mating and dying in the same evening. Second, the female never changes from a dun to a spinner but lives, lays eggs, and dies as a dun. Only the male changes from a dun to a spinner, and it does so on the wing. The male and female have atrophied legs so neither can rest on the water upright. When emerging, because of their lack of fully developed legs, the duns must escape rapidly or die. Fly-fishers must realize the characteristics of this hatch when they tie patterns and when they fish the hatch.

I recently tied a White Fly Emerger for the hatch and tested it on south-central Pennsylvania's Yellow Breeches Creek. I tied it like the Baetis and Isonychia emergers we talked about earlier and had a great deal of success with the pattern in tandem with the White Fly dry fly. I caught four trout on the emerger pattern for every trout on the dry fly.

I experimented more with the emerger pattern and added some crinkled Z-lon just before I used a whip finish to complete the pattern. Crinkled Z-lon looks like regular Z-lon except it has a curly look to it. I tied a small loop of this material less than a half-inch long just behind the eye and leaning back over the wing pad to give the effect of a partially emerged dun.

I tested the pattern one late-August evening on the Little Juniata River. The white fly hatch had already been on for more than a week, so I expected a horde of fly-fishers in the area, and I tried to arrive early so I could get a productive spot to fly-fish. But when I arrived I didn't see one other angler on more than a mile of water. What happened? Had the hatch already ended?

I stood in mid river trying to spot risers when the first white flies appeared just above the surface. Soon dozens more joined the group already emerged and a major hatch occurred—and I had the entire productive stretch to myself.

Too good to be true? You bet! I looked to the near shore and spotted another angler, who proceeded to move into the river only forty feet upstream. Soon four other of his friends joined him, and I had anglers fishing within twenty feet of me. Where just a few minutes ago the river seemed void of anglers, I now had five of them within a few feet of me. I looked downriver for a half mile and saw no other anglers; evidently I had taken the spot preferred by these fly-fishers so they attempted to crowd me out.

I looked up to the sky and thought if there's a God up there, he should reward me for suffering this frustrating intrusion. While the anglers near me flailed away with various White Fly patterns, I tied on a tandem with a White Fly and the White Fly Emerger, tied just two feet behind the dry. I spotted what appeared to be a heavy riser and cast the setup just a couple of feet upriver. The White Fly sank and I set the hook. The trout stayed deep, then moved toward the surface and I saw that he had taken the emerger pattern. A few minutes later I netted the heavy eighteen-inch Juniata brown. The other five anglers nearby began to complain that they had no strikes on their dry fly.

I saw another heavy riser and cast the tandem rig a couple of feet above that trout. It hit too, and I soon released a seventeen-inch brown this time. Now the five anglers began to mutter to themselves.

Three other Juniata River browns took that emerger before the first and only one took the dry fly. God had answered my prayer and I backed out of the stream to a chorus of murmurs from the nearby anglers who had crowded in on me. In the hour we had fished next to each other those five had not one trout to show on a dry fly. Do you think this emerger pattern works?

White Fly Emerger
> HOOK: Mustad 9671, size 12 or 14
> THREAD: Light reddish brown
> TAILS: Dark ginger hackle fibers

WING CASE: Dark ginger hackle

HACKLE: Dark ginger hackle

Tying Notes: I weight each pattern with lead wire, tie on some dark ginger hackle barbules for the tail, dub in a tan angora body two-thirds of the way up the shank, then tie in about thirty long hackle barbules. I take these fibers or barbules from the biggest, most webbed hackles at the back of the neck—usually those you never use. I tie the fibers in by their butts, with the tips pointing back over the body of the emerger. I cut off the butts, dub the front third of the body or the thorax with more black angora, then pull the hackle fibers over the top of the thorax and tie them in just behind the eye. Next, divide the tips of the barbules equally, tying one half on one side of the wing case and the other half on the other side. These barbules copy the legs of the emerger. If the legs appear too long, cut off the excess. Dub a bit more angora on the thorax than you did on the rear two-thirds of the body. This enlarged thorax gives the impression of a dun emerging from the nymphal shuck. Just before you make your final whip finish, add a piece of doubled crinkled Z-lon and tie it in at the eye. Keep it short.

Emerging Green Caddis Pupa

The Clark Fork just below Anaconda, Montana, holds an abundance of caddis hatches. I arrived on the thirty-foot-wide river just before 6:00 p.m. in early July. For years this part of the river held contaminants from upriver sources, but the river has been recuperating for several years and caddis hatches now abound. No sooner did I arrive at the stream than a heavy brown caddis hatch began. Only a few trout rose to adult winged caddis and after a half hour of waiting and looking for risers I tied on an Emerging Brown Caddis Pupa. I tie the pattern on a Tiemco 2457 hook in sizes from 12 to 18. I also add weight to the body by adding .015 lead wire to the shank of the hook to help sink the pattern.

I began casting across stream, letting the wet fly make its swing or arc, and getting set for the action. For the next hour the brown trout in that section of the Clark Fork wouldn't leave that pattern alone. More than two dozen trout hit that pattern before darkness and a waning hatch ended the feeding frenzy.

While thousands of caddis flies emerged that evening on the upper end of the Clark Fork, only a few trout rose to the adult. Most fed on caddis emergers.

When I arrived back in Pennsylvania later that week, I began to tie up some soft-hackle caddis pupa imitations to cover the increasing number of times I saw trout chasing the caddis pupa and not the adult. I dubbed a body of ultra-translucent nymph dubbing on a weighted Tiemco 2457 hook and added four or five turns of a woodcock or grouse hackle to imitate the legs and wings of the emerger. If you prefer you can add two mallard wing sections to either side to copy the wings of the natural.

I tried the pattern the next afternoon on my home stream, the Little Juniata River. At that time, more than a decade ago, this river held a tremendous hatch of green caddis flies in early May. For weeks you could expect to see clouds of these downwings and feeding trout in every stretch. More recently, however, this particular hatch has drastically diminished.

Alex Black accompanied me that day. He's a noted wood carver and has distinguished himself with the many beautiful ducks and geese he's so expertly carved. I tied on a Caddis Emerger and immediately began casting to some splashing rises. I cast the weighted pattern across stream, mended the line slightly and followed the fly though its arc. On one of the first casts the line tightened and I set the hook on a small brown trout. Several more casts and another strike. Most of the trout hit the pattern when it made the swing or arc. I missed many of the strikes, almost all violent attempts to snare the emerging caddis. For every trout I landed that day, I missed two more. Action continued for more than four hours that afternoon, and Alex and I quit confident that we had finally figured out these trout and this downwing hatch.

What makes the emerging caddis pupa so continuosuly effective? Because trout prefer feeding on this underwater natural over the quick-escaping adult on the surface. If you see these splashing rises it's a dead giveaway that trout are chasing emerging caddis pupa. If you see these rises, use an emerging pupa and work it just in front of the splashing rise.

Twitching the emerger often works. One day on the Little Juniata River I experimented with an emerging Green Caddis Pupa. I fished the pattern on a dead drift for 500 casts then twitched the same pattern for 500 additional casts. I averaged two strikes when I twitched the wet fly to every one when I fished the pattern on a dead drift. That's a significant difference and a point you should remember when you fish this soft-hackle pattern. By twitching the pattern just in front of feeding trout you can often get it to strike.

Do you have difficulty trying to determine whether trout feed on the caddis adult on the surface or the emerger just under the surface? Then try the tandem on your larger caddis hatches. Tie on a high-riding fluttering caddis for your dry fly and a weighted emerger for your wet fly. By weighting the emerger you'll sink the wet fly just a few inches beneath the surface—where trout feed on the natural. And by using a downwing caddis dry as your lead fly you'll catch those trout rising to adults on the surface. Any strike to the emerger pattern will sink your dry fly. If you're using the emerger as the point fly on a tandem rig, before you lift up the flies to cast again, twitch both of them.

Tie up these soft-hackle patterns with body colors of green, brown, black, gray, olive, tan, cream and yellow in sizes from 12 to 16. If you begin using these during caddis emergences, you'll increase your success tremendously. I said earlier that I often miss a lot of trout when I use a caddis emerger pattern. To help overcome this problem, I often offset my hook point.

You can imitate caddis emergers with Gary LaFontaine's Emergent Pupa, but I've found the Emerging Green Caddis Pupa almost as effective and much easier to tie.

If you've watched caddis flies emerge, you already know that the change from pupa to adult takes place in the surface film. If your

regular caddis emergers fail you, try a floating emerger. Fish this
pattern on the surface. Again, watch for strikes when this pattern
makes its swing. You'll find the dry emerger very similar to the Emerging Caddis Pupa, but with a strand of poly yarn for the wing on a dry
fly hook.

Emerging Green Caddis Pupa
>   HOOK: Tiemco 2457, size 12 to 16
>   THREAD: Green
>   BODY: Grayish green dubbed Sparkle Yarn
>   HACKLE: Four or five turns of a very small black and brown
>   woodcock or grouse hackle. Add weight to the body to sink
>   it just beneath the surface.

Gary LaFontaine's Emergent Pupa
>   HOOK: Mustad 94840 sizes 12 to 16
>   THREAD: Green
>   BODY: Green Sparkle Yarn dubbed, and pale tan to pale
>   green antron yarn tied on top and on bottom, covering the
>   underbody
>   WINGS: Dark brown hackle fibers tied on either side of
>   body and deer hair tied in on top.
>   HACKLE: Black marabou wound around the shank.

*Tying Notes: Tie in a piece of tan to pale green Antron yarn on top of the shank and another
piece underneath the hook, both with the butts pointing toward the eye of the hook. Dub the
body with the green Sparkle yarn, then cover the body on top and bottom with the Antron
you tied on the top and bottom at the bend of the hook. Bring both pieces over the body and
tie them in behind the eye of the hook. Tie in a few dark brown fibers on either side of the
body.*

Dry Emerger
>   HOOK: Mustad 94833
>   THREAD:Olive

BODY: Olive green Antron
WINGS: Pale gray poly yarn
HACKLE: Grizzly

Midge Pupa

Garry Sandstrom runs the Morning Hatch in Tacoma, Washington. Every chance Garry gets, you'll find him fishing on the Yakima River or one of central Washington's many productive alkaline lakes. As I suggested in *Great Rivers—Great Hatches,* he's one of a growing number of fly shop owners who not only runs an efficient shop but also excels as a fly-fisher. Garry first introduced the Black Midge Pupa to me on Nunnally Lake in central Washington. That introduction to Western lakes proved very frustrating for me—until Garry showed me his midge pupa pattern.

New Mexico's San Juan River. The Black Midge Pupa works well just below Navajo Dam.

The Midge Pupa worked so well on those high-desert lakes of the West that I pledged never to fish another lake or river without a good supply. Several years later, I fished the Green River at Flaming Gorge in Utah. Hank Boehm of Park City drifted the McKenzie boat downriver from the reservoir for a half mile before we began to fly-fish. I looked upward in awe at the high overhanging cliffs, then downward at trout swimming ten feet below in gin-clear water. As I scanned the surface of the river I saw thousands of dark gray midges emerging. Hank coaxed the boat into a deep eddy and asked me to try my Black Midge Pupa. I tied it on a three-foot leader behind a Patriot and watched the action unfold. In the crystal-clear waters I saw three heavy trout race for my pattern. I set the hook and battled a heavy rainbow.

More than a dozen heavy trout took the patterns. I said "patterns" because heavy Green River fish bent some of the hooks. Halfway down the seven-mile drift I had run out of the four Black Midge pupal patterns I had with me. I vowed never to run out of this vital pattern again.

Pupal patterns work especially well on Eastern and Midwestern waters from November through April. Next time you hit a pesky hatch of midwinter trout rising to a hatch of midges, try the midge pupa.

A size 24 Dark Grey Midge with a trailing shuck works when other patterns fail.

Garry Sandstrom recommends you vary the depth you fish the pattern. He often uses a strike indicator on lakes and moves the indicator to change the depth.

Carry plenty of these midge pupa in gray, black, and olive. Look for midge hatches on Western waters like the Cache la Poudre and Fryingpan rivers in Colorado, the San Juan in New Mexico, and the Green in Utah. On the Cache la Poudre and San Juan, midges appear daily from November through April.

Black Midge Pupa
    HOOK: #12-#18 Tiemco 2457
    THREAD: Black
    BODY: Black Antron
    RIBBING: Fine copper wire. Wing case of white poly or Z-lon
        tied in like short spinner wings.
    THORAX: Black angora, dubbed

Tying Notes: Tie in the white poly and make it extend an eighth-to a quarter-inch to the right and left of the shank. Dub a liberal amount of black angora behind, over top of the wing case. After finishing the body and applying the ribbing, tie in a piece of white Z-lon just behind the eye of the hook. Dub the thorax with muskrat, then bring the piece of Z-lon over top of the thorax and tie in at the eye. Let the Z-lon extend over the eye and an eighth inch beyond.

Stillborn Midge

Doug and Dan Daufel have tied flies commercially for the past five years. The young age of these identical twins from Dayton, Ohio, belies their tremendous fly-tying ability. They tie some of the best patterns I have seen in my forty-plus years of fly-fishing and tying flies. Recently the two tied up some of their new patterns for me. In that box they included Tricos tied backwards (the tail extends out over the eye); some Slate Drake dry flies; and a Stillborn Midge pattern. I placed the stillborn imitation in my midge collection and completely forgot about it until I fished on Arizona's Little Colorado River with

Craig Josephson of Johnstown, Pennsylvania.

Craig and I hiked downriver near the lower end of the X Diamond Ranch property and began fishing. The Little Colorado in this area is slowed considerably by several beaver dams, and throughout that late-May afternoon several heavy trout sipped insects off the surface in that slow water. After a frustrating half hour without any strikes, I finally tied on the Stillborn Midge pattern the Daufel twins had tied for me. I tied it two feet behind a Patriot dry fly and tugged on the line slightly to pull the midge just under the surface. I didn't have to wait long. Within seconds the dry fly sank, I set the hook, and a heavy rainbow fought to free himself of the size 20 midge pattern.

Greer Lodge in northeastern Arizona—what a spectacular setting for a week of fly-fishing! The hosts at that lodge served up some of the finest food and hospitality that I've experienced in all my years of Western fishing. Behind the lodge you'll find several ponds loaded with rainbow trout up to twenty inches long. The lodge entertains many angling groups throughout the year and allows all guests to fly-fish on some of these ponds. Craig Josephson and I spent a frustrating evening trying to catch trout on these ponds. Near dusk they came alive with trout rising to small midges, but it took us until the second evening of fly-fishing to figure out that these trout were feeding on emerging midge pupa and stillborns. Not until I tied on a Stillborn Midge did these hefty rainbows begin hitting the pattern. Craig and I landed ten trout that evening on a Stillborn Midge pattern.

Since those episodes, I make certain I carry plenty of these midge patterns with me—especially on Western waters. But don't overlook Eastern limestone streams, even in the dead of winter. On almost every winter morning midges appear and trout rise on Spring Creek in central Pennsylvania. The Stillborn Midge works well on those cold, blustery days.

I mentioned earlier that midges appear every day from

November through April on the upper section of Colorado's Cache la Poudre River. You have to experience this late-winter, early-spring hatch to really believe the enormity of it. Craig Shuman of Federal, Washington, accompanied me to the river at noon. Already dozens of trout rose in every slow section of the river to an overabundance of dark gray midges. I tied on a size 20 Stillborn Midge and cast above the first riser. The pattern stayed near the surface and on the third cast a twelve-inch rainbow grabbed it. In a small pool maybe a dozen rainbows fed freely on naturals. That Stillborn Midge with a black body took seven of those risers that afternoon. Those fortunate enough to live near the Cache la Poudre River can experience tremendous midge hatches and rising trout for more than four months during the winter.

Stillborn Midge
>   HOOK: Daiichi J220, size 20
>   THREAD: Black
>   BODY: Black tying thread ribbed with fine copper wire.
>   White Z-lon tied on top and extending over back and front
>   THORAX: Black angora, dubbed

Tying Notes: Tie in the Z-lon at the bend of the hook. Let a piece as long as the shank of the hook extend back over the hook. Pull the Z-lon over top of the completed body and secure with the ribbed copper wire. Let the Z-lon extend out over the eye of the hook about half an inch.

Chapter 5
Patterns for Fishing on Top—Matching the Hatches

Dick Mills and I gathered our fly-fishing gear and headed for Loyalsock Creek for an early-spring fishing trip. On our way down a steep bank to the stream the sky darkened and an unexpected early-spring snow squall hit. As we entered the chilled water I scanned upstream and downstream in a desperate, almost despondent, search for any surface activity. Certainly no insect would appear on this cold late-April morning. We stood in the stream for more than an hour trying to decide what to do next when Dick noticed a single rise fifty yards upstream. Shortly I noticed another rise, then another, and soon more than ten trout fed on surface food. What insect would appear under these conditions and bring this many trout to the surface on such an inclement day? I leaned down near the surface and scanned it for any indication of floating insects. A dark grayish-black mayfly floated past, then another. Soon the entire surface seemed filled with these dark duns too dazed and cold to take flight.

I took one look at the natural and told Dick to tie on a size 14 Quill Gordon. Soon Dick and I headed off in different directions, casting over pods of rising trout.

Before that hatch ended that afternoon we had landed more than twenty trout that rose to Quill Gordons. What an afternoon! What a hatch!

If you've fly-fished for any time, you've also fished over some great hatches. Hatches in the East like the quill gordon, hendrickson, green drake, and sulphur bring trout to the surface for insects.

In the Midwest you'll find great sulphur hatches, hendricksons, and blue-winged olive duns. The West also boasts many great hatches like the Western green drake and pale morning dun. We've included patterns for all of these — and many more in Chapter 10.

Tying Patterns for the Hatches

In Chapter 1, I mentioned Sheldon Seale of Ontario, Canada, as an exceptional fly-tier. I have adopted his method of tying many dry flies. When tying parachute-type dry flies, he first ties a post of poly yarn for the wing. Sheldon makes several thread wraps around the base of the poly yarn to prepare it for hackling. At this point Sheldon shapes the wing to look like a natural. He then ties on the tail at the bend of the hook. After Sheldon secures the tail he makes one or two turns under and behind the tail, which elevates the tail slightly and makes it look more lifelike. He then ties a body of the appropriate color up to and in front of the wing. He finishes the pattern by tying in a hackle at the eye and winding that around the poly wing. He winds the hackle around the post or wing and ties it off at the eye. To make certain the hackle doesn't slide off the wing Sheldon makes the first turn higher than the rest.

But, poly posts on parachute-type dry flies sometimes don't stand up well. After I place these dry flies in a compartment for a few days the poly yarns droop. If you want to use your patterns from year to year and you plan to tie dry flies parachute-style, then you might want to use deer hair instead. I've had great success with these posts and they last from year to year.

You might want to try tying some dry flies in a comparadun style as a sparkle dun. It's easy and effective, especially when you tie it in smaller sizes like sizes 16 to 20. To tie this easy pattern, tie in some gray Antron yarn just behind the eye of the hook. Make certain you use a piece long enough to make the wings and a shuck extend back beyond the bend of the hook. Cut off some of the shuck that you've substituted for a tail, then dub in some superfine poly for the body. Make several wraps of the dubbing in front of the Antron yarn wings. Next, cut the wings to proper length and shape them so they resemble the wings of a comparadun. In other words, fashion them so they form a semicircle. Add a few drops of cement to the base of wings to help hold them in place.

Tandem Connection

You can use most of the floating patterns listed in this chapter as lead flies in the tandem rig. If you're fishing a hatch, then match that hatch with the dry fly and use a nymph or emerger as the point fly. Let me illustrate. When the sulphur or pale morning dun appears, use a size 16 dry fly (I don't like to go any smaller than a size 16 as the dry fly or strike indicator) and use a Sulphur or PMD emerger or nymph as the underwater pattern. With this system during a hatch you'll catch trout rising to the dun and chasing nymphs and emergers. I've referred to this tandem setup as a bi-cycle.

Sinking Your Dry Fly

You see trout rising throughout the riffle in front of you. You see other telltale signs of trout feeding, like a swirl, indicating a trout chasing one of the sulphurs that just emerged on the surface. You have no wet fly or emerger pattern to copy the heavy sulphur hatch now occurring, only a dry fly. What do you do now? Look at the following events that occurred during some of the great hatches.

Green Drakes emerged by the dozens in front of us that evening on north-central Pennsylvania's Driftwood Branch. Once in a while we'd see trout chasing one of the emerging green drakes. Craig Hudson, Mark Campbell, Tom Barton, Don Perry, and I all used a large Green Drake pattern to match the hatch — and we all became frustrated. Trout resolutely refused any of the dry flies we cast over them. In a fit of frustration I tugged at the size 10 long-shank Green Drake pattern and pulled it a few inches beneath the surface. Within seconds a trout struck. Two more casts and another trout hit that "underwater dry fly." Craig and the others joined in and began sinking their Green Drakes. They, too, shared in the success that tactic brought us that evening. The five of us caught more than forty trout during the hatch — all on sunken dry flies. A year later I had a chance to fish the green drake hatch on Penns Creek. This famous central Pennsylvania limestone stream holds the heaviest drake hatch I've ever witnessed. In fact, many times the hatch and the spinner fall occur with such intensity that I've quit fishing rather than compete with so many naturals on the water. This particular evening, duns emerged in such great numbers that I sat back and watched the hatch progress. I then remembered the year before on the Driftwood Branch and sank the dry fly pattern. Within minutes I began catching trout. A nineteen-inch brown took that sunken dry fly that evening before I quit.

But sinking that dry fly pattern works on many other hatches. Recently Mark Jackson experienced his first hatch of white flies in the high waters of the Little Juniata River after a heavy thunderstorm. Mark saw thousands of white flies emerge, but few trout rise. He then remembered what I had told him about sinking the pattern when trout refuse your dry fly. Mark decided to do just that! He tugged at the White Fly and sank it a couple of inches beneath the surface. In the next hour Mark landed three heavy trout and missed more than a dozen more. Mark had used a floating dry fly for more than an hour without any success. But by submerging that pattern, Mark turned a potentially frustrating match-the-hatch episode into an eventful one. The same tactic works well during a sulphur hatch. I've often seen trout swirl at emergers and totally ignore duns on the surface. On many occasions I've tugged at my parachute Sulphur to sink it beneath the surface just a foot or two upstream from a feeding trout. Many times these trout take the dry fly just under the surface. Twitching the pattern once it has sunk sometimes seems to help.

We'll examine a few of the hatches here. You'll find patterns for these and other major hatches across the United States in Chapter 10.

I hoped this second trip to one of the premier rivers in the East was better than my first visit. Three years earlier I fished the Delaware River just below Hancock, New York, for an entire barren day. In five hours of fishing I had not seen one trout surface. Bob Sentiwany of White Haven accompanied me on this second trip to the same area. Bob assured me that we'd see some hatches and some rising trout this time, in late May.

We entered a long, fairly deep riffle at 4:00 p.m. and Bob pointed to several heavy trout already feeding in front of us. Now all I had to do was determine which pattern to use and how I could reach the trout with it. We both scanned the surface and saw some large pale yellow mayflies emerging in the riffle. One remained on the surface too long and disappeared with a large swirl.

The pale yellow body, tannish yellow wings, and two tan tails helped me identify it as a gray fox. Bob and I both tied on size 12 patterns and began casting to some heavy fish now feeding sporadically in the riffle. Bob caught the first trout, which he netted and released, a fifteen-inch rainbow. I cast the pattern over a rising fish five times before it came to the surface. When it did it grabbed the pattern, I set the hook, and the trout began to take out line. Before I knew it I was into my backing, and I waded downriver to keep up with the heavy rainbow. It shook one more time and broke loose. Ten other trout took Gray Foxes for Bob and me that evening before the hatch ended.

You'll find this same hatch on many Eastern and Midwestern waters. Pine Creek in north-central Pennsylvania has a great hatch.

Once the hatch begins you can expect to see these large mayflies appearing for a week or more. In the riffle at the head of Cemetery Pool, just a few miles above Waterville, more than ten trout fed on mayflies struggling to free themselves from the surface. Fred Templin and I had just arrived at the stream and saw trout surface feeding throughout a 100-yard section of water in front of us. For several days I had fished this sporadic hatch all afternoon with a great deal of success. Now I wanted to share this matching-the-hatch experience with someone.

For more than three hours that late-May afternoon, Fred and I caught trout during the hatch of gray foxes. Even though the hatch was less than concentrated, enough gray foxes appeared to bring trout to the surface. Once gray foxes appear, you can expect to see them for a week or more. The long time the hatch appears, the time of day it emerges, the light color of the imitation, which makes it easy to see, and the large size of the natural all combine to make this an exciting hatch to fish. The large size of the insect and its delay in taking flight sometimes coaxes even lunkers to the surface. When you find a hatch of gray foxes you're in for some exciting fishing.

Once you find this hatch you can have some great fishing for a week or more — even in the middle of the afternoon. Until seven years ago the Little Juniata River boasted, at best, a mediocre hatch of gray foxes. But by 1989, the hatch came on strong on the river. I can remember one trip on the river, on May 26, 1990, with Frank Chaplin of Philipsburg, and Ed Gunnett and Danny Deters of Williamsburg. Gray Foxes appeared all afternoon, as well as occasional sulphurs and green drakes. But most of the trout keyed in on the gray fox and hit the imitation freely. The four of us released more than fifty trout that afternoon — all caught on the Gray Fox pattern. With a sporadic hatch like the gray fox you can sit back and watch for risers then fish to them. Trout usually take a parachute-style Gray Fox readily.

You'll note that all three events described occurred on fairly large rivers or streams. You'll find this mayfly on many bigger waters, but also on some smaller streams. For example, the Bald Eagle near Julian, Pennsylvania, holds a great hatch of gray foxes. But by the time this hatch emerges on this smaller stream, water temperatures often reach the low seventies.

Have you ever been confused trying to identify whether the hatch emerging is a gray fox or a march brown? Some entomologists now classify the gray fox mayfly (*Stenonema fuscum*) as identical to the march brown (*Stenonema vicarium*). In several studies, scientists identified gray fox nymphs, which they raised to maturity. They identified these same nymphs as march browns in the adult stage. They also found no difference in the eggs between the two mayflies. I still see a distinct difference between the two. The wings and general body coloration vary considerably when comparing the gray fox with the march brown.

You can expect gray foxes to emerge as early as the middle of May. Hatches continue throughout the rest of the month, and sometimes well into early June. Duns most often emerge from afternoon until evening. On occasion I've hit heavy hatches of duns just at dusk. Spinners most often appear just before dusk. I match the dun and spinner with size 12 or 14 patterns.

Western rivers like the Colorado and Cache la Poudre in Colorado and the North Platte in Wyoming hold a hatch that looks almost identical to the Eastern gray fox. The Western hatch (*Heptagenia solitaria*) appears in late summer, usually in late August and early September. On the Colorado River just below Kremmling, gray fox duns emerged from late afternoon until dusk. Trout readily feed on stragglers on the surface and they enthusiastically take a size 14 Gray Fox. That evening hatch produced some of the best matching-the-hatch excitement on a recent two-week trip I took to

Colorado.

Where will you be fishing from mid-May through early June? Will you look for a green drake, sulphur, or light cahill hatch in the evening? Or will you fly-fish your favorite stream that holds a good gray fox hatch in the middle of the afternoon? Additionally, if you're fly-fishing on a Western river in late August don't forget the gray fox.

Little Blue-Wings

For several years Dick Mills and I opened New York's trout fishing season on the fabled Beaverkill. The season usually begins on April 1 and cold weather and cool water temperatures often greet early-season anglers. On many trips to this fabled water those cool days and cold water deterred trout from actively feeding underneath, let alone taking any insects on the surface.

One of those meetings on the Beaverkill stands out more than the others. That day, when I checked the water temperature at the Hendrickson Pool, I recorded a forty six-degree reading. This might seem exceptionally cold, but we hit even colder temperatures in years past. Shortly after noon, several little blue-winged olives braved the cold spring air and appeared at the riffle at the head of the pool. Soon more dazed duns join the first few, and a decent early-April hatch began. By midseason standards the half dozen trout that fed on duns on this early-spring day seemed pale by comparison. However, each one that took the tiny naturals rose for a size 20 Little Blue-Winged Olive.

If you've fished for any time you'll find little blue-winged olive duns exceedingly common on streams and rivers across the United States. In fact, this hatch possibly constitutes the country's most widespread hatch. Not only will you find the hatch on many trout waters across the country, but also you will see two distinct emergence times — spring and again in fall. This species (*Baetis tricaudatus*) has two generations per year, so if you catch the hatch in spring, you can expect it to return again in September and October.

I returned that same year to fish the Beaverkill and Willowemac in late September, hoping to see the fall hatch of these small but important mayflies. The little blue-winged olive proved the hatch to match on that fall trip. Water temperatures and weather conditions had improved tremendously from the early spring episode and trout rose eagerly to a size 20 Little Blue-Winged Olive.

Central Pennsylvania also boasts great little blue-winged olive hatches in September. Andrew Leitzinger of Collegeville and I arrived at one of the region's prime trout waters, the Little Juniata River, early in the morning on a late-October day. The fields bordering the river still held a heavy frost, a reminder of the cold night before and a harbinger of the winter to come. This was Andrew's first trip to this fertile limestone river and I wanted him to see some of the great hatches and heavy brown trout this river holds. But, realistically, could we expect to see any hatch this late in the season? Hadn't all the hatches ended until next March? And, of course, without a hatch would we see any rising trout this late in the season?

For most of the morning we used wet flies and streamers, hoping that midges, stoneflies, caddis flies, craneflies, or mayflies would appear in the afternoon. (In October and November if insects appear, they do so most often at the warmest time of the day — usually 1:00-4:00 p.m.) We picked up a half dozen healthy brown trout and decided to head upriver around noon. Several loud gunshots near the river reminded me that I should have forgone fly-fishing for grouse hunting that day, rather than freezing on a stream at a time too late in the fall for any hatch to appear.

Upriver at our new location a few small, dark gray mayflies appeared on the surface. I captured one, examined it carefully, and decided that it was one of those tiny mayflies anglers call the little blue-winged olive dun. It didn't take trout long to notice this fall bonus and several browns took up feeding positions in front of us. Both of us tied on size 20 Little Blue-Winged Olive dun imitations with dark brown Z-lon shucks. I add these shucks, extending back over the tail, to copy the mayfly leaving the nymphal shuck. Before the hatch ended around 3:00 p.m., Andy and I picked up more than a dozen trout by matching that late-season mayfly. Just as the little blue-wings diminished in numbers a second, larger mayfly, the slate drake, appeared. Both of us switched to a size 14 Slate Drake and caught a few trout on that pattern before the hatch ended abruptly when the late-afternoon sun dipped behind the high mountain to the west. Within minutes the air temperature dropped ten degrees and the hatch ended on this late-October day.

What happens when the day you've planned to fish the hatch turns out to be one of those raw, cold fall days not fit for an angler to brave? If you've experienced several days of relatively warm weather and the stream temperature has risen into the low to mid-fifties before this cold day, get out and enjoy the hatch. Often on inclement early-fall days, little blue-wings appear on the surface but they can't escape because of the cold weather. On these cold, overcast days I've seen duns literally cover the surface.

The little blue-winged olive isn't confined to the East. If you do any fishing on Midwestern waters like the AuSable, or New Mexico's San Juan then you already know that both hold spectacular little blue-wing hatches. I arrived just below the Navajo Dam on the San Juan in late February with Phil Camera, Chuck Rizuto, and Mike Manfredo. Phil fishes the San Juan a dozen or more times a year and I consider him an expert on the river. Phil has written a book on synthetics and he created Larva Lace. Chuck also knows the river and its hatches well. He and Roy Stoddard wrote an excellent book on the San Juan.

I spent the entire morning of the first day fishing the dark gray midge hatch just below the dam. By noon, Phil, Chuck, and I moved downriver several hundreds yards to fish the little blue-winged olive hatch. Already, little blue-wings appeared near shore and several heavy rainbows took up feeding positions within inches of the near shoreline. I tied on a size 20 parachute Little Blue-Winged Olive dun and cast upriver thirty feet to a heavy riser. Probably the first four casts had micro drag — the heavy trout ignored the pattern completely. Then, on the fifth cast, a good drag-free one, the rainbow, almost in slow motion, came up and grabbed that size 20 pattern. The trout fought only briefly and I netted it and returned it to the San Juan.

That afternoon I caught five heavy trout on the Little Blue-Winged Olive dun. The hatch appears almost all year long on the San Juan. But March, April, September, and October are the best times to meet the hatch.

Tie the pattern to match the dun on a size 20 hook. If you look closely at the natural, you'll see that the body has an olive-gray color. I usually use an olive-gray polypropylene or I soak muskrat fur in an olive dye for a couple of minutes.

I said earlier that I use dark brown Z-lon or Antron to simulate an attached nymphal shuck. Extend the shuck over the tail and make it as long as the shank of the hook.

Tie some of your Little Blue-Wings sparkle-dun style, with gray Antron wings and olive-gray superfine poly dubbing. You'll find this an effective pattern when naturals emerge.

Green Drake/Western Green Drake

I arrived in Missoula, Montana, just two hours earlier, rented a car, and headed for a section of the Bitterroot River fifteen miles south of Missoula. I arrived shortly before noon, and for almost half an hour I stared at the raging river. How would I catch any trout in this water — especially with a dry fly? What fly should

I use? Where in the world should I fish this high, snow-fed river? I scheduled my trip to the Bitterroot and twenty other Western waters in late June so that I could complete the manuscript for *Meeting and Fishing the Hatches*. I had a deadline — the publisher wanted the manuscript in three weeks — and I had to experience, first-hand, hatches, rising trout, and fishing success. I had hoped to meet and fish some of the great hatches on these Western waters, my chances looked rather slim after I stared at the high, cold water of the Bitterroot. Nothing I did seemed to work.

The fast-flowing river mesmerized me until I saw a splash from a rising trout just ten feet in front of me — then another and another. Soon I had five heavy trout rising within easy casting distance. I scanned the surface and saw a large, dark green mayfly attempting to escape the river and the clutches of a trout. I grabbed one of the escaping mayflies and examined it carefully. It had dark gray wings and a dark green body ribbed with yellow. Green Drakes, I thought, and I grabbed for an imitation that I had tied just before I left for the trip.

I hurriedly tied on the pattern, since I didn't know how long the hatch would last, and cast toward the closest rising trout. No sooner had the Green Drake landed on the surface than it disappeared in the mouth of a heavy cutthroat trout. I landed the fish and cast toward another rising fish. This cutthroat also took the pattern without hesitation. Before that hatch ended in early afternoon I caught and released more than a half dozen heavy trout on the Bitterroot. What a greeting to Western fly-fishing! What a way to start a trip! Barely a half hour after I first set foot on a Western river I fished a fabulous green drake hatch.

Since that first encounter I've fished the Western green drake many times on Henry's Fork in Idaho. The hatch there, too, begins around the end of June. Hatches start in the morning and usually continue sporadically for a couple of hours. Hatches on

Henry's Fork are heavy and usually bring some large rainbows to the surface.

One of the sparsest hatches I've seen occurred on the McKenzie River above McKenzie Bridge in central Oregon. Ken Helfrich, one of the top guides in the United States, first floated me down the upper end of that river. In its upper reaches McKenzie rainbows go crazy for green drake naturals. As we drifted through some of the most scenic land in the United States, Ken and I saw a few drakes appear on the surface. Soon enough appeared so that some heavy trout began feeding on them. On the fast trip though that upper end I hooked a heavy eighteen-inch rainbow on the Western Green Drake and landed the fish two sets of riffles and two pools downriver.

Probably the longest hatch of Western green drakes occurs on the Roaring Fork and Fryingpan rivers in Colorado. The drake hatch begins on the Roaring Fork near Glenwood Springs around June 25. It moves upriver a few miles each week, moving up a major tributary, the Fryingpan River, and finally reaches the section below the Ruedi Reservoir around the end of August or early September. So from late June until early September you can fish this hatch. On any day the drake emerges on a two- or three-mile section of the river.

Roy Palm, owner of Frying Pan Anglers in Basalt, and I hit the green drake hatch in mid-August several miles below the Ruedi Reservoir. Roy has fly-fished the Frying Pan for more than thirty years and he knows each section of the river and exactly where the drake hatch is every day. Roy handed me a deer-hair Green Drake pattern to try. As we entered the water shortly before noon, a few of these huge mayflies already appeared on the surface. Huge rainbows, now accustomed to the daily hatch, began feeding immediately on stragglers. Roy and I took turns casting to rising trout and we landed seven heavy fish before the sporadic hatch ended.

The Eastern green drake appears a few weeks later than its Western counterpart. In West Virginia, on the Elk and Cheat rivers you'll find good hatches in mid- to late May. In late May, fly-fishers match the hatch on Pennsylvania's Penns Creek and the Little Juniata River. By early to mid-June, anglers fish green drake hatches on the Delaware and Beaverkill.

I've often had difficulty catching many trout on the Green Drake pattern though Harvey's Green Drake has performed better than most other imitations. If you don't think you have many choices on what pattern to use during the hatch just visit Penns Creek during a hatch. You'll find anglers using hundreds of different patterns, some closely resembling the drake and some that don't look the least like the natural. If you observe closely when the drakes appear, you'll find that some trout prefer to feed on a smaller sulphur hatch. I often sit back before I begin to fish and watch the surface to see what's happening. One day on the Little Juniata River I counted eight trout feeding on a sulphur hatch while only two fed on the green drake hatch. I tied on a Sulphur and caught a half dozen trout on the pattern. Later I tied on a Green Drake and in an hour's time caught only one trout. Remember, when you fish this hatch watch to see if the trout are really feeding on the drake.

I'll always remember the largest trout I ever caught during the drake hatch on Penns Creek. Trout totally refused the dry fly during the hatch. In a fit of frustration I tugged at the dry fly and sank the pattern just under the surface. Within seconds a heavy brown trout hit that submerged fly. In a few minutes I landed a nineteen-inch brown trout that had taken that sunken dry fly.

I've grouped these two patterns together, although the two naturals have little in common. The Western green drake appears at midday, while the Eastern green drake emerges most often at dusk. Both, because of their large size, bring lunkers to the surface to feed.

Light Cahill

Barry Serviente owns Anglers Art and sells new and used fly-fishing books to thousands of fly-fishers and collectors worldwide. Just after *Pennsylvania Trout Streams and Their Hatches* was published in 1990, I went to an autograph session Barry organized in Carlisle, Pennsylvania. More than a thousand book collectors and anglers attended that fair that morning. Around noon an irate fly-fisher stopped by to talk with me. He insisted that Pennsylvania, and Penns Creek in particular, held no light cahill hatches and insisted that I correct my reference to that hatch in *Pennsylvania Trout Streams and Their Hatches*. When I told him I had no intention of changing my reference he became even more annoyed and said that in all his years of fly-fishing he never saw a light cahill hatch on Penns Creek.

Believe me, and thousands of other anglers who have witnessed the hatch, Penns Creek and many other waters hold hatches that anglers commonly refer to as light cahills. Often you'll find these mayflies appearing from late May through much of June and July. On those evenings when few other insects appear, the light cahill emerges in sporadic numbers.

Great hatches remain with us as lifetime memories. As fly-fishers we rarely forget those great episodes when a hatch appears, trout rise to the insect, and most important, we have an effective pattern to match that hatch. I had only begun fly-fishing a year before, but the first light cahill hatch I encountered has remained a vivid memory for more than three decades. Lloyd Williams and Tom Taylor accompanied me to Elk Creek in north-central Pennsylvania. I had finally coaxed Lloyd to resume fly-fishing after hiatus of more than fifteen years.

By 8:00 p.m. on this small stream thousands of light cahills emerged all at once. As luck would have it, the Light Cahill was one of the few dry flies I had in my fly box. That hatch, that evening, that match will always be remembered for its intensity and for the number of trout we caught.   When I prepared the manuscript for *Meeting and Fishing the Hatches* I decided to fly-fish the Bitterroot in southwestern Montana, and I hit a mayfly hatch appropriately copied by a size 14 Light Cahill. Matching that hatch that July evening on the Bitterroot near Victor remains a vivid memory now twenty years later. Brown and rainbow trout in the fifteen- to twenty-inch category hit that dry fly that evening, and the action lasted for more than two hours.

Because of the hatches it matches and the success I've had with the pattern, I consider the Light Cahill as one of my top ten dry fly patterns.

Possibly the best evening I ever experienced fly-fishing was on an early-June evening on central Pennsylvania's Little Juniata River. When I arrived at the river a cool breeze blew upriver and a misty overcast held the late-spring temperature down to the low sixties. A steady if sporadic hatch of light cahills (*Stenacron canadense*) already paraded down the far riffle leading into a deep pool. At least a dozen trout had already taken up feeding positions in that riffle. I tied on a size 14 Light Cahill and began casting to risers.

Fred Templin had agreed to meet me at this section of the stream around 7:00 p.m. By the time Fred arrived I had already caught ten trout on the Cahill. That evening the two of us caught and released close to forty trout on the Light Cahill.

The tying description for the Light Cahill is in Chapter 10.

Sulphur/Pale Morning Dun

Jerry Meck and I floated down the scenic Kootenai River tucked away from many fly-fishers in northwestern Montana. Dave Blackburn, a guide on the river, agreed to float Jerry and me down an eight-mile section near Libby. He skillfully drifted us though a two-mile section of rocks and rapids before we stopped to fish. On this late-June morning a fine drizzle fell and the temperature had difficulty rising above sixty degrees.

By the time we reached the third long riffle, a few pale morning duns began emerging. Soon more and more duns surfaced. Pools that appeared void of trout just minutes before now became feeding stations for more than fifty heavy rainbow trout. The drizzle and cold air temperature prevented many of the pale morning duns from escaping rapidly and they rode the surface for several feet before they attempted to fly. Trout ignored my conventional PMD pattern, so I quickly tied on a PMD comapradun with a dark brown Z-lon shuck attached to the rear. On the second cast a fifteen-inch rainbow hit the pattern. In that one glide more than a dozen trout took that mutated PMD pattern. A short drift down to the next pool, the three of us saw another pod of heavy rainbows taking pale morning dun emergers. Again the PMD with a Z-lon shuck proved the pattern of the day.

For years I used the high-riding conventional pattern — until that episode on the Kootenai River.

For forty years I relied on a conventional high-riding Sulphur pattern during the hatch. Within the past two years I've switched to a comparaduns and parachute patterns with a deer-hair post, and my success ratio has increased considerably.

In the East and Midwest you'll hit productive streams and rivers with sulphurs appearing for a good three weeks. When I fish over several trout that continuously refuse my parachute pattern I resort to using an emerger or nymph with the dry fly. If they refuse the emerger pattern I switch to a nymph.

Try tying some Sulphur patterns with Antron wings and superfine poly dubbing. The sparkle dun, as many anglers call it, works exceptionally well on trout that have experienced a considerable amount of angling pressure.

Blue-Winged Olives

I wrote about the episode in *Pennsylvania Trout Streams and Their Hatches*. It happened in early July on an extremely cool, dismal, overcast day on the catch-and-release section of Penns Creek. As I began to fly-fish, two other anglers left the stream in disgust over the poor conditions at this time of year. But always remember: When you're looking for midsummer blue-winged olive hatches fish on the lousiest days. No, I don't mean those days when you hit a heavy thunderstorm, but those cool, overcast May, June, and July days when mayflies can't take flight and trout sense that the duns on the surface won't escape quickly. Add a drizzle and you have the proper ingredients for a tremendous day of matching the hatches in midsummer.

That day in early July was the single greatest occasion of matching the hatches in my forty years of fly-fishing. Blue-wings dotted almost the entire surface of Penns Creek and trout went on a feeding frenzy. Several size 16 Blue-Winged Olive dun patterns proved the correct match for more than thirty trout.

But you'll also find great blue-winged olive hatches on Western rivers. I'll always have fond recollections of the fantastic blue-winged olive hatch on the Metolius River in central Oregon. Jay Kapolka and I traveled to this fabled river in late May. Jay, Dick Turner, Gary Kish, and I had fished the upper end of the river near Camp Sherman just a few days before with little success. We now returned four days later and on a chilly, drizzly morning several miles downriver. As Jay and I arrived at the river little blue-wings already dotted the surface of this great river. Thousands of these duns struggled to take flight, but most failed. By 10:00 a.m. pale morning duns joined the little blue-wings, creating a smorgasbord in the eddies for feeding rainbows. By now Jay had a dozen trout feeding in the food line in front of him. Jay's Pale Morning Dun pattern duped several of those risers before they switched to a third mayfly, the blue-winged olive dun.

Jay came upriver to see if I had any more success and on what pattern. I handed him a size 14 Blue-Winged Olive dun and he headed downriver to the next pool to give it a try. Within minutes both of us began catching fish on blue-wing patterns. The multi-hatch episode on the Metolius lasted for more than three hours and Jay and I caught heavy rainbows during the entire period. Don't ever overlook those drizzly, overcast, cool late-spring and summer days when you expect to see blue-wings on the water.

Blue Quills

Jerry Meck and I had just fished over a pale morning dun hatch all morning and had little to show for it. That late-June day just a few years ago, Henry's Fork seemed to hold fewer trout than it had two decades ago. We decided to give the stream another chance and headed out for an afternoon of fishing. On almost every occasion that I've fished it, Henry's Fork produces hatches. Others have often called it an insect factory, because of the abundance of aquatic insects. That afternoon Jerry and I fished as a concentrated hatch of Blue Quills appeared on the surface. Although fewer trout than I expected rose, we had a great afternoon of matching the hatch with a size 18 Blue Quill imitation.

Blue Quills appear throughout the United States and have become one of my favorite patterns. You'll find hatches of the genus this pattern copies (*Paraleptophlebia*) appearing from April through October almost daily. Eastern and Midwestern streams hold their share of these hatches, especially in late April.

George Harvey has fly-fished on central Pennsylvania's Young Woman's Creek for decades. He enjoys this small fertile, stream and its great hatches. However, on this late-April afternoon neither George nor I expected the intensity of the blue quill hatch that appeared. We had fished much of the morning and had few strikes. George and I decided to hit one more section of the stream before we headed home. As George approached a small pool with a long riffle above he began seeing some blue quills emerging. We both tied on Blue Quill imitations and looked for rising trout. George didn't have to wait long; within minutes the pool in front of him came alive with a dozen or more rising trout. Trout after trout took George's Blue Quill pattern.

Meanwhile, downstream a hundred feet, I saw the same intense hatch but only a few trout rose in the pocket water in front of me. George beckoned me to come upstream and fish the pool in front of him. When I arrived a half dozen trout still picked off escaping duns. Before the hatch ended George and I had caught and released fifteen trout in that pool and riffle, water that before the hatch seemed void of any trout.

No matter where you plan to fish make certain that the Blue Quill goes with you. This pattern matches so many widely distributed hatches that it's imperative to take some with you.

Definitely tie some of your Blue Quill patterns sparkle-dun style. This pattern, with dark gray superfine poly dubbing for the body and gray Antron for the wings and tail, works well all season. Also tie some of your imitations parachute-style, with a dark gray deer-hair post.

Hendrickson/Western March Brown

For the third week in April the weather turned dull, dismal, and dreary. As Mike Manfredo and I entered the McKenzie drift boat the air temperature struggled to reach fifty degrees. What a horrible day to match a hatch! Both of us prepared for the cold float trip by donning heavy winter jackets.

Ken Helfrich of Springfield, Oregon, skillfully drifted us

through a set of rapids on the McKenzie River several miles above Eugene, Oregon. Shortly after noon we had drifted more than a mile and had only one trout. But then the action began; within minutes the bottom of the river gave up thousands of Western March Brown nymphs in an explosive hatch that lasted for more than an hour. As we arrived at the first riffle after the hatch had commenced Ken pointed to dozens of trout rising to newly emerged duns, which had difficulty escaping the McKenzie's surface because of the cold, damp conditions.

Ken had rigged a March Brown dry fly on a dropper and a March Brown wet fly as the point fly. If the dry fly sank, it meant we had a strike on the wet fly. Ken showed Mike and me the recast method of fly-fishing from a boat with the two patterns. We'd let the patterns drift downriver below us, then lift them up and drop them back in the water nearer the boat. The dry fly sank more quickly than with the tandem method I recommend but it did produce many takes. Mike and I continued to catch and release McKenzie rainbows for more than two hours on that inclement day. What a hatch! What a day!

New York's Beaverkill boasts a tremendous number of great hatches. From early April until October you'll see insects emerging on this fabled stream. I mentioned earlier one opening day on the Beaverkill when Dick Mills and I hit a decent hatch of little blue-wings. But the hendrickson mayfly presents one of the best and earliest hatches to appear on the stream.

More than twenty years have passed since Dick Mills and I entered the appropriately named Hendrickson Pool just before noon near the end of April. Within minutes an unbelievably heavy hendrickson hatch appeared on the surface. The cold water kept some of the trout from rising, but both Dick and I had plenty of risers to attempt to catch. That hatch that day continued for more than two hours. Almost every part of the stream held dozens of struggling duns attempting to escape from the surface. Near 3:00 p.m. the hatch ended and only a trout or two still rose for the hendricksons still on the surface. What a day of matching the hatch!

The hendrickson and Western March Brown aren't closely related. However, both hatches appear early in the fishing season. The Western March Brown begins its annual appearance on Western Oregon rivers in late February and continues into May. Both hatches are similar in color and appearance, with tannish-brown bodies. Anglers find great March Brown hatches on other Western rivers like the Yakima in central Washington and on the Kootenai in northwestern Montana.

Dark Brown Sparkle Dun

For several years I've advocated the importance of copying a small dark ephemerellid, *Serratella deficiens*. I've encountered the hatch on many Eastern streams in early June. It's one of the smallest ephemerellids I've encountered, but it appears in heavy numbers and brings trout to the surface. Few fly-fishers, however, ever prepare for this hatch and even fewer attempt to match the hatch. I've fished over hatches in mid- to late afternoon on many occasions and had just mediocre success with a conventional high-riding imitation.

Greg Hoover, who co-authored *Great Rivers—Great Hatches*, relates a story about the hatch of these dark brown duns that he and several friends encountered on Spruce Creek. Greg and his friends resorted to using a Dark Brown Sparkle Dun imitation and caught more than sixty trout that afternoon. He said all four anglers caught trout that rose to naturals on the Dark Brown Sparkle Dun.

Try this same type of pattern but with an olive-yellow body tied in a size 16 for the sulphur hatch. Trout that refuse a Catskill-type Sulphur might take the sparkle dun.

The division between flies has become somewhat blurred in the past few years with so many new patterns, hybrids, and new materials on the market. Some anglers call comparaduns with shucks for tails, sparkle duns. Others refer to a pattern as a sparkle dun if it has a wing and tail of Antron yarn. Whatever you call it, make certain you carry sparkle duns in some of the smaller sizes.

Dark Brown Sparkle Dun
> HOOK: Mustad 94833, size 16 or 18
> THREAD: Dark brown
> TAILS: White Z-lon
> BODY: Dark brown poly
> WINGS: White Z-lon

Tying Notes: Tie on the Z-lon first. Take a piece of white Z-lon and make a loop or double it for the wings. Extend the Z-lon over the body and out over the bend of the hook. Make certain it extends beyond the bend about as long as the length of the shank of the hook. Cut off about half of the Z-lon that now copies a shuck. Dub fine dark brown poly and wrap for the body. Make several turns in front of the Z-lon wings to make them stand upright. Cut and shape the wings and move the Z-lon so it makes a semicircle.

Dark Gray Midge

Several years ago Craig Shuman set up a series of mid-April speeches for me in Fort Collins, Colorado, and Tacoma, Washington. Interspersed between the talks, were several fishing trips. On all these early-season trips one insect took on significant importance — a dark gray midge.

Our first trip took us to the catch-and-release section of the Cache la Poudre River just outside Fort Collins. By the time we arrived in late morning the hatch had already begun. Craig, Eric Pettine, and Jim Garrett and I each selected areas where a dozen or more trout rose to what seemed like an unending supply of dark gray midges. I stayed near Jim for a while, taking photos of five heavy trout he caught on his Gray Midge imitation.

After taking photos, I hurried downriver to a section where five trout fed freely on the dying, mated midges. I tied a size 24 Gray Midge onto a 5X tippet and began casting. Occasionally a trout would take the imitation — not regularly — since these trout had seen many anglers and dozens of patterns in the past months.

I finally tied on a size 24 Gray Midge with a white Z-lon shuck. Midge patterns normally don't contain a tail. Adding a shuck it not only copied the midge escaping from its pupal case but it also gave buoyancy to the floating pattern. Two trout took this pattern almost immediately, probably because they hadn't seen a pattern like it before. By the time the hatch ended all four of us had picked up several trout and had fished over rising trout for several hours.

You'll find midge hatches on many streams and rivers in the West. On our trip to Tacoma, Craig Shuman also set up a trip to Rocky Ford Creek several hours east of the Seattle-Tacoma area. Garry Sandstrom of the Morning Hatch in Tacoma accompanied us. Garry handed me a size 24 midge pattern and pointed to a few rising trout. That small pattern caught three of those heavy rainbows that morning.

But possibly the best hatch matching for the dark gray midge occurs on the San Juan River just below the Navajo Dam. In late February you'll see midges emerging much of the day. Phil Camera, a fly-fisher and outdoor writer, and Mike Manfredo accompanied me on my maiden trip to that river.

If you've fly-fished the San Juan River, you know that many anglers already know of its productivity. We counted more than twenty cars parked in the upper parking lot at 9:00 a.m.

Mike headed downriver while Phil and I headed toward the dam and some of the slower water. As I arrived at a small pool and riffle I noted a half dozen heavy trout feeding consistently on dark gray midges. Upriver from me I saw maybe ten anglers flailing away at his or her little section of river and at trout rising to this midge hatch. I first tried a size 24 Dark Gray Midge while Phil tied on a Griffith's Gnat. Both adequately copied the midge hatch that day — but both failed to catch any trout.

In the first hour of fishing the five or six huge trout rising just upriver a few feet completely frustrated me. I cast over each riser with several perfect casts without any success, then moved onto the next one. For that first frustrating half-hour I had only one heavy rainbow even come up to inspect my pattern.

Finally in desperation, I tied on a Gray Midge pattern with a white shuck. I watched the midges emerge on the river closely and I saw many of them take an inordinate amount of time escaping from their pupal shuck. I surmised that few trout had seen this pattern before so I might have a better chance of landing one. On the second drag-free cast over a riser he came up, and in what seemed like slow motion, took the midge. I set the hook gingerly on the heavy fish; it only fought for a few minutes and I landed an eighteen-inch rainbow.

That morning I duped four trout into taking that Gray Midge with the Z-lon shuck. Now that might not seem like a lot to you, but before I used the shuck pattern I hadn't landed a trout. Make certain you tie some of your favorite floating midge patterns with shucks.

Dark Gray Midge
      HOOK: Mustad 94833, sizes 12 to 24
      THREAD: Dark gray
      TAILS: (optional) White Z-lon
      BODY: Eyed peacock, stripped
      HACKLE: Grizzly

Downwings

Up to this point we have mentioned little about caddis flies. This order, Tricoptera, might be able to withstand a greater degree of pollution than some other orders of aquatic insects, especially mayflies, and you'll find caddis flies emerging from mid-April through September. On many streams you'll find the heaviest caddis activity occurs from late April until mid-May. I often call this time of the fishing season "caddis time." Usually the early mayfly hatches like the blue quill, quill gordon, and hendrickson have ended by early May. For the next two weeks you'll find plenty of downwings appearing.

Unlike the mayfly, the caddis goes through a complete metamorphosis. Its pupal stage lasts a couple of weeks. As I noted earlier, after the male and female mate, the female dives underwater and deposits the eggs. Some species drop the fertilized eggs in flight like many mayflies, while others actually swim underwater to place them. The eggs develop in a few weeks and the newly hatched larvae build cases to protect their fragile bodies. Unlike the mayfly nymph, which has a hard exoskeleton, the caddis larva has only a thin integument covering the greater part of its body. Only the legs and head of the larva are heavily protected, because these parts usually extend from the case.

To construct a covering, the larva uses the sand, pebbles, stone, sticks, or any number of things found in the stream. Each genus is usually specific in selecting building materials. In some genera, however, the larva moves about freely and builds no case. An example of the latter is the green caddis *(Rhyacophila lobifera)*. Imitations of this larva usually work well.

Most species, however, do build cases. The grannom *(Brachycentrus fuliginosus* and related species) builds its case of sticks and is usually found in backwater areas of streams. Another important caddis, the dark blue sedge *(Psilotreta frontalis)*, found most often in fast water, builds its case of sand and pebbles. Several genera, like *Hydropsyche* and *Chimarra,* are called net spinners because they build small fibrous nets to collect food.

As the larva feeds and grows, it adds to its case. About two weeks before it emerges as an adult, it goes into a pupal stage. In this stage, the case (sometimes called a cocoon) is almost completely closed except for a small hole that allows some water to enter. During this stage the adult develops. After about two weeks the pupa, encased in a protective membrane, swims to the surface. At the surface it breaks the covering membrane and flies to the shore. You can usually tell a hatch has just occurred when you see these transparent pupal cases floating in the water.

Adult caddis flies usually live longer than mayfly adults, perhaps a week or more. Since emerging adults are capable of mating, no change occurs from dun to spinner, as it does in mayflies. At emergence and during the egg-laying process, trout seize emerging adults eagerly. Since the wings of the adult are folded back over the body in a tent-like fashion, the wings of your imitations, whether wet or dry, should be shaped similarly. Wet fly patterns imitating the emerging caddis perform exceptionally well during a hatch.

Al Gretz of Punxsutawney, Pennsylvania, and I met on the Kootenai River just below Libby, Montana, for an evening of fly-fishing. Al visits Western rivers every chance he gets, but this trip marked his inaugural outing on the Kootenai. We arrived at the calm, still river hoping for rising trout. As we scanned the fast water and pool above and the riffle below, neither of us saw any sign of surface feeding. But that didn't last long. Within minutes a large tan caddis began emerging in the riffle below us.

Al raced upriver to a deep riffle and began casting to two dozen trout actively feeding on downwings. I headed downriver where a deep riffle undercut the near bank. In front of me ten

Kootenai rainbows fed on emerging tan caddis flies. I cast a few feet above the first riser, which quickly sucked in the pattern and shook violently until it freed itself. A couple of feet upriver the next heavy rainbow surfaced in that riffle. It also took the tan caddis eagerly. The next trout refused the Tan Caddis so after several attempts I tugged on the pattern until it sank just a couple of inches. As the Tan Caddis moved within a foot of this more selective riser I gently twitched the pattern to suggest movement. It hit that pattern savagely.

Two hours after the tan caddis hatch had begun, it ended with a whimper. But not before the Kootenai had surrendered more than twenty trout to Al and me.

Many of the great Western rivers host spectacular caddisfly hatches, and many of them appear in midsummer. Let me explain.

Richie Montella had just expertly guided Bryan Meck and me eleven miles down the Bighorn River for the float trip of a lifetime. From late morning through early afternoon Bryan and I fly-fished over pods of heavy brown trout rising to a pale morning dun spinner fall. And from early afternoon until 5:00 p.m. a gray *Baetis* covered every eddy along the river. Again, pods of trout poked their noses through the surface, scooping in five and six duns at a time. A size 22 Blue Dun imitation made that trip even more memorable.

But the culmination of that spectacular day occurred just a mile or two upriver from the Bighorn access. At 7:00 p.m. a dark caddis, almost black with an olive cast, began emerging. Trout surfaced in every riffle to this new supply of naturals. As Bryan tied on a size 16 Black Caddis, huge trout, some in the twenty-inch class, fed in a deep riffle in front of him. Bryan began casting as I sat in the boat and watched. We had already fly-fished for more than ten straight hours and I had to rest for a while.

Bryan coaxed that first heavy brown to strike within minutes. It exploded out of the water, shook violently, and threw the

Black Caddis imitation. Bryan didn't lose the next five trout on that pattern — all over fifteen inches long, and all taken on that dark downwing. What a sensational ending to a memorable day!

You can read about the emergence characteristics of caddis flies in Chapter 3.

Tandem Connection

Craig Josephson fished the Yellow Breeches in late June with an unusual tandem connection, a fluttering Green Caddis dry with an emerging Green Caddis on the point, an excellent way to fish streams and rivers that hold good caddis hatches. If trout chase the emerger during a hatch, they'll strike the wet fly; if they're feeding on top, they'll take the dry fly. You can use the tandem in other ways during caddis hatches. If you want to see the floating pattern better, use a Patriot or other larger upright-wing pattern with a caddis emerger or larva.

General Tying Instructions

If you've tied flies for a while, you already know there are many ways to copy caddis flies. First, no caddis pattern has a tail. However, with the advent of new synthetics, you can add Z-lon to some of your patterns to suggest the emergence of the caddis adult. Besides, adding a tail adds some buoyancy to the downwing pattern. If you look at the body of a caddis fly you'll see they're short and definitely ribbed, so rib your imitations. Keep each wrap separate, suggesting the ribbing and don't make the body too long. Shucks have grown in importance recently in fly-fishing, because they suggest nymphal or pupal cases still attached to the mayfly or caddis fly. Fly-fishers add these to many mayfly patterns. More recently some fly tiers have begun to add them to their caddis fly patterns. I tie most of these shucks with a pale tan Z-lon.

I prefer elk hair to deer hair for the wings of most caddis

patterns, but elk hair is not as easy to tie in. When cutting the hair off after tying it in, clip it at an angle so you can add the hackle and complete the head. Elk hair floats well and produces an excellent downwing pattern.

If you add hackle in front of the wing, make certain it is short. If you're tying a size 12 Green Caddis, use a size 16 hackle. If you use a larger hackle, you might want to clip it off on the bottom.

Many anglers prefer another type of floating caddis pattern. They dub a poly body, then palmer-hackle the body. The Henryville became a famous pattern with this type of body. Some anglers prefer lower-riding patterns and omit the hackle altogether. Without any hackle, this type of downwing allows you to sink the pattern, if necessary, just under the surface. As with mayfly spinners, you'll find caddis flies in colors of cream, tan, yellow, orange, cinnamon, green, olive, black, and gray and in sizes from 12 to 20. So I have a match for every caddis hatch – all colors in all sizes in several Wheatly-type boxes.

Next time you see a caddis hatch grab one and examine it. If you look closely at the body you'll see it's small and often noticeably segmented. Try to copy the natural as closely as possible.

Note that the discussion of the Black Caddis includes a different way to tie a caddis adult. It's easy and extremely effective, with a strand of antron used for the wing and extending beyond the bend of the hook. I call it Charlie Meck's Black Caddis, but I'm sure others have tied it this way before.

Tactics for Caddis Hatches

When fishing caddis fly hatches remember these two tactics: movement and depth. Movement refers to twitching or skittering the dry fly and twitching the emerging pupa. Depth refers to where in the water column you're fishing the pattern. If trout refuse your dry fly, then sink it just under the surface. If that doesn't work, try an emerging pattern. Let's examine both tactics in more detail.

Several years ago I fished a grannom hatch on Spruce Creek in late April. I cast over a half dozen rising trout and all refused the dry fly. In frustration I lifted my rod tip and moved the downwing across and in front of a rising trout in a skittering motion. At the first movement, a brown trout took the pattern. Within a half hour six more trout took that moving pattern. Don't overlook this method, especially if trout have refused a drag-free float.

While fishing the Green Caddis on the Little Juniata River one day, I varied the movement of the submerged emerging pupa pattern. I tied on a soft-hackle wet fly and alternated retrieves, fishing one with a dead drift and the next with a twitch or jerking motion. In more than 500 casts during that particular experiment, I caught twice as many trout on the pattern I twitched than I did using a dead drift. Vary the movement of wet and dry flies when you fish caddis hatches.

As with movement, depth also plays an important part in fishing a caddis hatch. Unlike mayflies, adult caddis flies usually escape the surface rapidly. Because of this quick getaway, trout often shun the adult and prefer to chase the underwater emerging caddis. Trout will take the dry fly, especially when the adult female comes back to the surface to lay eggs. But trout often seem to prefer an underwater pattern.

"The bi-cycle is the best way to fish the emerger," says Tom Finkbiner, Who has been helping anglers catch trout on Pine Creek during the cream caddis hatch for years. Western anglers have also used this method for years. With the bi-cycle you use a dry fly, then attach a tippet to the bend of the hook of that pattern. I usually prefer a two- to three-foot tippet, depending on the velocity and depth of the water. Tie the wet fly on the end of the tippet that is attached to the dry fly. I add a bit of weight to the emerger pattern when I tie it to keep it under the surface. When you're fishing a cream caddis hatch you can use a high-floating dry caddis and attach a cream caddis emerger to the tippet. With this method you cover trout coming to the surface and those feeding just under the surface, and with just a few minutes of practice you'll find it extremely easy casting the two flies simultaneously.

Black Caddis and Grannom

Craig Shuman and Jack Mitchell have guided on Washington's Yakima River for several years. Ask both of them what time of year they enjoy most on the river and without doubt both would say the last two weeks in May. Why? The Yakima, along with the Bitterroot in Montana and the Yellowstone in the Park, as well as many ohter Western rivers, harbor great hatches of black caddis or, as the local call it, the "Mothers Day caddis," since they begin around the second Sunday in May.

Washington's Yakima River in mid-May holds a fantastic grannom or black caddis hatch.

I hit the black caddis hatch on the Yakima recently with Craig Shuman and Jack Mitchell. Al Novotny of Casper, Wyoming, was along to film a video on the Yakima's great fly-fishing. Al has produced many award-winning outdoor films, as well as numerous travel videos, and he currently produces the Kodak series of video trips. Al, his wife Carol, and his son Jarrod came to the Yakima River to complete a production on the Kittitas and Yakima valleys. As a major part of this video Al wanted to include a float trip on the Yakima River, and Craig and Jack invited Dave Engerbretson and me to fly-fish the river.

We arrived for the first day of filming to a cloudy, almost muddy river with few caddis flies in the air and on the surface. But by the time Jack Mitchell piloted the drift boat less than three miles, it happened. First a few black caddis flies appeared, then thousands, and trout responded, even in the murky water, by rising in every eddy. Along much of the far shoreline rainbow trout took up feeding positions, waiting for the next dark downwing to appear overhead. Jack Mitchell maneuvered the boat into an ideal position for the two of us to cast. Dave and I each tied on a size 16 Black Caddis and began casting to at least a dozen rising trout. On the first drag-free float a fifteen-inch streambred rainbow hit the downwing. Within minutes several more trout responded to our imitations. Jack resumed the float downriver to another shoreline that held more trout eagerly rising to the caddis hatch. Here, too, we caught several trout before we continued our downriver trip.

For the next three days, that hatch appeared on the Yakima every afternoon and early evening. And every day the trout re-sponded to the hatch by rising all afternoon.

Travel thousands of miles to the East and you'll find caddis fly hatches with the same appearance. In fact, the same patterns I used on the Eastern and Midwestern hatches worked well out West.

Penns Creek boasts a black-bodied downwing that appears near the end of April, which anglers call a grannom. This hatch, better copied with a size 10 pattern, offers early-season matching-the-hatch opportunities. The grannom appears a good month earlier than the famous green drake hatch on Penns Creek, but if conditions are right, it can bring the same hefty browns to the surface.

Many other Eastern waters hold grannom hatches in late April. Fish the likes of the central Pennsylvania's Spruce Creek or the Little Juniata River in late April and you'll likely hit a hatch of grannoms most effectively copied by a size 16 Black Caddis or Grannom pattern.

I'll always remember the first grannom hatch I hit on Sugar Creek in northwestern Pennsylvania. In late April, Jack Busch of Erie, Pennsylvania, invited me to fly-fish this small, productive stream with him. Jack had fly-fished Sugar Creek the past few years while a hatch of grannoms appeared and had enjoyed fantastic success. When I met Jack, he showed me a vial of grannoms and advised me that the hatch had begun a day or two before.

When we arrived at the stream, Jack showed me evidence of the hatch—thousands of black-bodied downwings crawled on every branch near this small freestone stream. For the next five hours, Jack and I waited for grannoms to emerge or to return to the water in their egg-laying ritual. Not until 3:00 p.m. did an additional supply of caddis flies emerge. While these emerged from the bottom of the stream, yesterday's hatch returned to the water to lay eggs. A half dozen trout began feeding in front of me in a small riffle. Before the feeding frenzy ended, that afternoon more than ten trout took that size 16 Black Caddis pattern.

Have you ever tried shucks on your caddis patterns? Bryan Meck and I fly-fished the Missouri River near Helena, Montana, recently with professional guides Pat Elam and Mike Bay. Black caddis flies here also filled the air on that mid-July morning. Both Bryan and I tied on a size 14 Black Caddis and began casting to heavy risers. For a half-hour trout refused both patterns—until Bryan tied on a caddis pattern with a pale tan Z-lon shuck. He cast over what appeared to be a heavy riser, and it took the downwing on the first drift. The brown trout headed out toward the middle, and Pat followed it with the drift boat. In a whole day of fly-fishing the Missouri, no one would match that twenty-two-inch brown trout Bryan caught on the Black Caddis with a trailing shuck. That Black Caddis pattern saved that day and made me a believer in the value of shucks.

You can tie all your adult caddis imitations like the one I suggest below. By tying in the wing and the shuck from the same piece of antron, you'll find it easy to tie and a dynamite pattern.

Black Caddis
> HOOK: Mustad, 94833, size 10 to 16
> THREAD: Black
> TAILS: (optional) Add a tan Z-lon shuck
> BODY: Black poly, dubbed. (optional) Wind a dark brown
> hackle in at the bend of the hook and palmer it to the
> eye. Clip off the barbules on top.
> WINGS: Dark brown deer or elk hair
> HACKLE: (optional) Dark brown hackle

Tying Notes: If you hackle your caddis pattern, make it two sizes smaller than you would on a mayfly of the same size. For example, if you're tying a size 14 Black Caddis, use a hackle you'd ordinarily use for a size 18 mayfly pattern. This allows the pattern to ride even lower on the water.

Charlie Meck's Black Caddis

>   HOOK: Mustad 94833, sizes 10 to 16
>   THREAD: Black
>   TAILS and WINGS: Dark brown antron yarn
>   BODY: Black superfine poly, dubbed and ribbed with a dark
>   gray thread.
>   HACKLE: A small dark brown hackle (for a regular size 18
>   pattern)

Tying Notes: Take two pieces of dark brown antron yarn and tie in with the yarn extending back over the bend of the hook. Extend the other end of the antron out over the eye about the length of the shank of the hook. Take the other end, which is extending out over the eye of the hook, and make several turns with your dubbing in front of it so it bends backward at an angle. This will be your wing. Trim the end to approximate the wing length of the natural.

Tan Caddis

A size 16 Tan Caddis has taken more trout for me from June through August than any other downwing pattern I've ever used. It consistently caught trout on such disparate waters as the Firehole River in Yellowstone National Park, the Clark Fork near Anaconda, Montana, and the Lackawanna River near Scranton, Pennsylvania.

Nick Nicklas, Jerry Meck and I fly-fished the Firehole in late June recently. Even in the nearly eighty-degree water heavy rainbows rose to a number of tan caddis in a riffle entering a sizable pool. Nick, Jerry and I tied on a size 16 Tan Caddis and fished the riffles of this productive trout river. Ten Firehole trout took that downwing on that late-June afternoon.

The Tan Caddis also works exceptionally well on Northeastern streams and rivers during the summer. For years many anglers thought of Pennsylvania's Lackawanna River as a cruel joke. Mine acid prevented any trout from living in its lower ten miles. But an end to mining, sewage treatment, and other cleanup projects affected this river tremendously in the past three decades. About twenty years ago, some local anglers like Jim Misiura discovered some streambred brown trout in the river, and in the two decades since, Jim has caught brown trout as long as twenty-four inches in the Lackawanna.

Jim invited me to the river in early June two years ago. We entered the river near the town of Archbald. Just across the river an abandoned mine poured its acid-tainted water into the Lackawanna. I wondered how this section of the river could hold any fish, but in front of me two heavy trout rose. Only a few gray foxes appeared that evening along with a variety of caddis. I relied on my old summer standby—a size 16 Tan Caddis. That caddis pattern on that pool-and-riffle section fooled four heavy Lackawanna River brown trout that evening. No other pattern I used that evening, including one to match the emerging gray foxes, produced any strikes.

Tan Caddis

> HOOK: Mustad 94841, size 14 to 18
> THREAD: Tan
> TAILS: (optional) A light tan Z-lon shuck as long as the shank of the hook.
> BODY: Tan poly dubbed
> WINGS: Brown deer hair or elk hair
> HACKLE: (optional) Tan, cut off underneath

Tying Notes: On many of my caddis, I cut some of the hackle off underneath to make the downwing float lower on the surface.

Green Caddis

For years, several angling friends began the matching-the-hatch season on the Little Juniata River with the early-May green caddis hatch. At the time, twenty years ago, that hatch appeared for more than a week in numbers heavy enough to bring even the most wary brown trout to the surface. During a typical caddis hatch, it wasn't uncommon to catch fifteen to twenty trout. But the hatch has diminished to some extent and so have the number of trout rising to it.

You'll find green caddis abundant on many Eastern and Midwestern waters in early May, so be prepared with plenty of downwings in sizes from 12 to 20.

Tulpehocken Creek flows through Reading in southeastern Pennsylvania. In its lower reaches the "Tulpe" warms. A forty-eight-foot-deep impoundment, the Blue Marsh Dam, cools the stream so that it holds a good number of trout. Because of the shallow dam you'll find temperatures in July and August often in the high seventies, and even warmer on occasion.

I had an opportunity several years back to fly-fish the stream in early May with Dick Henry, a great fly-fisher and an excellent outdoor writer. That overcast, cool, early-May day we caught heavy rainbows on a size 16 copy of an adult green caddis.

But you'll find green caddis hatches on many other streams and rivers and at different times of the year, so it's important to carry patterns in sizes 12 to 20.

Every morning during the summer many Eastern and Midwestern streams and rivers hold great green caddis hatches. In July and August most Eastern limestone streams have trout rising to the hatch. Often I'll head out for a morning trico hatch and end up with a green caddis and trico hatch. On those late-summer mornings I often catch more trout on the downwing than I do during the spinner fall.

Green Caddis
> HOOK: Mustad 94833, sizes 12 to 20
> THREAD: Olive green

TAILS: Tan Z-lon the length of the hook shank
BODY: Green, grayish green, or olive poly
WINGS: Medium to dark deer hair or elk hair
HACKLE: Light brown

Simple Salmon

If you've fished Western rivers like the Deschutes in central Oregon in late May when the salmon fly emerges, you know what excitement this hatch brings. Fish dozens of other rivers like the upper end of the McKenzie near Eugene, Oregon, and you'll see the same hatch at about the same time of year. Travel to the Firehole River in Yellowstone Park and you'll find the same huge stonefly hatch in late June. The Yellowstone River near Gardiner, Montana, boasts a tremendous hatch of salmon flies in early July.

I intercepted the salmon fly hatch on the Yellowstone River just downriver from the Park several years ago. Here, because of the extremely cold water, the salmon fly emerges in early July. I remember shaking some of the bushes near the river and seeing hundreds of salmon flies falling onto the surface. Soon more than a dozen cutthroats fed on these huge stoneflies. Just at dusk, thousands of these stonefly adults returned to the river to deposit their eggs. The trout apparently sensed their return and immediately fed on huge dying adults. Any pattern closely copying the adult worked well that evening. I used a Simple Salmon, and the trout took it eagerly.

Jerry Meck and I recently fly-fished the Firehole River in late June with prominent guide Nick Nicklas. Nick gave Jerry and me a handful of patterns effective on West Yellowstone-area rivers, and he included several large downwing patterns he called Simple Salmons. They looked like a large caddis pattern with a burnt-orange body.

Nick said that in late June the lower end of the Firehole holds some salmon flies. Jerry and I tried the Simple Salmon pattern and both of us picked up trout in the first riffle. For the next hour we caught several more heavy trout that rose to that downwing pattern.

Simple Salmon
> HOOK: Mustad 94831, size 8
> THREAD: Orange
> BODY: Burnt orange poly, dubbed
> WINGS: Dark elk hair

Tying Notes: Tie the pattern just as you would a size 14 caddis pattern. Dub in poly for a size 14 pattern, then tie in a wing. In front of the first wing dub in some more poly, then another wing, until you finish at the eye. The final product gives the impression of a continuous wing—not five or six separate segments.

Patriot Downwing

For years anglers have used attractor patterns. I often prospect with them myself and have found them especially productive when no hatch appears on the water. The bright colors of the Wulff Royal Coachman and others often prompt trout into striking.

For many years anglers used, nothing but attractor patterns for almost the entire year. Joe Daugherty begins and ends the season with the Wulff Royal Coachman. So did my old friend Lloyd Williams. Look at the end of his tippet any time from late May through October and you'd probably find a Wulff Royal Coachman attached to it.

But through the years I have seen only one or two downwing patterns like the Trude that might represent a downwing attractor pattern. Don't downwing attractor patterns work?

It's been almost 15 years since I tied my first Patriot Downwing. At the time, I gave that pattern to my teenage son to test on a northern Pennsylvania trout stream called Oswayo Creek, which I still consider one of the finest freestone streams in the East.

My son Bryan and I attended a conference of the Pennsylvania
Outdoor Writers Association in Coudersport, Pennsylvania, where
members and guests could select from a number of fishing trips.
Bryan chose to travel with several anglers to the Oswayo Creek, and
before he left I gave him a Patriot Downwing to test for me. I'll
never forget when he returned home with that sixteen-inch brown
trout that he had hooked on the attractor downwing pattern--the
only trout taken on the trip.

Patriot Downwing
> HOOK: Mustad 94833, sizes 12 to 18
> THREAD: Red
> TAILS: None
> BODY: Smolt blue Krystal flash with a midsection of red
> tying thread
> WINGS: White or brown deer hair tied downwing
> HACKLE: Brown

Cream Caddis
> One of the most spectacular early-season caddis hatches
occurs on Pine Creek in north-central Pennsylvania. It usually
begins around May 1 and continues for more than a week. Locals
call the hatch the "green egg sac caddis." Others refer to it as the
"cream caddis." Tom Finkbiner of Slate Run has fished the hatch
for many years and suggests a soft-hackle emerger in the morning
during the hatch, and a dancer, or dry fly pattern, in the evening
when the egg-laying adults come back to the water. For his dancer,
or high-water pattern, Tom uses a ginger tail and a body of ginger
hackle. Tom says that skittering or dancing the pattern often
prompts the trout into striking. For his standard or low-water
pattern, he ties a light tan body and cream hackle on a size 14 dry
fly hook.

You'll find this same cream caddis prevalent on many Eastern streams from late April until mid-May, so tie the downwing in sizes from 14 to 16.

Cream Caddis

 HOOK: Mustad 94833, size 12 to 16
 THREAD: Cream
 BODY: Cream
 WINGS: Light deer hair or elk
 HACKLE: Pale ginger

Bryan Meck catches a brown trout on a Green Caddis with a shuck.

Chapter 6.
Patterns That Copy Mayflies That Return to the Water

Mayflies that return to the water to lay eggs make up an important source of food for trout. Anglers often call these mating mayflies spinners. They often return above a fast section of a river or stream in the evening, mate, lay eggs, then fall spent onto the surface. Mayfly adults lay eggs in one of several ways, but many die spent or sit upright for a while on the surface before dying. Trout often gorge themselves on this enormous supply of food. If you've fly-fished for any time at all, you know how frustrating spinner falls at dusk can be. First, you can't see the pattern on the surface; second, you'll often find trout unusually selective when feeding on spinners. Determining the spinner fall

When Western green drake spinners fall on the surface it's time to use a spent-winged spinner.

and a proper match for it tests even the most skilled fly-fisher. It could be one of hundreds of different mating adults. Getting the proper float also presents problems with spinner falls. With even the slightest amount of micro-drag, trout often ignore even the best spent-winged spinner imitation. I prefer to fish the spinner fall with a spinner pattern tied on a ten- to twelve-foot leader with a three-foot 5X or 6X tippet. This long, fine tippet helps prevent micro-drag.

If you incorporate a slack-leader cast in your presentation, you're prepared for the spinner fall. To execute such a cast, on the final false cast, stop the rod short and aim it three to four feet above the water. As the line comes down, bring the rod down by your side. Making a slack-leader cast produces s-curves in your leader (but not your fly line), each of which helps prevent micro-drag.

Spinners often fall in sections of a stream with several different current speeds. Trout tend to select one of these locations where it's almost out of the question to get a suitable drag-free float. Sometimes when I fish pocket water where I find several current speeds and have difficulty getting any float drag-free, I fish downstream. Stand upstream from the rising trout, cast the pattern a foot or two above the rising fish, stop the line short to execute a slack-leader cast, and look for the strike. You'll miss more trout this way, but you'll also get plenty more strikes.

In late May, Andre Lijoi, Jim Herde, and I fished over several spent-winged spinners. Two distinct formations of mating adults formed above the riffle in front of us. For the first half of that spinner fall, trout occasionally took our Sulphur Spinner patterns—but only when we floated the imitation perfectly drag-free, and most often when we fished upriver from the risers and let the imitation drift down over the trout.

No sooner did the three of us begin taking a few fish than the trout began refusing the Sulphur Spinner pattern completely. I noticed a larger spent mayfly on the water and suggested that we switch to a Ginger Quill Spinner pattern. Within minutes after switching to a size 14 Ginger Quill Spinner, Andre Lijoi caught four trout. Jim Herde fished over several trout rising in the flat water below, because he thought he could achieve a longer drag-free float. We ended that evening triumphant that we had matched two spinner falls and caught more than a dozen trout.

Tandem Connections

During heavy spinner falls I prefer to fish the spinner imitation by itself. However, if you have difficulty following the spinner pattern, use the tandem method. Tie on a larger pattern like the Patriot and tie the spinner imitation two feet behind the lead fly.

If you plan to use a sinking spinner, you might want to tie it behind size 12 or 14 Patriot or other easily detectable dry fly.

Attractor Spinners

Ann McIntosh of Monkton, Maryland, runs a bed and breakfast near the famous Gunpowder River, and you'll frequently find Ann fishing the Gunpowder. But she doesn't stop there. She often travels to central Pennsylvania to fly-fish the Little Juniata and other nearby limestone streams. Ann recently returned from a trip to the South Fork of the Snake River in Idaho and several spring creeks near Jackson Hole, Wyoming. You read part of her letter concerning the trip in Chapter 7.

For several years Ann has enthusiastically used a Patriot dry fly with much success on Eastern, Midwestern, and Western waters. While Ann stayed at the 4 Lazy F Ranch, her guide, George McCullough, tied up some size 14 Patriot Spinners for her. Yes, I said spinners. The next morning Ann decided to use the Patriot Spinner, and guess what? On the first ten casts Ann caught three cutthroats, all over fourteen inches long on that Patriot Spinner.

Patriot Spinner
> HOOK: Mustad 94833, size 12 to 24
> THREAD: Red
> TAILS: Brown
> BODY: A midsection of red thread and smolt blue krystal flash
> WINGS: White poly yarn tied spent

Upright Spinner Imitations

For days I had fly-fished the sulphur spinner falls. As darkness approached I had difficulty following the tan spent-winged pattern. Also, just at dark, sulphurs emerged as last night's duns fell as mated spinners. During the height of the sulphur hatch and spinner fall many anglers complain that they don't know which of the two trout will feed on. When trout feed on emerging duns, they often completely refuse a spent-winged pattern; when trout feed on dead spinners, they totally reject the dun pattern. During many spinner falls, you'll find some spinners floating downriver with wings upright, not spent. To compensate for those spinners that ride the surface in that configuration and to copy the sulphur dun at the same time, I tie a yellowish-tan-bodied spinner with white upright wings of poly yarn. This pattern adequately copies both the dun and the spinner and works well during an emergence or fall.

Sulphur Spinner Dun
> HOOK: Mustad 94833, size 16
> THREAD: Pale orange
> TAILS: Light deer hair
> BODY: Orangish-tan poly, dubbed
> WINGS: White poly yarn, tied upright
> HACKLE: Pale ginger

Tying Notes: You can make spent-wing patterns easy or complicated . Generally the patterns consist of poly or Z-lon wings, split or regular tails, and usually a body of poly. Many tiers add Krystal Flash or Sparkle yarn to the wings to help them locate the spinner and make them more like the wings of the natural.

Spinner Colors

In a lifetime of fly-fishing and attempting to match spinner falls, you'll certainly encounter many mayfly adults ranging from size 10 to 24 and in colors from white to black. To overcome many of my frustrations when spinner falls occur, over the years I've collected thousands of spinner imitations. I placed these spent wings in three Wheatly boxes with sixty-four compartments. I've included patterns from size 10 through 24. In each size I have compartments for spinners in eight shades ranging from white to black. With this system I rarely encounter a situation where I can't copy a spinner fall.

If you have to choose from a more limited selection of body colors and sizes, I recommend the Light Cahill, Trico, Dark Olive Spinner, Sulphur-Pale Morning Spinner, Dark Brown Spinner, Rusty Spinner, and the Dark Red Spinner. If you've fished enough spinner falls, you know how many times you've seen dark brown and dark red spinners on the water.

With the patterns we'll examine, you'll have a variety of productive body colors. I suggest tying the Light Cahill with cream and pale yellow bodies; tying the Dark Olive Spinner dark olive-black; tying the Dark Brown Spinner dark brown; tying the Dark Red Spinner dark reddish-brown; tying the Sulphur Spinner tan; tying the Trico cream and dark brown; tying the Quill Gordon Spinner dark gray; and tying the Rusty Spinner rusty brown. You'll find patterns for these and other spinners in Chapter 10.

If you tie the patterns in enough sizes, you'll copy most of the spinner falls you'll encounter. For example, if you tie a size 12 or 14 Sulphur, you'll also copy the ginger quill spinner; with a size 12 Dark

Red Spinner you copy the hendrickson spinner, the red quill, as well as the spinner of the slate drake and the white-gloved howdy.

Light Cahill Spinner

Mark Jackson of Hollidaysburg, Pennsylvania, began fly-fishing two years ago, but you couldn't tell that from his fly casting. Mark casts more like somebody who's been matching the hatches for a decade or so. In the short time he's fly-fished, Mark enjoys fishing spinner falls. From June 20 to July 10, you'll find Mark matching a cream cahill spinner fall that occurs almost nightly on the Little Juniata River.

The cream cahill fall occurs like clockwork every night. You can expect the duns to emerge and spinners to fall from 9:00 to 10:00 p.m., well past dark and well past the time most anglers quit fishing. At this time of year on the Little Juniata River, I've seen many fly-fishers quit just before the hatch and fall begin. Trout eagerly feed on these duns and spinners some evenings until near midnight. On most occasions, you'll find no other angling competition for this tremendous spinner fall. But you have to contend with my nemesis—total darkness.

I first encountered this important mayfly only several years ago on the Little Juniata River while fishing with Andre Lijoi of Hanover, Pennsylvania. At 9:15 p.m. we decided to hike back to my car. As we exited the pool we had just left, I shined the light on the water and saw a half dozen cream cahill spinners floating past. I shined the light upriver and saw more. Andre and I hurriedly tore off our imitations, tied on a size 14 Cream Cahill, and headed back to the riffle at the head of the pool.

By the time we arrived back at the riffle almost total darkness had set in. Against the last hint of sunset I saw a dozen or more trout feeding on the increasing supply of cahill spinners. I cast toward one rise that appeared to be a heavy trout and I tried to follow the fly. I set the hook on several rises close to the spinner pattern but felt no trout. A few casts later I set the hook, felt weight, and I finally landed a sixteen-inch brown. I continued to fish and set the hook, sometimes with success, most times without, well past 10:00 p.m. Six trout took that Cream Cahill before I quit—again. Andre fared much better, picking up several heavy browns during the spinner fall.

A week after I initially hit the great hatch-matching activity after dark, I invited Kathy and Ken Rictor to fish the same spinner fall. Kathy set the hook on the first trout well past 9:00 p.m. but both continued to catch fish over rising trout until 10:00 p.m. Since most of these spinners fall after dark, fly-fishers must listen for rises and look closely for any sign of a rise in the half-light.

This cahill spinner fall occurs nightly from late June until mid-July—almost three weeks of great midsummer fly-fishing!

Carry Light Cahills and Cream Cahills in sizes 12 to 20 and in body colors from white to cream to pale yellow to match other summer spinner falls.

Light Cahill Spinner
> HOOK: Mustad 94833, size 12 to 20
> THREAD: Cream
> TAILS: Cream hackle fibers
> BODY: Cream to pale yellow poly
> WINGS: White poly yarn

Pale Morning Spinner-Sulphur
Bryan Meck and I floated Montana's Bighorn with expert guide Richie Montella, who has floated the river thousands of times, witnessed innumerable hatches, and seen hundreds of twenty-inch trout caught. As we entered the river just below the dam, we saw dozens of other boats maneuvering for fishing space. Richie kept

drifting downriver for more than three miles before he guided the McKenzie boat toward the bank and told us to get out.

As Bryan and I looked upriver, Richie pointed to a pod of rising trout. At least fifteen heavy brown trout made slight dimples in only a foot or two of water. I noticed some pale morning spinners on the surface and saw trout in the pod take them regularly, so Bryan and I tied on size 16 Pale Morning Spinners. After four or five casts I placed the spent-winged pattern just in front of a heavy riser. It took the imitation on the first drift and I landed a seventeen-inch brown trout.

Bryan cast to the next riser in the pod while I watched. He, too, caught a heavy brown on a Pale Morning Spinner. He now cast to another riser in the pod and quickly caught and released a second heavy trout.

Before we re-entered the boat to drift downriver, Bryan and I caught fourteen of those trout that had been rising for spinners. That Pale Morning Spinner proved its value on Western waters from late May to early August.

The same spinner pattern that caught all the trout on the Bighorn River matches the sulphur spinner falls in the East and Midwest, where sulphur spinners create great hatch-matching opportunities. Sulphurs appear almost nightly on most Eastern and Midwestern trout streams from mid-May until mid-June. Last night's duns become tonight's spinners. Often anglers hit a dun emergence and spinner fall on the same night. On occasion, the dun and spinner fall occur at the same time; on other nights, the two occur within minutes of each other. It's imperative, therefore, that you carry patterns to copy both the dun and the spinner.

How can you prepare for either or both hatches that appear so close together? Tie on a pattern to copy the dun as the lead fly and one to copy the spinner as your point fly. That way you're prepared to fish both hatches. If only the dun appears while you're fishing, you can cut the spinner pattern off; if only the spinner appears, use both but use the Sulphur dry fly as an indicator. You'll also find a pattern to copy the dun and spinner earlier in this chapter.

Sulphur-Pale Morning Spinner
    HOOK: Mustad 94833, sizes 12 to 20
    THREAD: Tan
    TAILS: Tan
    BODY: Pale to medium tan poly
    WINGS: White poly yarn

Dark Olive Spinner
    For the past ten years I've found the dark olive spinner one of the most frustrating yet rewarding midsummer spinner falls. You already know how highly selective trout become on most spinner falls. Trout often refuse spinner patterns for three important reasons. First, trout ignore the pattern because it's too large or too small. Second, trout often refuse any that do not closely resemble the body color of the spinner natural. Third, trout often reject any spinner pattern displaying any drag, even micro-drag.

    For several years I had baffling experiences with the dark olive spinner fall of an exciting but often overlooked species, *Drunella cornutella*. Bob Budd and I fly-fished several heavy spinner falls on Eastern waters, always with frustrating results. Not until I changed the body color on my dark olive spinner did I begin to catch trout consistently. The body of many of these spinners of the genus *Drunella* takes on a dark olive, almost black hue. To get the correct color, I mix ten parts of black poly with one part of dark olive poly.

    I tied several of these patterns and took them with me on a fishing trip in late June. Bob Budd met me on the Little Juniata

River for a night of match-the-hatch fishing, hopefully over a spinner fall. I expected the dark olive spinner fall to occur that evening so I gave Bob a couple of the new spinner patterns with the darker body.

We didn't have to wait long for the spinner fall. Within minutes after we arrived, a size 16 dark olive spinner blanketed the surface. Dozens of trout cooperated by rising to the food supply, and on his first cast covering a rising trout, Bob caught a foot-long brown trout on the Dark Olive Spinner. That evening Bob and I caught more than fifteen trout on that pattern.

You'll find these dark olive spinners common on many streams and rivers across the United States. Follow the tying description in Chapter 10.

Trico Spinner

Vince Marinaro fished trico spinner falls on Falling Springs in south-central Pennsylvania for years. One late-July day Barry Beck, Dick Mills and I met Vince on the stream just prior to the trico spinner fall.

In the early 1970s when we fished Falling Springs, it held one of the heaviest trico falls in the East. More recently, the stream has fallen on bad times, with urbanization and farming, and the trico, although still a major hatch, has diminished dramatically. Thanks to the local Trout Unlimited chapter and a greenway group, the stream has partially recovered and future prospects for the hatch look bright.

That day, more than twenty years ago, trico spinners began falling around 8:00 a.m. and continued for more than an hour. All of us sat back and watched Vince cast to a couple of heavy rainbows that systematically sipped spent wings on the surface, then moved back down toward the bottom and waited for more. Vince kept casting to the constant risers but they continued to refuse his pattern completely.

After an unproductive half-hour, Barry Beck shouted over to Vince, "Why don't you tell the trout who you are and maybe they'll take your spinner imitation." Vince began to mumble a few inaudible and probably not complimentary words to us and to the trout that hadn't cooperated and continued to fish over the risers.

After that episode we all began to fish to the spinner fall—and all of us did poorly. Fishing pressure during this hatch makes these trout extremely selective. After several weeks of the spinner fall, trout on streams with heavy angling pressure see hundreds of spent-winged imitations. Not until I tied on a size 20 Wulff Royal Coachman did I catch a trout.

The memory of that early encounter with the trico stayed with me for years, and in late 1980s I got reacquainted with a man I consider the dean of American fly-fishers, George Harvey. Over the years, George has become a trico aficionado. In an average year George fishes the trico spinner fall from thirty to forty days. George first fished the trico hatch on Falling Springs in the early 1930s—well before many anglers knew the hatch existed. He developed a productive Trico Nymph and a Trico Spinner to fish those early hatches.

With the advent of Krystal Flash and Sparkle yarn, George began experimenting with these two synthetics for wings. He found that he could follow the spent-wing imitation much better and trout often preferred the brighter wings. He also found that trout on heavily fished streams, after seeing the same patterns for weeks, would reject most patterns for something a bit different. That's why his Trico Spinner pattern, tied with wings made completely of Sparkle Yarn, works so well.

Several years ago, Bryan Meck and I fly-fished what I then called the "mother of all hatches"—the trico on the Missouri River. Trico spinners fall in such great numbers during the height of the hatch in August that you have little chance to catch trout on your small Trico Spinner.

Pat Elam and Mike Bay guide on the river and have seen unbelievable, blizzard-like trico hatches for weeks. They've seen dead trico spinners by the millions on this tailwater. Pat and Mike often suggest fishing this spinner with a bouquet or cluster pattern. Tie the pattern on a size 16 hook that suggests two or three trico spinners in a cluster. Tie a tail at the bend of the hook and another at the eye. Tie two or three sets of wings. Remember another important feature when fishing extremely heavy trico spinner falls: when trout feed on these diminutive spinners they do so in a definite rhythm. Just ask Paul Antolosky and his wife Pat. They've seen this rhythmic feeding so often on the Missouri that they time their casts over rising trout. So when you fish the trico spinner fall on any water where it appears in heavy numbers, look for this feeding rhythm and use a bouquet or cluster pattern.

If you ask a group of fly-fishers which hatch often frustrates them most they'll probably tell you it's the trico. The hatch lasts for at least two months on many waters, and often brings unmatched angling pressure. Why? Anglers can depend on trico spinner falls for much of August and September. It therefore behooves you to use patterns which might be a bit different from what they have seen over the past number of weeks.

Doug and Dan Daufle, the twins from Dayton, Ohio, at just over twenty years old, have tied flies for more than ten years and now tie commercially some of the finest flies I've ever seen. They began tying reverse Tricos a year or so ago and found the pattern extremely productive. They tie the tail out over the eye and the head at the bend of the hook, an innovation that helps their Trico outfish regular Trico patterns by a considerable margin.

Carry patterns copying the male trico with you. Usually after female tricos fall for thirty minutes to an hour the male spinners begin to fall. Males can continue to fall an hour or more after the females have stopped. You'll find patterns for the regular tricos in Chapter 10.

Trico Cluster
> HOOK: Mustad 94833, size 16
> THREAD: Dark Brown
> TAILS: Pale dun (tie in pale dun hackle fibers at the bend of the hook and at the eye to suggest two tails).
> BODY: Cream poly, then dark brown poly; then tie in white poly wings. In front of that tie in some dark brown poly, a set of poly yarn wings, more dark brown, then cream, and add a tail at the eye.

Dark Brown Spinner

What a spectacular float trip we had down the Yakima River! As recounted earlier, expert guides Craig Shuman and Jack Mitchell invited Dave Engerbretson and me to fly-fish and help them film a video about central Washington and the Yakima River. For five days Dave Engerbretson and I fished and floated eight miles of the river, each day fishing for nearly ten hours.

For the first three days we hit spectacular grannom or black caddis hatches. Trout responded to the hatch, despite the murky water, by rising in pods along the shore. As we floated downriver, Dave and I cast almost continuously to trout that took the size 16 Grannom.

By the fourth day and the third float down the same section of the river, we found that the grannom hatch had diminished considerably. For the next few days, Dave and I would rely on a sporadic pale morning dun hatch to see rising trout.

As we exited the water on the Yakima the final day of the video production, we sat by the shore and reminisced about our tremendous fishing experience. As we did, I looked skyward and noticed an unbelievable number of spinners ten to fifty feet in the air. I finally captured one of these adults and showed it to Jack Mitchell. Because of its undulating motion in the air, dark brown body color, and three tails, I assumed it to be a spinner of one of the very common blue quills (*Paraleptophlebia* species). I urged Jack to try a size 16 or 18 Dark Brown Spinner on his next few float trips.

About a week or two after Dave Engerbretson and I left the river, Jack phoned me back in Pennsylvania to report that during the past week some of his fishing clients had done well on the Dark Brown Spinner spent-wing pattern. Jack became a believer in the value of this particular spinner pattern.

If you've fly-fished on Eastern and Midwestern trout waters in early spring or in midsummer, you know the value of the dark brown spinner. Most quality trout streams host heavy blue quill hatches in mid-to-late April. If you're fortunate enough to hit one of these spinner falls and you match it with a size 18 Dark Brown Spinner, you're in for a great experience. You'll find tying descriptions for this spinner fall in Chapter 10.

Quill Gordon Spinner

My first day on the Bitterroot River was my first day on any Western river. I stood there in awe of the swollen water on this late-June morning. I had no guide—no local expert to show me what to use and where to fish. By chance that first morning, a sporadic hatch of large Western green drakes appeared with a smattering of pale morning duns. On that first trip I landed more than a dozen heavy rainbows, browns, and cutthroats on Green Drake patterns.

I tried my luck again later that evening. This time I entered the river near Victor, Montana. For the first hour I saw no hatch and stood there staring at this snow-fed river. Then I noticed one dimple, then another, and another. Soon I had a half dozen heavy Bitterroot browns rising in front of me. I scanned the surface to see what excited these fish. Just upriver I saw a dark gray spinner on the surface. As I looked toward shore I saw more of these size 12 spent-wings. For the past couple of days a *Rhithrogena* species had emerged. Now, after laying its eggs, the adult had fallen, spent, onto the surface.

I quickly tied on a Quill Gordon dry fly, clipped its wings and cut the hackle off the bottom. It now closely resembled the naturals floating past me. I didn't have to wait long to see if the pattern worked. A heavy brown sucked in the Quill Gordon Spinner on the first drag-free float I made over it. That evening six heavy brown trout took that spinner pattern.

Always carry a generous supply of Quill Gordon Spinners with you—even if you fly-fish in other countries. Several years ago, Mike Manfredo of Fort Collins, Colorado, and I fished New Zealand's South Island for almost a month. From late January until late February we traveled from one fabulous river to another seeking the island's greatest trout waters. We hit just about all of the famous rivers and some of the not-so- famous ones. We had good days and some extremely bad ones. But one thing surprised us—we had very few hatch-matching opportunities. In twenty-five days of fly-fishing, Mike and I hit legitimate hatches or spinner falls only three times. When those few occasions occurred and we matched a hatch or spinner fall, we did exceedingly well. Trout seemed eager to take a natural on the surface and if you had a close match, they quickly took it.

I'll never forget that morning Mike and I drove to Lumsden for an early breakfast. Just before we reached the town, we crossed the 100-foot-wide Oreti River. I glanced at the river and saw a couple of rises, so I asked Mike to stop the car and we scanned the river for more risers. Just upriver from the bridge, Mike and I counted five heavy trout taking something off the surface. Mike parked the car, we hurriedly grabbed our gear, and assembled it as we headed down the steep bank leading to the river. The same five trout continued to rise as we moved into the heavy water well below them.

In two weeks Mike and I had learned one important lesson about New Zealand fly-fishing: You cannot get close to these trout. If you get too close you put them down for a long time. On some rivers Mike and I belly crawled more than fifty feet before we could cast to rising trout. Even then, the trout acted spooky.

I checked the surface of the Oreti for any sign of food and saw several fairly large dark gray spinners floating past me. Mike and I both tied on Quill Gordon Spinners and began casting to risers well upriver. Within minutes a heavy trout took my size 12 spent-wing and fought for more than fifteen minutes before I netted it. A few shots of dry-fly spray to the spinner and I cast to the next rising trout. This fish, too, took that spent-wing on the first drag-free float over it. That morning four heavy trout, all over twenty inches long, took that Quill Gordon Spinner before the fall ended.

Quill Gordon Spinner

      HOOK: Mustad 94833, size 12 to 20
      THREAD: Dark gray
      TAILS: Dark gray
      BODY: Dark gray poly or an eyed peacock quill, stripped
      WINGS: White poly yarn

Rusty Spinner

The more I fly-fish throughout the United States, the more I'm convinced that the little blue-winged olive dun frequents more streams and rivers than any other mayfly species. One of the most common little blue-wings (*Baetis tricaudatus*) has more than one generation per year. Usually you'll find this little blue-winged olive emerging in good numbers in March, April, and May, depending on where you live, and then again in September and October. On the San Juan in New Mexico you can expect a hatch of these small but important mayflies almost every month of the year.

I'm sure every fly-fisher who's matched hatches for more than a decade has encountered a size 20 little blue-wing hatch. I've seen great hatches on New Mexico's San Juan, on Silver Creek in Idaho, on the Firehole River in Yellowstone Park, and on hundreds of other trout waters. As anglers, we continuously match the little blue-winged olive—often with a great deal of success. But have you fished the spinner of this prolific species, the rusty spinner?

Often the rusty spinner falls in dribs and drabs just like the dark brown spinner. On rare occasions I've encountered heavy spinner falls, and on those days, a size 20 Rusty Spinner saved the day. On Montana's Bitterroot on a late-September afternoon, the Rusty Spinner worked when trout began feeding on small spinners; on Michigan's AuSable the same spinner pattern caught trout one late-September afternoon; on the North Fork of the Cache la Poudre near Fort Collins, Colorado, the Rusty spinner saved me from total frustration when I matched a spinner fall.

The medium to dark tan color of the body matches many different spinner falls you will encounter, so have a good supply of Rusty Spinners on hand in sizes from 10 to 20.

Rusty Spinner
>   HOOK: Mustad 94833, sizes 10 to 20
>   THREAD: Brown
>   TAILS: Dark brown hackle fibers
>   BODY: Dark brown hackle stem, stripped
>   WINGS: Pale polypropylene, tied spent

Weighted Spinners

The South Platte below Elevenmile reservoir southwest of Denver, Colorado, holds an unbelievable trico spinner fall from July through September. You have to see to believe the huge rainbows rising to these spinners. For a couple hours each morning huge rainbow trout cruise in slow, shallow water gulping every trico spinner within reach. You can see thousands of trico spinners on the surface during a morning's fishing.

Try fishing the trico hatch on the Missouri River near Craig, Montana. In *Great Rivers—Great Hatches,* I said I saw the mother of all hatches when I ran into that diminutive mayfly on the Missouri River. You have to actually see the enormity of the hatch to believe the number of trico spinners that fall on the surface.

If you've ever seen the trico hatch on the Bighorn in late August or early September you'll realize that big trout gorge them-selves on these small mayflies. Fish an eddy or backwater of the Bighorn while this spinner fall occurs, and you're in for some great fall matching-the-spinner activity.

Even on the lower end of the McKenzie River in Eugene, Oregon, you find a great trico spinner fall. Here, because of the mild fall weather, the hatch lasts until late October.

In fact, almost anywhere you go in the country you'll find good trico spinner falls from late July through September. On good trico waters you can depend on a hatch for ninety or more days, but after several weeks of seeing the same old Trico Spinner patterns trout become highly selective. On the South Platte trout often ignored my best copy even when it drifted completely drag-free.

I often wondered what happens after these naturals drift through several sets of pools and riffles? I surmised that after floating for awhile, these spent spinners sink, and trout that had not fed on the surface could feed on these submerged spinners for much of the day. Trout that had fed on spinners on the surface earlier might also move toward the bottom after the supply on the surface dwindled. This hypothesis remained a hypothesis for many years until I fly-fished several years ago on Falling Springs Run in south-central Pennsylvania with Gene Macri of Waynesboro. For years, Falling Springs had one of the heaviest and longest trico hatches in the East, along with hordes of fly-fishers fishing over the spinner fall daily.

Falling Springs in south-central Pennsylvania holds a good Trico hatch. Here, sinking the spinner pattern can sometimes be rewarding.

I had a deadline to meet. I had to complete the manuscript for *Pennsylvania Trout Streams and Their Hatches* within a month, and I still had more than twenty top Pennsylvania trout streams to cover. Gene Macri, an area authority on Falling Springs, agreed to fish with me. We planned a morning on Falling Springs Run just outside of Chambersburg, and I wanted to experience the fabulous trico hatch and spinner fall once more before I completed writing about this fantastic limestone stream.

Urbanization has not been kind to this small, productive stream. Within the past two decades the intensity of the trico hatches on Falling Springs has noticeably diminished. But even though the hatch has lessened, the trico still produces rising trout each and every morning from early July through much of October.

On this hot July morning, the spinner fall of these small mayflies barely lasted a half-hour. I no sooner tied on a trico spinner, cast it a hundred or so times, and hooked one trout, than the fall ended. Across the twenty-foot-wide stream, Gene continued to fly-fish. He landed his sixth trout before I had enough and wanted to find out what he did differently from me. Gene cast the female Trico imitation cross-stream, then purposely pulled it until the spinner imitation sank. How sacrilegious can one get? Who ever heard of sinking a spinner imitation? All I ever thought of was to fish that darned imitation on the surface.

I talked about the theory of sunken spinners at a seminar in Pittsburgh to the Penns Woods West Trout Unlimited Chapter. After my talk, Bill Simmeth told me about a recent experience. Bill fished on north-central Pennsylvania's Pine Creek when a fantastic red quill spinner fall occurred. For some minutes Bill cast his Red Quill Spinner over rising trout, but they all refused the pattern. But on one cast, the spinner pattern sank and Bill caught a trout, then seven more by purposely sinking the pattern.

But you'll often encounter problems when you fish a sunken spinner. First, you'll often find strikes at a sunken spinner very subtle and almost undetectable. Second, you might prefer fishing the weighted spinner just off the bottom, and how can you fish the pattern just off the bottom and detect even the subtlest strikes? You guessed it—with a tandem rig! Tie the weighted spinner to a six-inch piece of tippet behind the dry fly. On Falling Springs I often use a tippet less than a foot long between the point and lead flies. By using the tandem method, you can vary the tippet length to get the fly where you want it. Falling Springs and many other trico streams hold a good number of aquatic weeds, so you must fish the sunken pattern well off the bottom.

After watching Gene Macri catch those six trout, I almost forgot about using a sinking spinner—until this past year. Craig Josephson and I revisited Falling Springs one morning during the height of the trico spinner fall. During the entire two-hour fishing trip, neither Craig nor I saw any trout rise to trico spinners. Why? First, a late-evening thunderstorm the night before brought the water level up considerably. Second, few trico spinners fell that morning. After an hour of waiting and watching, I finally tied on a weighted trico spinner. I made a knot in the line and added a microshot to help the pattern sink and I tied the Trico on an eight-inch tippet behind the Patriot dry fly. On the tenth cast, the Patriot sank and I set the hook. A heavy rainbow had hit the spinner. A dozen more casts produced another strike on the submerged spinner. And within minutes another trout took the pattern. I didn't land one of these trout, but the fact that three of them eagerly took the sunken spinner should give you something to think about when no trout rises to the surface. The sunken spinner should prove invaluable to anglers fly-fishing waters with heavy trico hatches like those on the Missouri River in Montana and the South Platte in Colorado.

Still don't think the sunken spinner works? Ask John Newcomer of Chambersburg or Bob Duffus of State College, Pennsylvania. John is one of those skilled but quiet, modest fly-fishers. On a recent September outing, John fished a sunken spinner on a tandem rig on Falling Springs during a trico spinner fall. Bob Duffus called after that trip to tell me how effective the tandem rig and the sunken spinner worked. Bob said he sat back and watched John catch several heavy trout on the sunken spinner.

You might say that a sunken spinner has no long record of productivity, but for years the English have used a pattern called Patterson Sunk Spinner to copy drowned *Baetis* spinners on their chalk streams.

To sink the spinner pattern I make three adjustments. First,

I change the ingredients for tying the pattern. I use fur for the body rather than poly, and a wing made of twenty to thirty hackles tied in on top. Second, I usually add about five wraps of .010 lead to the body before I tie it. Third, if the pattern doesn't readily sink when I'm ready to use it, I add a micro-shot a few inches in front of the spinner.

You can use the sunken spinner on such diverse spinner falls hatches as the trico, sulphur, pale morning spinner, and the dark brown spinner (*Paraleptophlebia* species).

Sunken Trico Spinner

    HOOK: Mustad 94840, size 20 short shank

    THREAD: Dark brown

    TAILS: Soft cream hackle fibers

    BODY: Two or three turns of cream rabbit fur at the rear—
        tie the remainder of the body with dark brownish-black
        rabbit.

    WINGS: Tie in 20 to 30 hackle fibers on top and cut off the
        excess on either side.

Sunken Sulphur-Pale Morning Spinner

    HOOK: Mustad 94840, size 16 and 18

    THREAD: Tan

    TAILS: Tan hackle fibers

    BODY: Tan rabbit fur or angora

    WINGS: Thirty cream hackle fibers tied in on top

Sunken Dark Brown Spinner

    HOOK: Mustad 94840

    THREAD: Dark brown

    TAILS: Dark brown hackle fibers

    BODY: Dark brown angora or rabbit

WINGS: Cream hackle fibers

Tying Notes: To copy the undulating male spinner, make two turns of dark brown at the bend and finish the body with white fur. This copies the male Paraleptophlebia spinner so common on most United States trout waters.

Andrew Goldman releases a heavy brown trout caught on Pennsylvania's
Spruce Creek on a Bead-head.   Bryan Meck

Chapter 7

Topwater Patterns When There's No Hatch to Match

How many times have you carefully planned to fish a hatch and it never appeared or did so in feeble numbers? What do you do next? These situations require special patterns. Patterns that anglers call attractors often work well when there's no hatch to match. Patterns like the Wulff Royal Coachman, Goofus, and Patriot with their bright colors often bring trout to the surface. Unfamiliar with the Patriot? I developed this highly productive dry fly more than ten years ago, and since then, I've changed body and tail materials several times. The Patriot has saved the day for me on New Zealand's South Island and on trips throughout the United States.

The Goofus, too, has saved me from embarrassment on several trips to the Madison River in Montana. When few other patterns caught trout, a red-bodied Goofus did the trick.

The Adams has worked well on many waters. Recently when I surveyed more than 100 fly-fishers in Michigan and Pennsylvania, the majority said they preferred to use a gray-bodied Adams when there's no hatch on the water. I won't travel far without a good supply of Adams patterns. These gray-bodied flies match many of the large flies anglers call gray and slate drakes.

And the Wulff Royal Coachman consistently performs when many other patterns fail. How many times has this pattern out-fished all others on my favorite small mountain stream?

Tandem Connection
All patterns listed in this section in sizes 16 and larger make

188

excellent lead flies for the tandem rig. I select the Patriot by a wide margin as my first choice when no hatch appears, because in sizes 12 and 14 the Patriot floats well, and under most conditions it's easy to follow. When I employed the tandem rig on Utah's Green River, I used a size 10 Patriot. In the fast Western waters you'll often need a larger pattern. A good second choice is the Wulff Royal Coachman. Again, I use a size 10 when I'm fishing faster waters on the Madison in Montana and the Deschutes in Oregon. Although the Adams works well throughout the summer, it can be difficult to see and follow as the floating fly in the tandem rig.

We'll look now at each pattern and tying recipes for each.

Patriot

As I said, my first choice when there's no hatch to match is the Patriot. More than ten years ago, I read an article about trout and colors. In the article the writer said that the rainbow trout he studied had a preference for blue. I first concocted a pattern that looked a lot like the Royal Coachman but it had blue marabou where the Coachman had peacock. I carry a mechanical counter and I tested the Patriot against ten other old standbys like the Adams, Wulff Royal Coachman, and Light Cahill. I'd make 1,000 casts with each pattern over a period of a year on water void of rising trout. The Patriot out-fished every other pattern I used by at least two to one.

Mike Bay catches a trout on the Patriot on the Missouri River

I added smolt blue Krystal Flash to the body about five years ago. I remember that trip to the Youghiogheny River in southwestern Pennsylvania when I first used the Krystal Flash pattern. I gave one to Art Gusbar of nearby Somerset. Art looked at the pattern and suggested I name it the Patriot because of its red, white, and blue colors. Art tied on the pattern and on the second cast hooked a heavy rainbow that broke off almost immediately. Pat Docherty of Grafton, West Virginia, also fished with us that evening. When Pat saw the size of the fish Art had just lost, he tied on a Patriot and began casting. On the first cast Pat, too, hooked a heavy trout that he lost almost immediately. As we left the river that evening, both anglers asked me to send them a half dozen of these productive patterns.

Want more proof that the Patriot works on streams throughout the United States? As I mentioned earlier, Craig Shuman invited Dave Engerbretson, Jeff Edvalds, and me to take part in a video he planned for the Yakima River in southeastern Washington. Dave is a professor at Washington State University, teaches a fly-fishing course there, and in his spare time is the Western editor of *Fly Fisherman* magazine. Jeff Edvalds is an accomplished fly-fisher and a professional outdoor photographer. Craig and Jack Mitchell guide anglers on the Yakima seven months of the year. Al Novotny of Casper, Wyoming, directed the video. We had no sooner left the access area when Al began pleading with—no, directing— us to "catch a fish." I tried to tell him I couldn't catch a trout on command, but he insisted.

For the first hours of that initial float trip we hit a tremendous black caddis hatch and trout continued to rise for several hours to the size 16 downwings. By early evening the caddis hatch had lessened and few trout rose. I decided at that time to try my Patriot to see if I could bring any rainbows to the surface, and for the next two hours that pattern caught heavy Yakima River rainbows. By the end of a week's fishing on the Yakima some of the locals began tying and using the pattern.

Craig Josephson set up a late-May trip to fly-fish some of Arizona's top trout streams. Arizona trout fishing? Yes, Arizona has some unbelievable trout streams and rivers. Just think—drive 200 miles northeast of Phoenix in the White Mountains to fish the likes of the Little Colorado, the North Fork of the White, and the East Fork of the White rivers. Craig of Johnstown, Pennsylvania, Josh

David of nearby Lakeside, and I fly-fished one late-May afternoon after a short but heavy thunderstorm. I used a tandem with the Patriot as the dry and a Bead-head Pheasant Tail Nymph as the wet fly. Josh used a caddis pattern, and Craig tied on a Patriot. Directly upriver from Craig three rainbows rose. Craig cast to the nearest one and on the second cast hooked a twelve-inch 'bow. Two more casts and he caught the second trout, and the final rising trout took the Patriot a few minutes later.

On another day on our Arizona trip Craig Josephson, Josh David, Bob David, and I headed onto a thirty-mile dirt road leading into the White mountains. Craig had scheduled this leg of the trip so we could catch some native Apache trout. Only a few small streams in the area still hold native populations of Apaches, and from his studies of this species of trout, Bob David knows each stream well. I wanted to see how these Apache trout reacted to the Patriot dry fly.

We stopped at one of the six small streams holding native trout and began working our way through a dense thicket of pines. For more than a mile, tangles, branches, and trees prevented us from approaching much of the stream, let alone casting. But about a mile downstream we found the most picturesque, scenic setting I had ever seen. The heavy pine forest gave way to a cienega—a huge alpine meadow—that appeared to be at least a mile wide and four miles long. As we entered the opening, we saw wild Merriam's turkeys running for cover and nearly a hundred wild horses glaring at us. The small stream flowed through this opening. Imagine fishing four miles on a small stream and not once having to contend with small brush or other obstacles. We took turns casting into the miniature pools in this meadow. Craig caught the first Apache trout of the trip—on the Patriot. It measured only six inches long, but its beauty and the fact that it had grown up in this spectacular location made it worthwhile. Josh caught the next native Apache—again only six inches long but as magnificent as the first. My turn came next, and in the next pool another six-inch native smashed the Patriot. We took turns until an unexpected thunderstorm washed the meadow. What an experience, one none of us will ever forget!

And it's not just my friends and I fishing in exotic locations who take a lot of trout on the Patriot.

I recently received a letter from Jim Misiura, who fishes the Lackawanna River near Scranton, Pennsylvania, almost daily. Jim recently tied some Patriots to try on the river, and here, in his words, is how well the pattern worked:

"July 29 and 30 I used some Patriots on pocket water in Jessup. It was 3:30 p.m. when I started on the 29th. I fished until I lost my only two Patriots. I caught seventeen on the first, only two on the second before a tree claimed it at 6:30. I could hardly believe I would be able to top that day. That night I tied eight new Patriot patterns for the next day's fishing with Pete Kunis. I met him at 3:00 p.m. We fished more pocket water. I gave Pete four of the new flies, but he switched to a caddis before giving the Patriot a chance. Well, we both did good, although I did much better, with twenty trout to Pete's eight. Incidentally, I caught eighteen of those browns on the same fly, then switched to an emerger pattern and took the final two fish. On Sunday morning, I gave that fly and three others to a couple of guys from New Jersey. I'm sure they did very well with them."

How about experiences with this dynamic new pattern on streams outside of the United States? Several years ago, Mike Manfredo and I fly-fished on New Zealand's South Island for a month. Mike teaches at Colorado State University in Fort Collins and fly-fishes all over the world. I took more than two dozen Patriots with me on that trip but used all of them in the first couple of weeks. For the last two weeks Mike and I tore one of our blue knapsacks apart and tied some Patriots with the blue thread. On that trip Mike and I caught eleven of our twelve biggest trout on the Patriot. Trout up to twenty-eight inches long rose to the Patriot.

I often use the Patriot in a size 12 or 14 in tandem with a wet fly. I tie a wet fly on a leader behind the dry fly and use the Patriot as a strike indicator. When the Patriot sinks, a trout has struck the wet fly. If the dry fly floats drag-free on top, the wet fly drifts drag-free underneath. Throughout the summer I'll catch one out of six on the dry fly or strike indicator. I often use the Green Weenie or Bead-head Pheasant Tail Nymph as the wet fly with the Patriot. Consider this an experience with the Patriot.

I recently addressed a group of anglers at the Nemacolin Encampment at Beaver Creek in southwestern Pennsylvania. For three days about 150 prominent western Pennsylvania businessmen join in the fun and frivolity of angling and shooting. I spoke to them for a half-hour about many of the recent breakthroughs in fly-tying materials and advancements in fly-fishing techniques.

I showed them some of the new productive patterns like the Crystal Comparaduns, and midge and caddis patterns with trailing shucks. I showed them two of my favorite patterns when there's no hatch on the water—the Patriot and the Green Weenie. I also showed the anglers at the encampment how they could use the Patriot and Green Weenie in tandem by tying a thirty-inch piece of tippet at the bend of the hook of the Patriot. At the end of this second tippet I tied on the Green Weenie.

After my talk on patterns and techniques the anglers suggested that I head over to Beaver Creek and catch a trout for them. Wow! The pressure was on! After all the talk, I had to produce. I had an audience of a dozen anglers watching my every cast. Adding to my woes, the summer had produced precious few storms and a stream flow only a trickle of its spring volume.

I stood on the bank next to a small, deep pool that held

maybe a dozen heavy brookies, browns, and rainbows. With each cast, I became more desperate to prove to the onlookers that I could really catch trout on this Patriot pattern. The entire morning before the talk, only one or two anglers had taken trout, so I was fearful I would be among the majority who caught none. But on my fifth or sixth cast I saw a heavy brook trout leave its position near the bottom of the pool and move toward the surface. This huge brook trout slowly but deliberately opened its mouth just inches under the Patriot and then closed its mouth and moved toward the bottom of the pool. I struck! Five minutes later I released an eighteen-inch brookie in front of a group of interested anglers. Two more casts and another brook trout took the pattern. This one I missed.

That afternoon I landed several more heavy trout on both the Green Weenie and Patriot. By the next morning, most of the anglers who had watched the action the day before tied on a Patriot.

What stream would provide the ultimate test for the Patriot? If you've ever fished LeTort Spring Run in Carlisle, Pennsylvania, you know why I think any pattern that catches trout there deserves special recognition. Several months ago Mark Jackson of Hollidaysburg, Pennsylvania, fly-fished this frustrating limestoner. The cool, chalky waters ebb through a narrow channel clogged on both sides by fertile aquatic weeds. You not only have to contend with highly selective streambred trout, but also currents and weeds.

Mark fly-fished these hallowed waters one evening in late July. Mark brought some Sulphur patterns with him, and even though he fished in midseason, he still hoped he'd see a few stragglers emerging. Mark saw only three trout rise that evening, and then only infrequently. He tied on a size 14 Patriot and cast to the first riser. The ten-inch trout readily took the Patriot attractor. He then cast above the second and third risers with the same success. Can you believe that? Three trout rose on this fabled spring creek, and Mark caught all three on an attractor pattern? Some of the more famous names in angling who have written so capably about this cool spring water and have since departed have probably turned over in their graves after Mark's experience.

Recently I wrote an article on the Patriot for *Fly Fisherman* magazine. Within days after that article appeared letters from anglers who had tried the pattern started pouring in from Washington, Arizona, Maryland, and Pennsylvania extolling the value of this new attractor pattern.

Josh David of Lakewood, Arizona, told how he used the new attractor on Horseshoe Lake in Arizona with great success—so much success that he and a friend want to start tying the pattern.

My letter from Ann McIntosh of Monkton, Maryland, however, says it all:

"I want to commend *Fly Fisherman* for featuring Charles Meck's Patriot fly in the *Fly Tyer's Bench* column of the September issue. This letter is a plea to tackle shops to begin to offer the pattern. I hope Meck's article will increase its commercial availability. I have found the Patriot to be the most reliable attractor pattern in my box, having caught innumerable trout with it when *nothing else* would work. However, it's very difficult to purchase in large or destination fly shops, or by mail order.

"I first became aware of the Patriot when Charlie Meck came into Alan Bright's Spruce Creek Outfitters and gave me a #14 Patriot as I was homebound from a week's fishing in central Pennsylvania in June, 1993. My home water is the Gunpowder Falls in northern Baltimore County, Maryland. The fish are selective, wary, pressured, and prone to naturals—especially midges and nymphs. I suspected they would not accept the Patriot. I was wrong. They swatted it greedily, time after time—fish ranging from eight-inch young of the year to eighteen-inch adult browns.

"I have recently returned from a trip to Western waters. I had a dozen #14 Patriots custom-tied to take with me. My trip began fishing the pristine, private spring creeks of the Jackson Hole valley—part of the 4 Lazy F ranch. The largest fish I hooked (a twenty-plus-inch cutthroat) took the last Patriot I had.

"That night, George McCullough, fishing guide at the 4 Lazy F where I was staying, tied up some #14 Patriot spinners as well as a #16 Patriot emerger. The following morning I tied on the spinner and landed three fourteen-inch-plus cutthroats on my first ten casts.

"The ultimate Western water tribute to the Patriot came on a float trip on the South Fork of the Snake River in Idaho. The river averages 7,500 cutthroats per mile through the sixteen-mile gorge we drifted. My friend and I caught more than thirty cutts between us. I took the only brown trout on the Patriot dun, and two of the cutthroats. Carter Andrews (a guide from Jack Dennis Outfitters), was astounded. 'I can't get them to look at a Royal Wulff or a Coachman over here,' he announced. 'Usually these South Fork cutts want very precise imitations of the naturals!'

"I rest my case. I hope tackle shops will begin to sell the Patriot so I don't have to beg, bargain and cajole my favorite destination shops to custom-tie them for me, and I can find them when and wherever I need them!"

What a testimonial! The Patriot has produced all over the world.

The Patriot
> HOOK: Mustad 94833, sizes #10–#18
> THREAD: Red
> TAILS: Brown hackle fibers
> BODY: Smolt blue Krystal Flash wound around the shank.

Wind some of the red thread in the middle of the shank, similar to the Royal Coachman.

WINGS: White impala or calf tail, divided.

HACKLE: Brown

Tying Notes: Add a drop or two of cement to the body to hold it in place.

Wulff Royal Coachman

For nearly seven years I fly-fished almost daily with Lloyd Williams of Dallas, Pennsylvania. Lloyd's one of those anglers who doesn't believe in matching a hatch. He presents a strong argument that an angler needs only two or three patterns to fish successfully throughout the season. In early spring, Lloyd uses a Muddler Minnow. But from early June into early September Lloyd never changes flies. In fact, if you looked in the back seat of his car you'd see his fly rod broken down into its three pieces, with a fly still attached to the tippet. If you check that fly you'd probably find it was a Wulff Royal Coachman. Lloyd used the Coachman exclusively through those summer months and caught as many trout as many anglers matching the hatches, and Lloyd annually caught more than his share of lunkers with that Coachman pattern.

Not only on large streams and rivers, but also when he fished small mountain streams, Lloyd Williams preferred the Wulff Royal Coachman. With the white impala or calf tail wings, this attractor pattern shows up particularly well under a typical mountain stream's heavy canopy. Compared to a dark Adams or Slate Drake, you can follow the Wulff readily on the surface. Just recently Lloyd went to that place in the sky where you always fish the right fly and catch a trout on every cast. He will long be remembered.

Joe Daugherty of Lewisburg, Pennsylvania, also depends on the Wulff Royal Coachman throughout the fishing season. For more than a decade he's had great results with this attractor pattern even on such great match-the-hatch water as Penns Creek. From June through October you'll find Joe catching streambred brown trout on this famous Eastern limestone stream on the Coachman pattern.

Joe prefers to use a size 12 or 14 pattern. However, under low-water conditions in late summer I've seen him use size 18 or 20 patterns. On occasion on big Western waters like the Madison in Yellowstone Park, I've used a size 10 pattern. On one trip to the Madison, I caught the largest trout of the week on the Wulff Royal Coachman.

So far I've presented an argument for fishing the Wulff when no hatch appears. Will the Coachman catch trout during a hatch? Recently I presented a talk on tricos at the Izaak Walton Fly Fisherman's Club in Toronto. This group presents an annual forum with as many as 2,000 participants.

During my talk, I suggested that I often had problems catching trout on a heavily fished section with a conventional Trico pattern. Many in the audience agreed and asked what they could do. I suggested they use a different pattern. I then related a story about a trico hatch on central Pennsylvania's Spring Creek and what I did there one day. I remember vividly wading upstream to a 200-foot glide and seeing a dozen trout feed on spent female trico spinners. I still had the tandem Patriot and Green Weenie tied on and thought I'd cast the duo above the rising trout before I switched to a Trico Spinner. Three streambred brown trout feeding on tricos took that Green Weenie pattern within fifteen minutes.

Several years before that incident on Spring Creek, I had a similar experience, this time on Falling Springs in south-central Pennsylvania. Falling Springs for years held one of the heaviest trico spinner falls in the East. Clouds of spinners fell onto the surface for more than two hours. Because of its popularity, Falling Springs also had a considerable number of anglers fishing the fall daily. By mid-

August these Falling Springs trout had seen so many imitations they become extremely selective. Often the trout came up to a pattern, inspected it carefully, then bumped it with their nose. One day while fishing over thousands of spinners and becoming more frustrated by the minute, I tied on a size 18 Wulff Royal Coachman. That coachman picked up a half dozen streambred rainbows before the spinner fall ended.

Wulff Royal Coachman
> HOOK: Mustad 94833, sizes 10-20
> THREAD: Red
> TAILS: White calf tail
> BODY: Peacock with a red floss midrib
> WINGS: White calf tail, divided
> HACKLE: Brown

Adams
What pattern do fly-fishers prefer when no hatch appears on the water? Back in 1982, I conducted a survey of fly-fishers throughout the country and asked that question. Sixty percent of the anglers surveyed selected the Adams as their top choice when no hatch appeared.

George Harvey once said to me that an Adams would produce as many trout in midsummer as any hatch-matching pattern. I couldn't argue with him because this pattern really does produce, especially in June, July, and August. Why? Look at any stream in the Eastern United States and Canada. Many of those waters hold great slate drake, or *Isonychia*, hatches.

Look at many of the Western rivers. Throughout the summer you'll find many gray mayflies (*Rhithrogena* species) emerging on many of these rivers. What do Montana's Bitterroot, Madison, and Gallatin rivers have in common? These and many other

Western waters hold great *Rhithrogena* hatches throughout the summer. Examine the body of most of these mayflies and you'll see that the gray-bodied Adams copies them credibly. Look at the great rivers of the Midwest. Here you'll find gray drake hatches common. Again, the Adams works well.

A virtual insect factory, the Henry's Fork in Idaho hosts hatches almost daily throughout the summer.

Fish any of the lakes in the West holding good trout populations and you'll find the speckled-winged dun. This *Callibetis* species appears almost daily on many lakes, usually from late morning until early afternoon from May through August. A size 14 or 16 Adams copies this hatch adequately.

Recently Craig Josephson, Bob and Josh David, and I fished Sunrise Lake near Greer, Arizona. This lake, just 200 miles northeast of Phoenix, holds great rainbow and Apache trout populations. Josh David handed Craig and me a Peacock Lady and suggested that we try the pattern first. For two hours we caught trout on that odd-looking pattern. By 11:00 a.m., a speckle-winged dun hatch appeared on the choppy surface. Trout immediately began to feed on the duns, and I realized that a size 16 Adams during this sporadic hatch would have worked well.

Try the Adams in sizes 16, 18, and 20 and you'll see how effective these smaller patterns perform. Why do these smaller Adams work so well? Just about every trout stream worth a second look holds some blue quills. These mayflies (Genus *Paraleptophlebia*) emerge almost every day of the year. If you fish Henry's Fork in late June you'll see blue quills from late morning through early afternoon. Fish the North Platte near Saratoga, Wyoming, in late August and you'll again see blue quills appearing. Most Eastern, Midwestern, and Canadian trout streams also hold good hatches on almost every summer morning. Any trout stream worth fly-fishing should hold at least one blue quill hatch, and a small Adams suitably copies all blue quill species.

No wonder the Adams works so well. It copies hatches common in the East, Midwest, and West that appear much of the year. The next time you don't know which pattern to use, try the Adams.

Adams

     HOOK: Mustad 94833, sizes 12 to 20
     THREAD: Gray
     TAILS: Mixed brown and grizzly
     BODY: Dark gray poly, dubbed
     WINGS: Grizzly hackle tips
     HACKLE: One grizzly and one brown hackle

Humpy

     Phil Baldacchino owns the Kettle Creek Tackle Shop in north-central Pennsylvania. In his store, Phil features the top fly patterns matching the hatches that appear each week of the fishing season. When the hendricksons appear on Kettle Creek, Phil sells dozen of imitations of that hatch. When the blue quill appears, he features that fly. During the green and brown drake hatches, Phil displays dozens of those imitations. So while Phil features these flies in his display, what does he use during a hatch? Phil often ties on a red-bodied or yellow-bodied Humpy. Yes, a Humpy works even during a hatch.

Recently Phil and I fly fished on Kettle Creek when a hendrickson hatch appeared. I matched the hatch with a Red Quill and Phil tied on a red-bodied Humpy. During the hatch Phil caught as many trout on that red-bodied Humpy as I did matching the hatch with a Red Quill. Phil says the Humpy matches the reddish body of the male red quill. He finds the Humpy appropriate for fishing some of the hatches and also when no hatch appears.

Humpy

> HOOK: Mustad 94833, size 10 to 18
> THREAD: Red
> TAILS: Dark elk hair
> BODY: Red Floss
> WINGS: Light elk hair
> HACKLE: Badger

Tying Notes: Tie in about ten dark elk hairs for the tail. Tie in about twenty light elk hair fibers at the bend of the hook where you just tied in the tai, with their tips extending backward over the bend of the hook. Make certain you make these fibers fairly long, because they'll form the wings. Wrap red floss over the body then bring the elk hair over the top and tie off just in front of the eye of the hook. Shape the tips into two upright wings. Add two badger hackles.

Trout Fin

Talk about old patterns that really catch trout, and you've got to include the Trout Fin. I've used this pattern off and on for more than forty years, and when all else fails, including the Patriot, I often resort to this orange-bodied pattern.

John Weaver first shared the Trout Fin with me on a Northeastern stream. After I sat back and watched John catch trout in July and August with the Trout Fin, I asked him if I could see it. He not only showed me the pattern, but also gave me a couple to try. I tied one on that evening and have never been without the pattern since.

Why does the Trout Fin work so well, especially in late season? If you examine many trout streams in July and August you'll find sporadic emergences of mayflies with orange and pink bodies, the color of the body of the Trout Fin. Try this pattern if you run into one of those frustrating unproductive fishing days.

Trout Fin

> HOOK: Mustad 94833, size 12 to 18
> THREAD: Orange
> TAILS: Brown hackle fibers
> BODY: Bright orange floss
> WINGS: Impala
> HACKLE: Brown

Patriot Downwing

Many anglers use nothing but attractor patterns for almost the entire year. I talked earlier about Joe Daugherty, who begins and ends the season with the Wulff Royal Coachman. I also indicated that my old friend Lloyd Williams used an attractor practically the entire season.

But through the years I have seen only one or two downwing patterns like the Trude that represent a downwing attractor pattern.

It's been almost fifteen years since I tied my first Patriot Downwing. I gave that pattern to my teenage son to test on a northern Pennsylvania trout stream called Oswayo Creek, which I still consider one of the finest freestone streams in the East. As mentioned, Bryan and I attended a conference of the Pennsylvania

Outdoor Writers in Coudersport, Pennsylvania, members and guests could select from a number of fishing trips. Bryan chose Oswayo Creek and caught the only trout taken on the group field trip—and on the downwing attractor.

Patriot Downwing
>HOOK: Mustad 94833, sizes 12 to 18
>THREAD: Red
>TAILS: None
>BODY: Smolt blue Krystal Flash with a midsection of red tying thread
>WINGS: White or brown deer tied downwing
>HACKLE: Brown

A brown trout takes the Patriot.   Bryan Meck

Chapter 8
Patterns That Copy
Land-based Insects

It's July or August and many of your favorite hatches have ended for the year. What do you do now? What patterns work on these hot summer days when no hatch appears?

If you're fly-fishing any stream or river that meanders through a meadow, a grasshopper imitation might prove effective at this time. A grasshopper pattern saved the day for me on the Brown's Canyon section of Colorado's Arkansas River. On that hot afternoon no insect appeared on the surface and no trout rose. But the minute I began casting a hopper pattern, trout chased it.

Ask guides like Craig Shuman and Jack Mitchell on central Washington's Yakima River what they use in late summer, and they'll tell you how effectively grasshopper patterns work during late summer. Every day for several weeks, Craig and Jack find hopper patterns work extremely well along the banks of the Yakima.

Then there's August 25 on many Eastern trout waters. Almost like clockwork, you'll find a winged ant falling on the surface of many trout streams, starting a feeding frenzy that can last for a couple of days. I've kept records of this winged ant for the past 20 years, and it has always appeared on the surface within two days of that late-August date. If you carry dark brown and black ant patterns in sizes 18, 20, and 22, you'll find unbelievable matching-the-terrestrial episodes in late August.

Ask Bob Budd of Altoona, Pennsylvania, what patterns he most often opts for in July and August. He'll select an ant or a gypsy moth. Bob has used both patterns extensively and has continuously found them to be top fish-catchers in midsummer.

But you'll find many other terrestrial patterns effective in July and August. Beetles and caterpillar imitations work well at that time. I've even used white moth patterns to copy the adult of the spanworm caterpillar.

Tying the Terrestrials

You may, of course, have trouble following your ant or beetle pattern on the surface. They're not easy to detect. George Harvey ties a piece of bright yellow or orange feather on the top of his beetle patterns so he can follow them easier. I strike when I see a rise in the general vicinity of my terrestrial.

With the advent of some of the newer materials (discussed in Chapter 10) it's much easier to tie many of the terrestrials. Polycelon has made old ant patterns outmoded. Just tie on one of the cylinders for ant, beetles, grasshoppers, crickets, or caterpillars and you have an excellent imitation of these terrestrials. Rather than using deer hair for the beetle and ant, I now use this new plastic.

Tandem Connection

How can you possibly use a tandem connection with terrestrials? As you know, ants and beetles ride low in the water, and even if you add a bit of orange or red, you'll often have difficulty following the pattern. The solution? Tie on a large attractor pattern like the Patriot as the lead fly and tie on an ant or beetle about one to two feet behind it. You'll readily detect the attractor and more likely be able to know the approximate location of the terrestrial.

Fishing Terrestrials

On small streams, George Harvey often slaps his ant or

beetle pattern onto the water. Unlike mayflies, stoneflies, and caddis flies, terrestrials often fall onto the surface from a distance and therefore their sudden relocation often makes a more showy appearance than those emerging from the bottom. If you find no takers when your terrestrials land perfectly, try slapping the pattern like George Harvey does. Fish the shorelines along the stream or river thoroughly. Since winds often transport terrestrials from banks along the shoreline, trout readily look for them along the edges.

Beetles, ants, grasshoppers, crickets, cicadas, and cater-pillars make up a majority of this wind-borne food anglers call terrestrials. What terrestrials will work best for you? If you're fly-fishing in July or August and there's no hatch, you'll probably do well with an ant or beetle. In any case fly-fishers should carry some good terrestrial patterns with them. Patterns like the Green Inchworm, Gypsy Moth Larva, Ant, and Beetle make up a good selection of productive patterns.

Green Inchworm

George Harvey often tells the story about the first Green Inchworm pattern he created. In the early 1930s, during the summer, George worked at Fisherman's Paradise in central Pennsylvania for the state Fish Commission. The Commission designated part of Spring Creek as a special fly-fishing-only section and allowed anglers to keep one big trout. One day George instructed his daughter on the finer details of fly-fishing. That day she landed one huge fish after another on a simple cork pattern George developed and called the Green Inchworm. While hooking many trout, she also lost a lot of patterns and George's supply of cork caterpillars ran low. Charlie French, an executive of the Fish Commission at the time, watched George and his daughter fish. Charlie asked George what pattern his daughter was using so successfully. When George showed Charlie the cork inchworm, he asked George for one so he could fish. George said he only had two left and wanted to keep them for his daughter, and Charlie French left in a huff. The very next morning, George remembers, someone had placed signs along the entire section of Fisherman's Paradise outlawing cork inchworms.

That didn't bother George—he went home that evening and tied a new pattern—this time with green deer hair, a pattern that worked as well if not better than the cork pattern. Now, almost sixty years later, George uses the same Green Inchworm pattern during much of the summer. It floats well and looks like so many caterpillars found just above the stream. In June, when the green inchworms fall onto the water, you'll find the imitation especially productive.

Recently George Harvey developed a new method for tying the Green Inchworm that makes it even more lifelike and easier to tie. I describe this new technique under "Tying Notes."

You can now purchase green polycelon and use it for the inchworm body. All you have to do is place a couple of drops of Super Glue on the shank and hold the cylinder against the shank for a minute. Wrap a dark green thread from the bend of the hook to the eye to secure the inchworm and to simulate the segmentation.

Green Inchworm
>   HOOK: Mustad 94831, size 10
>   THREAD: Green
>   BODY: Deer hair, dyed green

Tying Notes: Take about twenty or thirty strands of the green deer hair, place it with the tips extending back over the bend of the hook, and the butt section toward the eye. Secure tightly with tying thread, then pull the deer hair toward the eye of the hook. Make certain you have strands of the deer hair on the top and bottom of the hook. Move up the shank an eighth of an inch or so and wrap some of the green thread around the deer hair to give the appearance of segmentation. Wrap some green thread around the shank just in front of the deer hair, then bring the deer hair toward the eye and wrap around it another eighth of an inch toward the eye. Continue this process until you've reached the eye.

George Harvey's new method for tying the Green Inchworm is as follows: He ties in a bunch of green deer hair near the eye with the butts facing forward and the tips extending out over the bend of the hook. George uses green tying thread and bright green floss. He ties the body securely back to the bend of the hook. He leaves the bright green floss at the bend. George then pulls the deer hair forward, making certain that half remains on top of the hook and the other half is on the bottom. He ties the deer hair in at the eye. He then ribs the deer hair body with the green floss.

Winged Ant

Almost like clockwork on many Eastern trout waters, I often find trout rising to winged ants around August 25. I have fished the hatch so often and have seen so many trout sipping the naturals that I'm convinced that this particular terrestrial behaves differently than most of its cousins. When you fish terrestrials you'll occasionally see a trout taking a natural beetle or ant. When the winged ant lands on the water in great numbers from late August through October you're in for some great fly-fishing—all day long. Trout take up feeding positions and rise to these transported terrestrials for hours. I have fished over trout rising to these winged ants for more than five hours at a time.

If you've fished this "terrestrial hatch," for any time, you know you'll find two distinct sizes of winged ants and two distinct body colors, so it's important to carry a variety of patterns with you.

I carry winged ants in sizes 18 to 22 and in body colors of dark brown and black so that I can copy the different winged terrestrials.

I can remember heavy winged ant "hatches" occurring from late August through mid-October. If you hit Indian summer-type weather in the fall, look for these winged ants on the water.

Since these ants are terrestrials you'll find the ant hatch most common on fairly open streams. Don't forget—when ants appear on the water for as long a period as these do, many sink. If you have no success with your floating pattern, then sink it—and use it on a tandem rig so you can detect even the slightest strike.

Winged Ant

    HOOK: Mustad 94833, sizes 16 to 24

    THREAD: Black or dark brown or cinnamon

    BODY: Black, brown, or cinnamon poly dubbed and tied
       in as two humps, or Polycelon or foam tied similar to the
       Black Ant.

    WINGS: Two pale gray hackle tips tied in just behind eye.

    HACKLE: Black or dark brown tied in between the two
       humps.

Deer-Hair Ant

For years on every trip to a favorite small stream, George Harvey has used a Deer-Hair Ant. He describes it in his book, *Techniques of Trout Fishing and Fly Tying.* This buggy-looking terrestrial has worked for me time and time again. After you catch a few trout with one of these ant patterns the hairs begin to split. After catching a half dozen trout the pattern looks like anything but an ant. But it seems that the more use and abuse you give the pattern, the more effective it becomes. Each of the broken hairs makes another simulated leg.

With the advent of some of the new synthetics, I most often

use them to tie my ant and beetle patterns. Polycelon or black cell foam makes an excellent body for ant patterns. I tie them in sizes 16 through 22 with body colors in cinnamon, brown, and black.

Deer-Hair Ant
> HOOK: Mustad 94833, Sizes 12 to 18
> BODY: Black deer hair

Tying Notes: Take a bunch of black deer hair about one and one half times as long as the shank of the hook. Tie in the butts at the middle of the shank with the tips pointing toward the bend of the hook. Move thread to the bend, tie in the deer hair and move thread back to the center of the shank. Pull deer hair tip back over the butt and again tie in at the center of the shank. Pull remaining deer tips to the eye and tie in. Make certain the two piles of deer hair form the two humps of an ant. Clip off excess hair at the eye. Pull out three hairs from the rear hump with a bodkin. These become the legs of the ant.

Poly Ant
> HOOK: Mustad 94833, sizes 12 to 18
> BODY: Black poly or Polycelon, dubbed into two humps on the hook, with the rear hump a bit larger than the front one.
> HACKLE: Add a black hackle after you complete the rear hump and before you start the front one.

Tying Notes: Substitute black poly for the deer hair and you get the Poly Ant. This version lasts much longer than the Deer-Hair Ant. You can dub the poly or use poly yarn. As I've mentioned, the new bodies made from Polycelon can't be beat for durability and a lifelike imitation.

Black Ant
> HOOK: Mustad 94833, size 16 to 22
> THREAD: Black
> BODY: Black foam strip
> HACKLE: Small black hackle in the middle

Tying Notes: Cut a narrow strip of black cell foam and tie in at the bend of the hook with the strip extending out over the bend of the hook. Wind your tying thread up to the middle of the shank. Wind the foam around the hook three or four times, then make several secure turns at the middle of the shank. This produces the first hump. Tie in a small black hackle and make three turns and tie this off at the middle. Now wrap the remaining piece of foam around the shank and toward the eye two or three times. Tie off and cut off the excess.

Beetle

Even if you've never tied a fly before, in a couple minutes you can create a Poly Beetle. The entire pattern consists of a piece of black poly yarn. It's simple to tie and extremely effective. You can tie either the Poly Beetle or a Crowe Beetle. You tie the former with several strands of poly yarn and the latter with deer hair dyed black. Just like the Deer-Hair Ant, the hair on the Crowe Beetle also breaks quickly. The new cell foam beetles come precut and make an extremely lifelike pattern.

Poly Beetle

The Poly Beetle is tied exactly like the Crowe Beetle, except you use black poly yarn rather than black deer hair. On a size 16 beetle, use three strands of the yarn (about three match sticks thick). Tie in the poly securely below the bend of the hook. If you wish, tie in a peacock herl at the bend of the hook to imitate the Japanese beetle. Wind the tying thread up to the eye of the hook and wind the peacock. Pull the poly up over the shank of the hook and tie in securely just behind the eye. Cut off the excess poly, but leave some to imitate the head. You'll really like this excellent pattern. It's simple and realistic, and it takes less than a minute to tie. Tie on hook sizes 12 to 20.

Cricket

Ken Rictor invited me to fly-fish for a day on Falling Springs Branch in south-central Pennsylvania. I scheduled the trip to coincide with the trico hatch on this fertile limestone stream. Ken and I fished on an area recently purchased by Falling Spring Greenway, and as we hiked downstream a few hundred yards we noticed thousands of hopper and crickets in the field. When we arrived at our destination, Ken tied on a cricket and I tied on a green-bodied hopper imitation. Before I had finished attaching my hopper pattern, Ken landed a typically brilliant Falling Spring streambred rainbow. Within minutes he landed another one of these extremely selective trout. That morning, when only one trout rose, Ken and I landed a half dozen Falling Springs trout on terrestrial patterns.

A rainbow caught in August on a green inchworm.

On occasion the cricket can work well. I often rely on the cricket in the middle of summer after a heavy downpour and when streams run higher than normal. Tie the cricket just as you'd normally tie a Muddler Minnow. With the cricket, use black poly or Polycelon for the body, black deer hair for the legs, and black goose quills on the side of the body.

LeTort Cricket
>   HOOK: Mustad 94831, size 10 and 12
>   BODY: Black poly, heavily dubbed (or black Polycelon)
>   WINGS: Black dyed goose quill sections, tied downwing
>   HACKLE: Deer body hair, dyed black and tied in similar to
>   the Muddler

Grasshopper

It happened one late-July afternoon just above Brown's Canyon on the Arkansas River in central Colorado. With a warm wind blowing downriver, I noticed several grasshoppers blown from a nearby field onto the water disappearing into the mouth of an Arkansas brown trout. I had only a couple of grasshopper patterns with me, but I tied one on quickly after I saw the startling results with the natural. I increased the leader to about twelve feet long, tied on a hopper, lifted my rod tip, and let the wind move the terrestrial back and forth across the surface. It took no more than two casts to produce a trout on that moving pattern. Almost every time the hopper skittered across the river a trout rose—no, chased—the terrestrial. For the rest of the afternoon twenty trout hit the hopper imitation. At a time when no aquatic insect appeared on the surface, a hopper imitation saved the day.

If you plan to fly-fish in July, August, or September on a stream or river near fields and grasslands, make certain you carry some hopper patterns with you. Fishing a Hopper, especially if you skitter it, can produce explosive rises.

Polycelon and other pliable plastics make excellent terrestrial bodies. Take a long cylinder of yellow or olive Polycelon and tie it in over the body. Secure the body with Super Glue and wind some tying thread to hold the cylinder in place and give it a ribbed effect.

Only once in my forty years of fly-fishing did I ever catch a trout that I had just previously lost. It happened during a sulphur hatch several years ago. The trout took my Sulphur imitation, shook violently, and broke the 5X tippet. I immediately tied on another Sulphur and cast to a riser in the same general vicinity where I had just lost the fly. A trout struck on the first cast and I landed a seventeen-inch brown. I unhooked the fly from the right side of the trout's mouth and detached another Sulphur from the left side of the mouth. The same trout had risen again just a minute after I lost it on the first Sulphur pattern.

Just recently Craig Josephson fly-fished on one of Virginia's finest, Mossy Creek, one evening. In July and August grasshopper patterns generally work well, so Craig tied on a LeTort Hopper. He saw a low bush overhanging the stream, so he cast the terrestrial up and under that obstacle. A heavy brown came splashing out and grabbed his hopper pattern, breaking off within seconds.

Craig headed upstream trying to fool more trout on another hopper pattern but had little success. Before he left the stream, he decided to make one more attempt under that same bush for that same trout. This time he used a hopper pattern with a different colored body. Again on the first cast that heavy brown hit the hopper pattern. This time Craig landed the fish and retrieved both of his hopper patterns. Just twenty minutes after he lost the terrestrial, Craig caught that same trout on the same pattern.

Ken's Hopper
>   BODY: Yellow to yellowish olive poly, dubbed heavily; or a cylinder of Polycelon glued, then wrapped on top of the hook.
>
>   HEAD AND WINGS: Use deer body hair dyed yellow and tie in just behind the eye as you would with the Muddler. Clip the butts, also as with the Muddler

Gypsy Moth Caterpillar

   For the past two decades much of the East and some of the Midwest and West have had to contend with the hugely destructive gypsy moth. The larvae have destroyed many hardwood stands in the East. Caterpillars hatch from eggs in mid-May, just in time to begin munching on fresh spring leaves. The caterpillars continue to grow until early July, when they go into a pupal or resting stage. In some areas of the East the black caterpillars fall onto trout waters in large numbers. Trout seem to prefer the younger caterpillars and often refuse the large ones in late June. I found May and early June the best time to fish the imitation. After that, the legs of the larvae seem to affect trout when they eat them.

Gypsy Moth Caterpillar
>   HOOK: Mustad 94831, size 10
>   THREAD: Black
>   BODY: Black Polycelon cylinder
>   HACKLE: A size 16 grizzly hackle palmered on the body.

Tying Notes: Place a drop or two of Super Glue on the shank of the hook and press the cylinder onto the shank for a minute. Tie in the grizzly hackle at the bend of the hook. Wrap the black thread up to the eye of the hook with five or six turns around the cylinder. These turns suggest segments on the caterpillar. Tie in the Polycelon at the bend of the hook and make several turns with the thread around the shank as you move the thread to the eye of the hook. Wrap the grizzly hackle around the poly where you previously wrapped the tying thread.

A size 12 white moth imitation works well on Northeastern streams in June and early July when the adult of the elm spanworm appears.

White Moth

Craig Josephson is a small-stream enthusiast and an accomplished fly-fisher on waters filled with tangles and undergrowth. He can cast into cramped areas like no other small-stream angler I've ever seen. Craig has fished small Laurel Run for more than 20 years. Craig's father is a member of a hunting and fishing club with a cabin on the stream. In his younger years, Craig used live bait to trick the brook trout on here, but it's been a decade since he started fly-fishing, and now he enjoys tricking these clever trout with a dry fly.

The two of us fly-fished this same stream twice in the past year, each time with the same disastrous results. After three hours of exhaustive fishing in April we had one strike and no trout. On the second trip, in October, Craig and I caught only two trout in two hours of fly-fishing.

With only two trout to show for almost six hours of fly-fishing, I resisted returning to that stream, but the following July I had an assignment from *Pennsylvania Angler* Magazine to cover the tailwaters of Pennsylvania. Two of these tailwaters flowed just fifty miles north of this small stream that Craig and I fly-fished the year before. We again stayed at his dad's cabin and fished the two tailwaters for several hours. These two tailwaters, the East Branch of the Clarion River and the Allegheny River, proved even worse than the small stream we fly-fished the year before. In a day of fishing the two tailwaters Craig and I didn't even see a trout, let alone have a strike.

We returned to the cabin after our pitiful day on the tailwaters, and Craig suggested we try his small stream one more time. Craig doesn't give up easily. He had first fished this small stream more than twenty years earlier, and he remembered how many times he caught brook trout and the many fond memories it has given him. Besides, he fly-fished it just a few years ago in early September and caught more than twenty trout.

After some urging, I agreed to give the small stream one more chance—and this definitely would be the last try if we failed again. A brief thunderstorm had just ended on the watershed and the stream became a bit discolored—better for us to sneak up on these wily trout.

We hiked upstream along a dirt road about a mile and then headed down a steep embankment to the stream. As we approached the brook we began to see hundreds of white moths flitting around near the water. As we approached a pool on the stream where Craig said we should start, one of these white moths landed on the surface. It rested there for ten seconds when it quickly disappeared in the splashing rise of a seven-inch brook trout.

I looked around the small stream and now saw hundreds of these white moths flying near the water. I handed Craig a size 12

White Fly pattern I use during the *Ephoron* hatch in late August. This White Fly pattern, tied by Russ Mowry, had large spent wings and I hoped it looked enough like the moth to excite these brookies. Craig told me to fish the first productive area while he headed downstream a hundred feet to cover an interesting riffle and pool there. On my very first cast, an impressive brook trout, huge for this small stream, came up quickly to suck in the White Fly. I struck too late and missed the first legitimate strike I had in three visits to this small stream.

Meanwhile, downstream Craig landed a six-inch brookie on the White Fly. Both of us headed upstream and Craig pointed to a deep, productive-looking pool with a large round boulder on the right side. He urged me to fish this pool thoroughly. On the first cast just upstream from the rock, the White Fly sank and I set the hook on a seven-inch native trout. Two more trout in that pool eagerly took that pattern that suitably copied the white moth, now so common along the stream. What's happening here? Four strikes in less than a hundred feet of water?

Craig took the next section upstream that held some interesting pocket water. And he quickly picked up two brookies on the "white moth" pattern. I moved up to the next small pool and cast to a rising trout. Before my line reached the surface it tangled in a hemlock tree and I tried to shake it loose. When I did, a dozen white moths moved out of the tree. Even after getting tangled, I picked up a trout in the partly discolored water.

For more than a mile, in two hours of incredible fly-fishing, Craig and I moved up this little stream and caught trout in almost every pool and riffle. It seemed that on this day, this small stream would redeem itself for the lousy outings we had experienced there before. It gave up its trout eagerly that day, almost as if it wanted to prove to Craig and me that it truly deserved the reputation of a topnotch small stream in the Northeast. In that mile of fishing,

Craig and I estimated that we caught forty trout and missed many more. Craig caught several trout over seven inches long.

What in the world produced the major turnaround on this small stream? One thing—one insect: the adult elm spanworm. And matching that insect with an appropriate imitation—the White Fly. In some parts of the Northeast this insect has devastated more forest than the gypsy moth. You'll find the ash-gray caterpillar foraging on leaves from mid-May until mid-June, and a gray caterpillar pattern in May should prove productive. From mid-to late June, the caterpillar enters the pupal or resting stage. From late June through much of July, you'll find the adult male flitting along in forested land, looking for an unmated female. Females can't fly as well as males and often find their way onto the water's surface, especially on windy days. If you're fortunate enough to find a trout stream near where many of these adults live, you're in for some great fly fishing—all day long.

Without the White Flies Craig and I used that evening, Laurel Run would probably have surrendered its healthy brook trout population only grudgingly. But these trout had fed on this white moth for weeks, and this source of food provided a bonanza on this small, heavily wooded stream. Fishing the white moth that evening proved the ticket to a successful matching-the-hatch experience—an event neither of us will ever forget.

If you encounter the larvae or caterpillars of this forest pest, you can use the pattern for the gypsy moth caterpillar described earlier.

If you ever see these white moths in late June or July, drop everything and go fishing. Tie the pattern I suggest and you, too, might be in for a fishing experience of a lifetime.

White Moth

     HOOK: Mustad 94833, size 10 or 12

     THREAD: White

     BODY: White poly yarn

     WINGS: White deer hair tied delta wing

     HACKLE: White hackle

Tying Notes: Tie the wings at an angle to imitate those of the adult moth. Tie the butts of the white deer hair outward. This makes the wings look heavier. Use size 16 white hackle for the legs. If you examine a white moth, you'll see that they have a robust body, so make the poly body fairly heavy.

Chapter 9

Larger Underwater Patterns

For several years I've considered *Pennsylvania Angler* one of the finest state-specific fishing magazines in the nation. Recently I wrote an article for that magazine called "Buggers, Muddlers, Ghosts, and Weenies," in which I discussed the patterns I use on opening day on Pennsylvania streams. Significantly, those patterns work on almost any stream in the nation and at almost any time. I've used the Green Weenie and the Wooly Bugger successfully from January through December from Oregon's McKenzie River to Maryland's Gunpowder River with equal success. On the other hand, the Muddler Minnow and Lady Ghost work especially well in the early season and in high-water conditions. Carry patterns of each for those days when your favorite stream or river runs high and no hatch appears.

Tandem Connections

In Chapter 4, I said that the Bead-head Pheasant Tail Nymph and the Green Weenie rank as my first two selections for point flies in the tandem rig. Larger patterns, especially those with added weight, require larger dry flies. If you plan to fish the Wooly Bugger or Bead-head Wooly Bugger, you'll need a larger dry fly. Go with a size 10 or 12 Patriot, Wulff Coachman, or a Yellow Drake. At the end of the drift with some of these larger dry flies, lift the rod slowly to imitate the fly moving toward the surface. I've caught many trout on just such a maneuver.

If you plan to try some of the larger patterns like the Bead-head Wooly Bugger, prepare yourself for some difficult casting. Tie some Wooly Buggers on smaller hooks and with less weight than the twenty or so wraps of .015 lead I use. The Bead-head Wooly Bugger does produce when fished behind a size 10 or 12 dry fly. However, I usually fish patterns like the Bead-head Wooly Bugger and the larger streamer patterns by themselves.

Bryan Meck lands a brown trout caught on the Green Weenie.

Green Weenie

Russ Mowry, Ken Igo, and Tim Shaffer of southwestern Pennsylvania first introduced the Green Weenie to me more than seven years ago. On a local trout stream, Loyalhanna Creek, in late March, Russ, Ken, and Tim caught some two dozen trout that afternoon while fly-fishers on either side of them caught none. That might not seem too exciting unless you actually experienced that day. In the middle of eight or nine other anglers these three anglers, using the Weenie, caught more than two dozen trout—while all the other anglers just feet away from them landed not a single

one. After that trip and that experience I went home and tied
dozens of Green Weenies, determined always to carry this pattern in
a special place in my fly box.

Josh David lands an Apache trout taken on a small
stream in Arizona's White Mountain's.

Need more proof that this simple pattern really works?
George Cook guides fly-fishers out of Poulsbo, Washington. If you've
ever seen those wide-angle Sage Rod posters of an angler casting a
perfect loop, that's George. He is one of the finest fly casters and
fly-tiers I know. Besides that, he's the consummate guide. Re-

cently, George invited Craig Shuman, Jack Mitchell, Jeff Edvalds, Dave Engerbretson, Al Novotny, and me to Isaak Ranch in central Washington for a day of fly-fishing on a trio of alkaline lakes. Al Novotny produces outdoor videos and wanted to include ranch fishing in one of his latest efforts.

George handed me a Damsel Fly Nymph to try first. "Twenty-five casts with that pattern then we'll try another one," George announced. I made twenty-five casts without one strike! George next handed me a dark Wooly Bugger-type pattern and urged me to try this fly for "twenty-five more casts." Instead of tying this second pattern on, I furtively tied on a Green Weenie. Why not try the Green Weenie on this Washington lake? It saved me from a barren day the year before on the McKenzie River in central Oregon. The Weenie has consistently saved me from frustrating days across the United States in all types of water and weather.

I quickly cast the Green Weenie so George couldn't see I had switched patterns on him. A slow retrieve for two feet and a heavy Kamloops rainbow hit. George saw the strike and seemed reassured that we would do well that day. I released the eighteen-inch 'bow and quickly made another cast so George couldn't see the Green Weenie. Maybe I retrieved the Weenie ten feet this time before another trout hit that ugly pattern. George unhooked my three-pound rainbow and did a double take when he saw the pattern.

Before the day ended George asked me for a couple of Green Weenies for anglers he planned to guide the next day.

George said later that he "hammered'em all summer long on the Green Weenie."

Mary Kuss, who teaches a fly-fishing class at the Sporting Gentleman in Media, Pennsylvania agrees. Several years ago I introduced her to this chartreuse-colored fly. In mid-May that same year Mary fly-fished on north-central Pennsylvania's Kettle Creek. She watched an angler catch a half dozen trout right in front of her, and when she found out he picked them up on a Green Weenie she quickly switched to one and caught three trout on her first three casts.

Recently Craig Josephson and I fly-fished on some exciting northeastern Arizona rivers. You'll read about them and how well we did with the Bead-head Wooly Bugger. But after two hours of great fishing with the "Bugger," both Craig and I lost our only patterns. I tied on a Green Weenie and caught more than a dozen more trout!

Craig also tried one of these smaller patterns on one of his favorite miniature mountain streams. While I used a Patriot dry fly, Craig used a Green Weenie tied on a Mustad 9672 hook. In deep pools, riffles and pockets Craig picked up native brook trout on that pattern.

The next week, I tried the smaller Green Weenie on Clarks Creek north of Harrisburg, Pennsylvania. I tied the Weenie eighteen inches behind the Patriot to keep it off the bottom. In each pool, even in slow sections, trout swirled around the Weenie each time. Occasionally one would hit and sink the Patriot.

Make certain you carry plenty of weighted and unweighted Green Weenies in Sizes 8 to 12. Tie some smaller patterns on Mustad 9672, size 12 hooks for small stream fishing. I tie these smaller Weenies with weight added to the shank and some with no weight.

Many anglers might laugh at the simplistic design of this top pattern, but they'll soon stop when they find out how many trout they catch with it.

Green Weenie

> HOOK: Size 10-12, Mustad 9672
>
> BODY: Cut off a five-inch piece of small or medium char-treuse chenille. Form a small loop with the chenille extending out over the bend of the hook then wrap the chenille around the shank of the hook up to the eye.

Tying Notes: I include a loop as the tail of the Green Weenie. I feel this loop makes the pattern move as it drifts downstream. I often add weight to the body. I add ten, fifteen, twenty, and twenty-five wraps of .015 lead, then color code the patterns. For twenty-five wraps I use orange thread; for twenty wraps I use a chartreuse thread, etc.

San Juan Red Worm

Phil Camera of Woodland Park, Colorado, has proven to be one of the most creative members of the fly-fishing community. Phil ties incomparable patterns and has worked for years with synthetics. In fact, a few years ago Phil wrote a popular book, *Fly Tying with Synthetics*. He also created Larva Lace and sells this material worldwide.

Recently Mike Manfredo and I had a chance to fish with Phil on New Mexico's San Juan, just below the Navajo Dam. Phil and I spent an entire morning fishing over a dozen heavy rainbows sipping dark gray midges. Neither of us moved more than a couple of feet from where we started four hours before.

At noon we met for lunch and discussed our afternoon strategy. We decided to move downriver and look for trout taking little blue-wings. Phil and I tied on size 20 Little Blue-winged Olive Duns and began casting to some risers near the far shore. Mike Manfredo headed downriver a hundred yards and tied on a San Juan Worm. I did a double take at the worm and began kidding Mike about the pattern. But not for long. By the end of the afternoon Mike had caught and released a half dozen heavy San Juan trout on that pattern.

Mike had to leave early but suggested that I try the San Juan Worm in the same general vicinity where he had all the strikes. In two hours of fishing with that ugly excuse for a pattern I picked up four heavy trout. Mike had finally convinced me that this pattern deserved a place in my compartment of productive patterns.

San Juan Red Worm
> HOOK: Mustad 37140, sizes 6 through 12
> THREAD: Red
> BODY: Orange Larva Lace

Tying Notes: Tie in the Larva Lace halfway down the bend of the hook. Take the red tying thread and cover the shank of the hook completely on your way up to the eye of the hook. Now take the Larva Lace and wrap it around the shank up to the eye. Tie off and cut off excess.

Wooly Bugger

Bob Budd and I fly-fished the lower Bald Eagle in September looking for a trico hatch. This is a large stream with plenty of deep holes, and it holds a good population of streambred and stocked brown trout. On this hot, late-summer morning the trico spinner fall ended only minutes after it had begun. What did we do after the hatch ended? I tied on a Green Weenie while Bob tried a Wooly Bugger.

I seldom thought of using that large sinking pattern in late summer. For the most part, before this experience, I used the Wooly Bugger the first week or two of the season, often when waters ran bank-full. But Bob Budd uses the pattern throughout the season— especially under high-water conditions, but also on large streams.

He tied on a large black Bugger this late-season morning, and only a few casts later a heavy trout Bob estimated at twenty-plus inches long hit the pattern.

Opening day on central Pennsylvania's Bald Eagle Creek several years ago presented some unique fly-fishing problems. Just the day before the season the stream flowed a foot over its bank. Bryan Meck, Ken Rictor, and I stood back the first morning and just stared at the stream. Hundreds of large worm-like insects floated past in the high water. I grabbed one and looked at it closely. The Bald Eagle and many other streams and rivers across the nation hold good numbers of fish fly larvae. High water flushed these three-inch larvae off the bottom and into the flooded waters.

After I saw the great number of fish fly larvae floating past me I tied on a gray Wooly Bugger I had made for just such an event. I began casting this large gray Wooly Bugger in some of the back eddies of this flooded stream. Within minutes the first trout hit that pattern. Within a couple of hours ten trout—in this high water—took that darned pattern.

Why does the Wooly Bugger work so well? It's my contention that this large pattern, in addition to copying the fish fly larvae, also imitates the hellgrammite, which is found in many streams throughout the United States. I've found fish fly larvae very common on small mountain streams, whereas hellgrammites usually inhabit fairly large streams and rivers.

Greg Hoover, an aquatic entomologist at Penn State, and I have seen good numbers of fish fly larvae on extremely small streams. This would suggest that a copy of this larva should work exceedingly well on these small waters, specially during heavy spring runoff. The adult fish fly emerges in June and July and resembles a large black moth-like insect with a heavy slate gray body.

If you plan to fish any small to moderate streams, you've got to carry some of the patterns copying the fish fly larvae.

If you examine the fish fly larva you'll see a two- to three-inch dark gray worm-like insect with plenty of short gray legs and a long black thorax and head. For several years I've tied a Fish Fly pattern just like a Wooly Bugger. This gray color far out-produces any other Bugger color, including the popular dark olive-bodied Wooly Bugger, especially on small and medium-sized streams.

Wooly Bugger
> HOOK: #8, Mustad 79580
> THREAD: Black
> TAIL: Black marabou
> BODY: Fine dark olive palmered with black saddle hackle

Tying Notes: Tie some of the Wooly Buggers with lead wire on the hook shank. For heavy water, I use twenty-five wraps of .015 wire.

Fish Fly Larva
> HOOK: Mustad 79580, size 8 to 12
> THREAD: Black
> TAILS: Dark gray marabou
> BODY: Fine gray chenille or vernille, palmered with a dark
> gray saddle hackle

Bead-head Wooly Bugger
Craig Josephson heard about some great Arizona fly-fishing on the Little Colorado River, so he contacted Gerald Scott, the river keeper at the X Diamond Ranch near Springerville, Arizona. The ranch encompasses about a mile and a half of prime Little Colorado River fly-fishing. In addition, right on the ranch you'll find a museum of local Western history well worth the visit.

When we arrived at the ranch, Gerald relayed some bad news: Anglers fishing the Little Colorado had experienced poor fly-fishing for the past three days. For the first hour we fly-fished that morning, Craig and I had to agree with Gerald's assessment. We didn't even have a strike for all our intense effort.

A nice Arizona trout caught by Craig Josephson on the Bead-head Wooly Bugger on the North Fork of the White River.

Then it happened! The river began surrendering its heavy browns and rainbows in every likely run and pool. What caused this instantaneous success? One thing—one pattern! After using that big underwater wet fly for only an hour it became one of my all-time favorite subsurface patterns. The Bead-head Wooly Bugger, complete with a tail of black marabou and Flashabou, seemed to entice every large brown and rainbow on the Little Colorado to strike.

Whether we fished the pattern near the bottom on a dead drift or cast the bead-head across stream and twitched it deliberately when it made its swing, we caught trout.

For the next three days of fly-fishing on northeastern Arizona rivers like the East Fork and North Fork of the White River, Craig Josephson and I found the Bead-head Wooly Bugger hands down our most productive pattern.

Ask Josh David how well the Bead-head Wooly Bugger works. He's been fly-fishing on the East Fork of the White River for several years and never saw a larger brown than the one that took a Bead-head and finally broke off on a huge rock.

Even on the upper North Fork of the White River near Greer, Arizona, the Bead-head caught trout. When Craig Josephson and I entered the river in late May, Craig commented how cold the water seemed. In fact, Craig's thermometer registered forty degrees at 10:00 a.m. For the next two hours we used the Bead-head Wooly Bugger and caught a dozen trout, even under those adverse conditions.

My son, Bryan Meck, first tied that pattern several years ago for opening day and early-season fly-fishing on Pennsylvania streams. But he found it extremely effective much of the year. Bryan feels that the Bead-head helps get the pattern deeper more quickly and that the trout strike at the Flashabou tail. I'm certain the shiny tail is a factor. I can often detect a glare off the tail even in a deep pool. I've found it especially effective on large Western rivers.

Bead-head Wooly Bugger
> HOOK: #8, Mustad 79580
> THREAD: Black
> TAIL: Five to ten strands of Flashabou over top of black marabou
> BODY: Fine dark olive chenille palmered with black saddle hackle
> HEAD: 5/32-inch copper bead

Tying Notes: Tie some of the Wooly Buggers with lead wire at the midsection. If I plan to fish heavy water, I use twenty-five wraps of .015 wire.

Muddler Minnow

The Muddler works well early in the Pennsylvania season, but would it work on a far-away stream in New Zealand? I changed the pattern slightly and added Flashabou on the tail, body and wings, certain that the reflection from this material makes trout strike the pattern. My first attempt with this new pattern happened on Dingle Burn on the South Island of New Zealand. A single-engine Piper Cub took Jeff Berry, of Newburgh, New York, and me over some unbelievably high peaks and into the narrow valley where this genuinely isolated river flows. We landed on what I considered a terrible excuse for a runway and headed toward the stream. The pilot promised to meet us five miles upstream at 6:00 that evening—"if the winds didn't pick up." If the winds blew too hard the pilot told us he'd come back tomorrow. Tomorrow? Yes, he told us we could find overnight shelter in an old sheepherder cabin several miles up the hillside.

Jeff Berry and I headed quickly toward the forty-foot-wide

stream. I stared at the rapid water while Jeff began casting. Finally, I tied on a Muddler with lots of Flashabou. I didn't have to wait long for the action. On a long drift through a deep, narrow riffle the Muddler stopped and I set the hook. The huge rainbow didn't move for a few seconds then began to fight. It headed downstream through another rapids, then through a deep pool and finally tired maybe a hundred yards from where I had hooked him. A twenty-four-inch rainbow had taken that Flashabou Muddler.

Before that memorable fishing day ended, I landed two more heavy rainbows on the Muddler, both more than twenty inches long. Three fish in several hours might not seem like a lot, but on many New Zealand streams and rivers it is.

Muddler Minnow

> HOOK: Mustad 79580, size 10
> THREAD: Brown
> TAIL: Mottled turkey quill sections with several strands of Flashabou
> BODY: Flashabou wrapped around shank
> WINGS: Mottled turkey quill sections, several black deer hairs, and several strands of Flashabou.
> HACKLE: Thirty to forty pieces of deer hair with the tips back toward the tail and the butts tied in forward. Trim off the butts to form a rounded head.

Peacock Lady

> I have fly-fished on dozens of Western lakes in the past few years, Washington lakes like Nunnally, Lennice, and Lenore. I had fly-fished the lakes on Isaak Ranch several times, but not once did I ever set foot in a belly boat. I swore to Craig Shuman, Jack Mitchell, Jeff Edvalds, and George Cook at Isaak's Ranch in central Washington that maybe in another life I'd try one, but not yet.

George Cook, the expert guide and skilled fly caster at the ranch, couldn't even convince me to enter one.

But when Craig Josephson and I met Bob and Josh David of Lakeside, Arizona, early Sunday morning on 10,000-foot-high Sunrise Lake, I had no choice but to finally try a belly boat. When we arrived, Bob and Josh already had four of these inner-tube type devices inflated and laid out—one for each of us. How could I refuse? Besides, Bob wanted me to catch some of the Apache trout in this White Mountain alpine lake. Bob works for the U.S. Fish and Wildlife Service at the hatchery in Whiteriver, Arizona, where he's been instrumental in raising Apache trout for stocking in the state. The program has proved a huge success in Arizona's lakes and streams.

A heavy mantle of snow lingered on 11,000-foot Baldy Mountain nearby in late May, and a strong wind produced white-caps on the cold lake. Talk about a duck out of water! Just try putting on fins, then getting into the "boat," then trying to walk with fins on your feet and the inner tube around your belly. Then, worst yet—trying to back into the lake. Now I know why I didn't like this device. After a half an hour of attempting to put on the fins, maneuvering into the boat, then walking backwards, I began paddling my way toward the deep end of the lake.

Before we entered the lake, Josh had given Craig and me a Peacock Lady he had tied the night before. I looked at the simple pattern, and frankly it didn't impress me. The long-shanked streamer hook had a peacock body, a long brown hackle at the front, and a shorter grizzly hackle near the bend.

I didn't listen to Josh's advice on how exceptionally well the Peacock Lady produced on this lake and began fishing a Green Weenie. Within minutes after entering the water, Craig landed a sixteen-inch rainbow on the Peacock Lady. A few minutes later, Josh landed another rainbow on the peacock pattern. Then Bob landed an Apache trout. For the first half hour, I never had a strike. Besides that, the wind had blown me to the far end of the lake. It took me more than an hour to paddle my way back to the middle.

Finally I had had enough. I admitted defeat and switched to a Peacock Lady. Almost immediately I started getting strikes and catching trout. A cast followed by a slow retrieve brought excellent results with that pattern. That morning on Sunrise Lake the four of us landed close to thirty trout—all on the Peacock Lady. No other pattern we tried worked. If you're planning a trip to any lake for trout, make certain you take plenty of Peacock Ladies with you.

Peacock Lady
>   HOOK: #10, Mustad 79580
>   THREAD: Black
>   BODY: Two or three strands of peacock wound up to the eye
>   HACKLE: Wind a small grizzly hackle at the bend of the
>   hook. The barbules of the hackle should be as long as the
>   gap of the hook. Wind a brown hackle with barbules
>   about twice as long as the grizzly hackle just behind the
>   eye.

Tying Notes: Tie some of the Peacock Ladies with lead wire. If I plan to fish heavy water, I use twenty-five wraps of .015 wire. Also try a bead head on some patterns. The weight and the bead head allow you to get deeper quicker.

Lady Ghost
I had a deadline to meet. I had yet to cover four Virginia rivers, three in Maryland, and four more in West Virginia. Greg Hoover, co-author of our upcoming book, *Great Rivers—Great Hatches,* was also traveling on assignment. While I covered those rivers in the Southeast, Greg drove to Michigan and Wisconsin to sample the top trout waters there.

I'll never forget the weekend in late August I spent on

Virginia's Rapidan River in the Shenandoah National Park. Two days of almost continuous rain made the trip an interminable, almost miserable, assignment. Washed-out roads made getting to the upper end impossible, so I arrived at the lower paved end and hiked upriver. And the river was in worse shape than the road. I had only two days to spend fly-fishing the Rapidan—now almost in flood stage. The river in this area holds a respectable slate drake hatch in June and again in early September. I had planned to test a couple of new Slate Drakes I tied particularly for this trip, but I now had to re-plan my strategy for the day. What pattern could I try under these adverse conditions? No dry fly! No terrestrial! What about using a Wooly Bugger, Muddler Minnow, or Lady Ghost streamer? I had only the Lady Ghost in my fly box at the time so the choice was made for me.

Huge boulders and rocks make up part of the Rapidan's character. Getting into a position to cast the streamer meant avoiding these huge obstacles. I found a small section where I could approach the river and began flinging the Lady Ghost. In this torrent, I expected to go through the motion of casting and retrieving, but I expected no trout. On the third cast, I felt a bump at the fly; on the fourth cast another one. I retrieved the fifth cast much more slowly and this time the line stopped. I set the hook and landed an eight-inch brook trout. Now, you might not think an eight-inch brook trout under these conditions merits any tribute, but that day, those conditions, that river, and the Lady Ghost were four unusual factors in an unbelievable day of fishing success. For the next three hours Rapidan brook trout, it seemed, felt almost obligated to strike that streamer pattern. Every brook trout in the next mile-and-a-half upriver stretch seemed to want that Lady Ghost streamer.

What a day under unbelievable adverse conditions! Now I carry a special assortment of Lady Ghost streamers for just such unfavorable conditions. For example, the Lady Ghost works well on snow-fed rivers of the West. This same pattern produced some heavy rainbows on Montana's Bitterroot in late June.

Whether you fish some of the Southeast's finest trout waters or the great rivers of the West, carry some Lady Ghosts with you. They just might turn a rainy day into a great fishing day.

I've revised the original pattern a bit so that it includes readily available materials.

Lady Ghost
> HOOK: Mustad #10, 3665A
>
> THREAD: Black
>
> BODY: Flashabou wrapped around the shank
>
> WINGS: Four badger saddle hackles under four peacock herls
>
> THROAT: Yellow deer hair underneath and white deer hair on top
>
> CHEEKS: Small reddish brown feathers with a darker tip from a ring-necked pheasant

Large underwater patterns work well on Abrams Creek in Tennessee.

Chapter 10
Patterns for the Hatches

What's your pleasure: parachute, comparadun or conventional?

Have you ever used a comparadun or parachute-type dry fly? Why do these dry flies work so well? I'm convinced it's because they present a lower profile on the water. Consider the following event that changed my thinking on these low-riding patterns.

Don Puterbaugh of Salida, Colorado, met Phil Camera and me on the Arkansas River several years ago. You'll find Don fly-fishing on that great central Colorado river almost daily. Don's one of the finest artists and fly-fishers I've known. He's illustrated many articles and several books, like Phil Camera's exciting new book on synthetics. Don met Phil and me one late-July morning to fly-fish the river just outside Salida. Don took us just below town where he had seen a sporadic pale morning dun hatch the day before.

As we approached the river, we noticed several decent brown trout feeding along the near shoreline. I cast to some of these risers, but for the first half hour that morning I had only one strike. Finally, Don Puterbaugh grabbed my Pale Morning Dun imitation, took out his scissors, and began cutting off the hackle on the bottom of the pattern. The lower the profile, he said, the better my chances of catching these Arkansas River browns. I didn't have to wait long to test his premise—more than a dozen browns hit that slightly altered pattern that morning.

This episode forever persuaded me that a low-riding pattern

works much better under many conditions than the conventional high-riding pattern I so often use. For years, George Harvey has resorted to snipping hackle off the bottom of some of his conventional flies. Test it for yourself. If your high-riding pattern fails to catch several rising trout, cut off the hackle on the bottom and see if the new lower-riding version works.

Comparaduns

Almost twenty years ago now, Dirk Blakeslee and I met on Pine Creek just above Waterville in north-central Pennsylvania for an afternoon of late-May fly-fishing. Pine Creek at that time of year held a great, if sporadic, hatch of gray foxes. In all my years of fishing, Dirk was one of the best fly-fishers I knew, and he has been one of the most vocal proponents of the comparadun almost since its inception.

As we arrived at the stream, we saw dozens of trout rising to gray foxes throughout the pool and the riffle above. On large water like Pine Creek and the Delaware River, you'll find this hatch appearing intermittently throughout the afternoon and early evening. Even though it's sporadic, the gray fox's size and its tendency to rest on the surface before taking flight tempts some heavy trout to the surface to feed. The gray fox appears for more than a week in late May and its size and the time of day it appears make it a favorite of many fly-fishers. At that time, Pine Creek held one of the best gray fox hatches in the Northeast, but because of mining pollution upstream, its gray fox population has diminished somewhat.

I always held some disdain for comparaduns until I fished that gray fox hatch that May afternoon with Dirk. He tied on a Gray Fox Comparadun while I rigged up with a high-riding Catskill-type Gray Fox. In the next two hours, Dirk made a believer of me on the value of a comparadun pattern. For every trout I caught on a hackled pattern, Dirk caught two. Finally I had enough, and asked Dirk for a comparadun. I immediately began catching more trout. Forty trout later, Dirk and I left the stream confident that the comparadun really worked well on highly selective trout. I made certain from that point on to fish the major hatches with a plentiful supply of comparaduns.

My next match-the-hatch opportunity with a comparadun pattern occurred in late September with a *Baetis* hatch. That cool afternoon on the Little Juniata River brought one of the heaviest hatches of this diminutive multi-brooded species that I've ever encountered. I selected a size 20 Blue Dun Comparadun to copy the small species and began casting to a heavy riser in the riffle in front of me. Before that small hatch ended that day more than twenty trout took the no-hackle pattern.

I opted for conventional patterns for the next few years until I took a float trip on the Kootenai River in northwest Montana in 1991. Halfway through our float, a heavy pale morning dun hatch appeared. A cold drizzle slowed the duns' escape from the surface, and as we drifted down a glide, we saw more than a hundred trout feeding on the small dazed duns. Rainbow after rainbow refused the hackled Pale Morning Dun imitation. In a fit of frustration I tied on a size 16 Pale Morning Comparadun and began casting to a half dozen risers just a few feet from the drift boat.

All these trout had just seen and refused my previous

pattern, but in the next half-hour I landed a half dozen trout. Yet I remained frustrated with the many refusals of this no-hackle imitation. Dozens of trout still rose in front of me so I hurriedly switched to a comparadun pattern with a Z-lon shuck at the tail. On the first cast, a heavy rainbow took the shucked pattern and ran upriver. In the next hour, I landed more trout than I normally would on a good day of fishing a hatch. A small comparadun with a Z-lon shuck had done the trick.

I add shucks to many of my comparadun patterns. Use the shuck instead of or with a tail and make it as long as the shank of the hook. Try to make the shuck the same color as the nymphal skin. You'll find shuck colors for all the major hatches later in this chapter. Little Blue-wings in size 20 and Blue Quills in size 18 produce well when hatches these two match appear.

Don Bastian had guided anglers in central and northeastern Pennsylvania for a number of years. Don's also an outstanding fly-tier, especially when it comes to comparaduns, which he ties in sizes 12 to 20. Don often prefers using the smaller comparaduns, in sizes 18 and 20, to match blue quills and blue-winged olive duns. While guiding other anglers, Don has seen numerous examples where hackled patterns just didn't take highly selective trout. On some of the slower sections of Fishing Creek in northeastern Pennsylvania, where he guides frequently, Don maintains that you can forget using hackled patterns. "These trout often opt for comparaduns over regular patterns," Don says.

Although the comparadun has been popular only for the past couple of decades, no-hackle patterns first appeared more than sixty years ago. In fact, George Harvey first tied and used no-hackle flies back in the 1930s. Comparadun patterns usually contain a outrigger-type hackled tail created by adding dubbing at the bend of the hook, a tapered body of poly or other dubbing, and a wing of deer hair. Fly-tiers shape the deer hair so that it makes a half circle.

When on the water, the hair on either side of the pattern effectively floats it. Like a parachute pattern, comparaduns ride low in the water. The longer I fly-fish, the more I believe that imitations that ride lower on the surface catch more trout.

Recently many fly-fishers and fly-tiers have begun using Antron yarn rather than the deer-hair wing. They call this pattern a sparkle dun and it has become highly effective (as we saw in Chapter 5). The Antron can be spread in a semicircle just like the deer hair, but it doesn't add the bulk to the pattern and doesn't tend to creep forward. Often the Antron extends out beyond the bend of the hook to make a shuck. If you prefer comparaduns, try Antron yarn for the wings and the shuck.

If you don't tie comparaduns, you'll find them readily available in most better fly-fishing shops. Once you fish these comparadun patterns over highly selective trout during a hatch, you may never use a conventional pattern again.

A parachute Sulphur dry fly tied with a trailing shuck made of Z-lon.

Parachutes

I had had enough of winter in the East. After weeks of snow, cold, and downright raw weather, I agreed to meet Mike Manfredo on New Mexico's San Juan River. Even in late February, this river just below the Navajo Reservoir holds at least two great hatches. All day you can expect to see midges in the flats just below the dam, and downriver little blue-wings fill the air most afternoons throughout the year.

Mike and I met Phil Camera and Chuck Rizuto at the river. Phil recently completed a book on tying with synthetics, and Chuck co-authored a book on the San Juan. All of us fished for several hours in the morning over a heavy gray midge hatch, but we waited until noon to head downriver several hundred yards to await a little blue-wing hatch. Within minutes after we arrived, we saw thousands of little blue-wings emerging. Soon, heavy trout began feeding on these late-February duns. Within inches of the shore, heavy rainbows fed on what seemed like an unending supply of little blue-wings. Just for this hatch, I tied up a dozen size 20 parachute Little Blue-Wings with a post of dark gray deer hair. I tied one of these small parachutes on and cast upriver just above a methodical, heavy riser. On the second good drag-free float, the big rainbow hit the fly almost in slow motion. Three more heavy trout hit that parachute pattern before the hatch diminished later that afternoon.

Recently I gave a series of talks to the Canadian Fly-fishing Forum in Toronto as part of the Izaak Walton Fly-Fisherman's Club's annual symposium, one of the finest I've ever attended. At that program I watched an accomplished fly-tier, Sheldon Seale, of Missinaugua, Ontario, tie a parachute Little Blue-winged Olive Dun using gray poly yarn for the wing or post. After I watched him, I tied a few with the poly, and trout really struck these parachute poly flies. But the poly quickly bends and doesn't have the durability of deer hair.

I'm certain my strike ratio with the parachute is much higher than with a conventional pattern. I've almost exclusively gone to tying parachutes rather than the high-riding Catskill-type patterns to match many of the hatches.

Russ Mowry of Latrobe, Pennsylvania, has tied parachute patterns commercially for a couple of decades, some of the finest I've ever seen. Contrasted with a comparadun pattern, the parachute does include a hackle. Contrasted with a conventional fly, the parachute's hackle is wrapped around the wing rather than around the shank of the hook. The hackle flares out around the wing. Some fly-tiers complain that the hackle they tie around the post creeps up the wing. To prevent this, wrap your first one or two turns of hackle higher on the post than the last few. The parachute, like the comparadun, rides low in the water. Tie some of the patterns listed later as parachute patterns.

What makes these low-riding patterns so effective? Look at a typical mayfly then look at the parachute or comparadun pattern versus the Catskill-type high-rider. Next time you fish when a mayfly hatch appears, look how low that natural rides on the water —similar to the float of comparadun and parachute dry flies.

Conventional Patterns

I've had plenty of old-timers refuse to change from their high-riding patterns that have worked for them for years. I mean those flies that usually have two hackles and ride relatively high on the surface. Many anglers refer to them as Catskill-type patterns.

"They've worked well for years. Why change them?" an old-timer once asked. Sure they caught and continue to catch trout. But try an experiment sometime. Do what Don Puterbaugh did on the Arkansas River that day he, Phil Camera, and I fished a sporadic pale morning dun hatch: If trout refuse your conventional pattern during a hatch, cut the hackle off on the bottom. Then see if rising fish don't strike this lower-riding pattern.

Of course, I've seen several instances when high-riding patterns come in handy. You'll find an August and September mayfly on many streams in the East and West. It's an unusual mayfly (a member of the Genus *Ephoron*), since the female never changes from dun to spinner and mating often takes place quickly after the duns emerge. During the emergence, mating, and egg-laying, these mayflies rarely fly more than a foot above the surface. Often male spinners move up and downstream in search of females flying just above the surface. Trout often jump completely out of the water for these roaming male spinners, emergers, and females coming back to lay eggs. I've often found a high-riding, long-hackled fly to be the best choice during this hatch.

After all this criticism of conventional patterns, you'd think I had stopped using them. But they continue to produce trout. I will continue to tie the Patriot and many other patterns in this conventional high-riding style, because they work!

Remember this as you read the chapters devoted to patterns and pattern selection: It's not only the fly but also how you tie and use it that make the difference.

Recent Innovations

Have you noticed recently the number of new patterns available to the fly-fisherman? An article in *Flyfishing* more than a decade ago alluded to the many new patterns and tying methods we have been bombarded with over the past twenty years. It's even more so today. The article grouped new patterns and methods into three categories:

1. New patterns that are not as good as the old standbys.
2. New patterns that are equal to but no better than older patterns.
3. Patterns that are truly revolutionary and are better than current patterns.

In Group 1, the author listed such patterns as the no-hackle flies, latex-bodied nymphs, and others. In Group 2, he mentioned the Matukas and the parachute dry flies. Remarkably, he suggested none for Group 3. Does that tell you anything about some of the recent "revolutionary" developments?

But, within the past decade since that article, several innovative materials and patterns have made their way to the market. Bead-head patterns have made a substantial impact on the fly-fishing scene, and I personally believe the Bead-head Pheasant Tail Nymph to be the top fish catcher today—bar none. Sparkle duns with Antron yarn wings and tail and sparkle caddis with Z-lon or Antron shucks have proved top fish catchers in the past few years. Fluorescent chenille in red, orange, and chartreuse have proved a valuable ally of the fly-tier. Polypropylene is another notable advance for the fly-tier. Don't forget Polycelon when you tie terrestrials. If you tie a lot of hoppers, crickets, ants, beetles, and caterpillars you'll find this foam an invaluable tying aid.

Here are five questions we should ask ourselves as discriminating fly-fishers before we jump at every new pattern, method, or material that comes our way:

1. If it's a change in the method of fly-tying, is the new method easier to tie than the older one?

2. Does the end product, the fly, more closely simulate the natural (if it's supposed to copy a natural)?

3. Is the material easy to obtain?

4. Is the finished product relatively durable?

5. And the most important question of all, does the pattern catch trout? Moreover, does it produce on a wide range of waters and over a good part of the season?

Let's look briefly at these criteria. Any method that makes tying a pattern easier (criterion 1) will get my attention quickly. That's why I prefer to tie a simple Poly Beetle most often. It's as effective as all the others but takes only a seconds to complete.

Anyone, and I mean anyone, can tie the Poly Beetle in a minute or less. The same goes for the Poly Ant. Also, using Polycelon cylinders for an ant or beetle makes a lifelike, durable, and easy-to-tie pattern. You'll find many examples of new methods of tying old patterns that really produce strikes throughout this book.

Look at the Sparkle Duns described in chapter 5. With a simple wing and tail or shuck of Antron and a body of superfine poly, you'll find this an extremely easy fly to tie. If you use it during the hatches, you'll also find it an excellent fish catcher. Sparkle Duns, however, do have some flaws—in sizes larger than 16 they don't float as well as the smaller sizes.

I feel parachute dry flies copy naturals better than conventional dry flies do (criterion 2). Some of the newer wing materials like Micro Web also fulfill criterion 2, because upright wings and downwing patterns made from this material copy the natural more closely.

Is the final product durable (criterion 4)? Comparaduns work well. I caught trout during a hatch on a comparadun when they outright refused any other type of pattern. But no mater how I tie a comparadun, I have trouble making the wings stand upright. Store a comparadun over winter and look at the wings. I told you how to tie a poly-winged parachute dry fly earlier. Again, one problem with this tie is that the soft wing loses its shape after a while. I much prefer a stiffer deer-hair wing for posts on a parachute pattern.

Finally, question 5 poses the ultimate criterion: Does the new pattern catch trout over a wide range of waters? The goal of any pattern is to catch trout. I once heard an old-timer say, "You have flies that catch anglers and flies that catch trout." Forget about flies that catch anglers; you want patterns that consistently catch trout.

Walt Young gave me a couple of his Bead-head Pheasant

Tail Nymphs, which remained in my fly box for several months before I used them. The day I did, trout refused to look at a half dozen patterns I tried, but when I tied on a Bead-head, I had six trout in a half-hour. That Bead-head pattern has worked on great trout waters across the country and has turned many otherwise frustrating, fishless days into productive days. The Bead-head patterns have proved so successful that when no hatch appears I start out using a Bead-head on almost every fishing trip.

Products like bead-heads, bugskin, Larva Lace, Krystal Flash, Sparkle Yarn, Poly yarn, Antron yarn, and Polycelon really work. We'll examine all of these.

Bead-head Patterns

As far as I'm concerned, the Bead-head has revolutionized fly-fishing. It is one of the top five products to come on board in the past fifty years. What makes a Bead-head pattern so effective? Does the glitter from the bead tempt trout to strike? Does the bead get the pattern down to the trout more quickly? Does the bead suggest to trout a bubble and an emerging insect? It's probably a combination of things. But they really work, and consequently, bead-heads have made an impressive entrance in the American market. Not until I actually fished the Bead-head Pheasant Tail Nymph and the Bead-head Wooly Bugger did I realize the potential impact this material would have on American angling. Beads come in various sizes from 3/32 to 3/16 of an inch and colors like copper, brass, clear, nickel, and black. I prefer copper beads for the Pheasant Tail Nymph and the Wooly Bugger.

The Bead-head Wooly Bugger with a Flashabou tail has proved a top fish catcher for the past two years on streams and rivers across the United States.

You'll find certain problems when you use beads. On some hooks the bead slides up and over the eye; on others you'll have difficulty getting the bead past the bend of the hook. (I crimp the barb of the hook before stringing the point through the bead.) I recently found a simple way to handle beads without dropping a lot of them on the floor. Put the bead, with the larger hole facing upward, on a tube of fly-tying wax. Place the hook point through the larger hole and move the bead to the eye.

For smaller patterns, I use a Tiemco 2457 hook. Up to size 18 it's easy to place the bead over the bend of this hook. For patterns like the Bead-head Wooly Bugger I use a size 8 Mustad 91780 hook.

After I place the bead just behind the eye of the hook I usually add weight, from ten to thirty turns of .015 lead wire up the shank just behind the eye. On smaller patterns I use .010 wire.

Materials for Tying Shucks

I reported earlier about my experience on the Kootenai River with a Comparadun PMD with a Z-lon shuck. One day on the West Yellowstone, Nick Nicklas gave me some of his innovative patterns. A Pale Morning Dun pattern he included in the box intrigued me most. It had all the normal accouterments for the PMD Comparadun pattern, but with something extra. Where you'd normally see a tail, Nick had tied on a shiny piece of Z-lon extending back over the body. Then a light went on: This pattern copied the critical stage in the transformation of a mayfly—a dun escaping from the nymphal shuck. Hadn't I observed stillborns for years? During each green drake hatch hadn't I watched dozens of drakes desperately attempting to escape from their nymphal shuck? Maybe trout recognize the vulnerability of a mayfly at this stage in its development.

I tested Nick's PMD pattern on the Kootenai River a week later. I related what happened on that trip earlier in this chapter—namely, the pattern worked to perfection and changed my thinking on shucks forever.

I went home after that trip and vowed always to carry a good supply of imitations like the Green Drake, Sulphur, and PMD with Z-lon shucks.

Shucks work like magic—sometimes. On other occasions trout refuse them. Would I now have to tie patterns for all the hatches with Z-lon shucks? How about a piece of material you could attach and detach when warranted? One day during a green drake hatch, Jim Ravasio and I fly-fished on the Little Juniata River. Neither Jim and I nor dozens of other fly-fishers had much success on that dull, dismal, cold afternoon. Four different mayflies including sulphurs, green drakes, little blue-winged olives, and slate drakes emerged in numbers. The first two species appeared in the heaviest numbers and trout seemed to focus on those. I watched drake after drake float past me and saw trout take none of them. Finally, a heavy brown rose quickly to capture a huge green drake dun wriggling to free itself of its nymphal shuck. I had prepared for just such an occasion by cutting some inch-long strips from pale gray panty hose. When I stretched these crosswise they curled up and resembled a nymphal shuck. I attached a piece of panty hose about as long as the shank of a long shank hook to the bend of the Green Drake fly. I pulled the detachable shuck up just under the black tail. On about the third good float over the spot where the brown rose, he again rose abruptly and grabbed the shucked fly. I called Jim Ravasio upriver to take a photo of the trout with the pattern in its mouth.

When Jim looked at the shuck, he asked if I had any dark brown pieces to copy the sulphur nymph. I pulled out a smaller dark brown version and gave it to him. Jim headed back downstream and began casting over a half dozen risers taking sulphurs. Before long Jim had caught and released all six trout rising in front of him.

I told a friend, John Randolph, editor of *Fly-Fisherman*

magazine, about the incident. John's one of the finest and most inventive writers, editors, and fly-fishers I've known. He suggested I write a story about the incident on the Little Juniata River with the detachable shuck. I called that article "Aw Shucks." This nylon shuck has saved me on many occasions during the past few years.

As I said earlier, shucks work on occasion—for some hatches and for some species. But whether you use the detachable panty hose shuck or tie the Z-lon patterns, make certain you carry some. As I've often said, shucks are another weapon in your arsenal of patterns.

Bugskin

Chuck Furimsky, who owns a leather shop called Ole Man Winter, is a skilled fly-fisher and one of the best fly-tiers I know. Chuck has experimented with all types and textures of leather and how they can be used to tie flies. For example, a new machine can press leather so thin that the final product feels like tissue. But the day I met him on Spruce Creek, I thought he had left the boundaries of sanity!

Chuck invited me to meet him on a private section of Spruce Creek to fish for a few hours. Just before I arrived, the usually clear limestoner became discolored by a sudden summer storm. I expected to see Chuck in the cabin relaxing and waiting for the stream to clear. Not Chuck! I found him fishing a section of the meadow a few hundred feet downstream from the cabin. Within minutes after I arrived, Chuck had caught and released more than a half dozen trout, so I walked over to him and grabbed the pattern attached to his 5X tippet. Chuck caught those temperamental Spruce Creek browns on something that looked suspiciously like the San Juan worm used on its namesake river in New Mexico, only Chuck tied his with thin red leather. After three more trout, I swallowed my pride and asked Chuck if he could give me one of those new patterns. Since that auspicious day, Chuck has tied patterns from tanned leather to copy crayfish, hellgrammites, stoneflies, nymphs, and leeches. I found the crayfish to be extremely effective. He dubbed the new extremely lifelike material "Bug-skin." You'll find Bugskin and Larva Lace available through Phil's Tackle, Box 4031, Woodland Park, CO 80866.

Larva Lace

A handful of my angling friends deride any fly-fisher who uses synthetic materials to build their flies. Some of them refuse even to use poly to dub dry fly bodies. I try to tell them that with the advent and onslaught of new materials they will be at a disadvantage if they don't at least test these new materials. My many visits to Western waters convince me that if I want to keep up with those anglers, I have to keep abreast of new materials.

In an article for a great new regional publication, *Fly-fishing Guide*, I examined some of the new synthetics like Larva Lace. The originator of Larva Lace, Phil Camera, wrote the book *Fly Tying with Synthetics*, and after I fished for a few days with Phil in Colorado, he gave me some samples of the new material and asked me to try it. Larva Lace is a hollow plastic material that comes in a variety of colors and sizes.

The Larva Lace Phil gave me stayed in my fly-tying room for almost a year before I had the urge to try it after Greg Hoover and I conducted an entomology course at Seven Springs. While on Laurel Hill Creek collecting insects, the class saw a number of bright orange caddis fly larvae. This larva emerges as the little black caddis in mid-April. Several anglers in the class surmised that if this larva was so common in the stream, they should have a fly to copy it.

We returned to the classroom to tie flies after our morning

on the stream collecting insects. Members of this class, including Ben Furimsky and Craig Josephson, asked what pattern would most appropriately copy this larva. Ben Furimsky grabbed some orange Larva Lace, slid it over the hook, and moved it beyond the bend of the hook. Then he tied in this relatively new synthetic, ribbed the Larva Lace with the tying thread, and dubbed in some tan angora at the head. The finished product looked amazingly like the natural. The beauty of these synthetics is that they effectively copy many naturals that would otherwise be difficult to copy. It's important for you to try these new materials—simply because they work and will make you even a more effective fly-fisher.

Poly Yarn and Crinkled Z-lon

Andy Leitzinger fly-fishes throughout the East, and he regularly takes vacation when the sulphur emerges. For several years he's had exciting results fishing a Sulphur dry with a Sulphur Emerger as the point fly. On several occasions during a sulphur hatch, Andy has landed as many as thirty trout in an evening, the Sulphur Emerger accounting for most of those trout. Andy ties the emerger with poly yarn to imitate the wing case. He makes a loop of the yarn on top of the thorax. I often tie in a short piece of poly yarn just behind the eye. Sometimes, to be sure, the looped poly pulls out after I've caught a couple of trout.

I've tied other patterns like the Hendrickson Emerger and they work as well as the Sulphur Emerger.

Recently I began tying some of my emerger patterns with crinkled Z-lon. I tie the emerger pattern like the Baetis Emerger in Chapter 4, then just before the last whip finish, I place a 1/8-inch loop of crinkled Z-lon over the top of the wing pad. An emerger tied this way works extremely well during the white fly hatch.

Of course you'll find poly yarn as the material of choice for spinner wings, and I also use it for bodies of white moths and Coffin Flies.

Sparkle Yarn, Krystal Flash, and Flashabou

Bryan Meck ties a Wooly Bugger with a bead head and a Flashabou tail. He feels that the sparkle from the Flashabou attracts trout. On a bright, sunny day I've noticed the shine from the bead head on the bottom of a stream.

But you don't have to use these bright materials just for tail material. I first used Krystal Flash when I developed the Patriot dry fly. For years I tied the body of this pattern with blue poly. With the introduction of Krystal Flash, I changed the body to smolt blue, which makes the body shine and produced more strikes than before.

I add Flashabou to many of my Muddler Minnow patterns. I add a few pieces to the tail and wings, and I wind several pieces around the shank of the hook. As with Krystal Flash and Sparkle Yarn, Flashabou works well for body material.

You can also add a few strips of Krystal Flash to the spent wings of spinners. I add a few strands of Krystal Flash with the poly yarn, especially when I tie the Trico. This attracts trout and also helps me follow the pattern on the water.

Polycelon

George Harvey likes to fish terrestrials, and in the 1930s developed the Green Inchworm. He fishes ants and beetles frequently. Recently he developed a great pattern to copy the caterpillar stage of the gypsy moth. Over the years I've found that trout seem to take smaller caterpillars and avoid larger ones; therefore, imitations of this larva seem to work best from May through early June. After that the caterpillars get too large.

George ties on a cylinder of black Polycelon then ribs the plastic with size 16 grizzly hackle. You can obtain Polycelon from any good sporting goods store. This material floats well and is virtually indestructible. The cylinders come in black, green, olive, and yellow, and they also make excellent bodies for grasshopper and caterpillar imitations.

Antron

Antron yarn has become a material of choice of many fly-fishers for spinner wings, shucks, caddis pupa, and wings on Sparkle Duns. Greg Hoover uses a medium gray Antron yarn to tie his effective Sparkle Dun pattern. (See Chapter 5 for complete tying directions.) Using Antron rather than deer-hair wings on comparaduns has several advantages. Antron is much lighter and does not bend forward the way deer-hair wings usually do. You'll also find Antron yarn much easier to clip and tie in than deer hair. For your patterns matching hatches smaller than size 14, try Antron yarn.

Although some anglers use Antron for spinner wings, I prefer poly yarn. If you want some sparkle in those spent-winged patterns, try this material.

Gary LaFontaine's caddis pupa patterns tied with Antron have proved a top fish catcher on streams and rivers across the United States. If you hit a hatch of caddis flies you want to have this pattern on hand.

I use Antron yarn for my caddis emergers. I dub the body, then double a piece of brown Antron yarn. I tie it in at the head and place one of the strands on the right side and the other on the left side to copy the wings of the merger. I add a turn or two of woodcock (soft) hackle.

The patterns we use to catch trout fall into several categories. Many of these copy various phases of the mayfly, caddis fly or stonefly life cycle. The nymph copies the larval stage; wet flies and emergers often copy the emerging stage of the insect; and the dry fly copies the dun or spinner stages. We looked at the life cycle of mayflies in Chapter 5, but let's review it here.

Nymphs

Nymphs hatch from fertilized eggs in a couple of weeks to as long as several months later. The nymph spends approximately a year (there are many exceptions) in slow, medium, or fast stretches of rivers and streams on rocky or muddy bottoms—many species are specific in their habitat. After almost a year of growing and shedding its outer covering many times (instars), the nymph is ready to emerge.

As the nymph lives and feeds for almost a year underwater, it is naturally a food source for fish. Since the nymph is the longest phase of the life cycle, trout have an opportunity to feed on this stage more than any other stage. Imitations of nymphs work well most of the year because trout feed on this stage almost daily.

In a year or so, the nymph emerges, and after several false dashes, it reaches the surface. Here it sheds its nymphal skin dorsally (a few do this on the bottom of the stream), and becomes a dun (often called a subimago). Skilled anglers realize that trout forage on emerging nymphs, so they imitate the nymph or an emerger, which is a hybrid between the nymph and the dun. Often the nymph works well just as the hatch begins. The emerger works well throughout. The best emergers are the Harrop Quill emergers or a plain soft-hackle wet fly, which is particularly effective when you find caddis hatches. Fish a soft-hackle emerger with a twitch during a caddis fly hatch and you'll enjoy the action.

Since the advent of Sparkle Yarn and Krystal Flash some flytiers add these materials as part of the wing pad to their nymphal imitations.

Emergers

How many times have I been frustrated by a hatch? Many times what I thought were risers to duns on the surface were in reality trout feeding on the emergers. The two largest trout I have caught on imitations in the United States both hit when I purposely sank a Green Drake dry fly and fished it just a few inches under the surface. This shows you that trout often feed on nymphs rising to the surface and on nymphs in the process of transforming into duns. Be sure to take this important phase of fly-fishing into consideration.

Nymphs change to air-breathing mayflies in a series of deliberate steps. Most often the nymph moves toward the surface and rests or rides in the surface film for a time while it splits its nymphal skin dorsally. Slowly the dun releases itself from the shuck of the nymph. First the wings appear and slowly move vertically, then the rest of the dun appears on the surface out of the nymphal skin. All this takes time, and while it occurs the nymph, emerger, and dun are vulnerable. What anglers often think is a rise to the dun may in reality be a rise to the emerger or nymph.

To tie an emerger, use the tail fibers listed later in this chapter. Use the same hook for emergers that you would for the dry fly if you want the fly to ride in the surface film. I recommend a wet fly hook if you plan to use the emerger pattern on a tandem rig or on a telltale setup. I even add five wraps of lead to the hook to make certain the emerger sinks just an inch or two below the surface. Tie in a short wing of gray turkey, Antron, poly yarn, or crinkled Z-lon. Slant the wing back at a forty-five degree angle over the body. With Antron and poly, you can loop the material to suggest wings evolving. Make the wings a half to three quarters the length of the body. If you want the emerger to float rather high in the film, use some floatant.

Duns

The nymph appears on the surface as an air-breathing dun. Many of these duns ride the surface for some distance before taking flight, and they are especially important to imitate with dry fly patterns. Patterns like the Hendrickson, Western Green Drake,

Green Drake, and many others have gained fame because they match insects that normally are slow to leave the surface.

The Hendrickson Pool on New York's Beaverkill. Many great mayfly hatches appear on this stretch of water.

When the dun finally becomes airborne, it usually heads for the nearest tree or bush close to the stream. Duns emerging early in the season sometimes rest on sun-warmed rocks or debris next to the water to protect themselves from early-season freezes.

Spinners

Although a few genera change from dun to spinner in an hour or less, and a few never change, most require one or two days. With a final molt, the dun shucks its outer covering and reappears over the water as a more brightly colored mayfly with clear, glassy wings. The female mayfly spinner, or mature adult (scientists call the spinner an imago), mates with the male spinner, usually over fast stretches of a stream and most often in the evening. The male appears over the stream first, waiting for the female spinner. After mating, the female deposits her fertilized eggs by one of three methods: (1) flying just above the surface, (2) sitting or dipping on the surface, or (3) diving underwater. How the spinner lays its eggs becomes important to the fly-fisherman. These spinners become more readily available as a source of food for trout if they lay eggs in either of the second two ways.

Some imitations copy even the egg sac found on spinners and caddis flies. The Beaverkill represents the female Hendrickson spinner. Grannom patterns often include a turn or two of peacock at the rear to imitate the egg sac of this early-season caddis fly.

After the egg laying is completed, many females fall onto the water, usually with wings spent (flat on the surface). Female spinners falling in great numbers on the surface can be either a blessing or a curse to many anglers. Often furious surface feeding occurs at this time. Moreover, this feeding frenzy often occurs around dusk. It's imperative that you know the type of spinner that might fall that evening and be prepared with appropriate spinner imitations.

Most spinner imitations copy the spent-winged variety and usually include a tail, body, and wings of poly yarn. Few contain any hackle, except some of the classic patterns like the Ginger Quill.

It's important to include imitations of some species with divided, upright poly yarn wings. Some sulphur species, for example, lay their eggs and remain on the surface with wings upright. Copies of spinners with these upright wings are much easier to locate on the surface at dusk.

Downwings

You'll find a complete discussion of caddis flies in Chapter 5, and you'll find pattern descriptions for some of the more common caddis flies later in this chapter.

Tying the Patterns

The following sections contain directions for tying patterns that copy mayflies, caddis flies, and stoneflies. Each recipe can be used for tying either a wet or dry fly. If you prefer using wet flies, substitute a heavier hook, less-buoyant body material, and hen hackle for the tail and legs. If the pattern you want to copy calls for a deer-hair tail and the natural has an amber tail mottled with brown, use fibers from a mallard or wood duck flank feather instead. Rather than use a body of dubbed poly, you might substitute fur or any other material that sinks more rapidly, to tie the wet fly. When the wings of the dun are dark gray and the dry fly calls for dark gray hackle tips, use mallard quill sections for the wet fly.

If you prefer to tie no-hackle patterns, you can copy the body material suggested and use deer hair for wings and tail. If you prefer comparaduns, omit the hackle.

Note several innovations in the following pattern descriptions. First, for all the major hatches I've included a shuck color. Second, you'll note a tying recipe for emerger patterns copying all of the major hatches. For most of the emerger patterns, I recommend poly yarn to imitate the emerging wings of the dun. You can also tie the emerger wings of Antron. You can also use short white, brown, or gray turkey feathers. Tie in the turkey as a short wet-fly-type wing just behind the eye of the hook. You can use a Mustad 3906B or a 94840 hook for the emerger pattern, depending on how far you want the pattern to sink. If you plan to fish it on the surface, use the 94840 hook. If you plan to use it with the telltale or tandem rig, use a 3906B hook.

You'll note that not all species have patterns for nymphs and emergers. I've included only the most common ones.

Eastern and Midwestern Patterns

ORDER EPHEMEROPTERA: Mayflies

Blue Dun or Little Blue-winged Olive Dun
Copies *Baetis tricaudatus* and some *Pseudocloeon* species.

A Little Blue-wing olive dun tied with a trailing shuck.

HOOK: Mustad 94840, sizes 18 and 20
THREAD: Dark Gray
TAIL: Medium to dark gray hackle fibers
BODY: Gray muskrat or medium gray poly, dubbed; for the
    Little Blue-wing Olive use olive gray poly.
WINGS: On smaller sizes (20) use dark gray mallard quills;
    on larger sizes use dark gray hackle tips; for the tandem
    use a dark gray deer-hair wing and tie the pattern as a
    parchute dry fly.
HACKLE: Blue dun

Rusty Spinner

>HOOK: Mustad 94833, sizes 18 and 20
>
>THREAD: Dark brown
>
>TAIL: Dark grayish-brown hackle fibers
>
>BODY: Grayish-brown poly, dubbed and ribbed with fine tan thread
>
>WINGS: Pale gray poly yarn, tied spent

Baetis Nymph

>HOOK: 3906B, size 18
>
>THREAD: Dark olive
>
>TAIL: Wood duck fibers, dyed dark olive
>
>BODY: Dark olive brown opossum
>
>WINGS: Dark gray mallard quill section
>
>HACKLE: Cree or ginger variant, dyed dark olive

Baetis Emerger

>HOOK: Mustad 3906B or 94840
>
>THREAD: Dark olive
>
>TAIL: Dark brownish-olive hackle fibers
>
>BODY: Dark grayish-olive muskrat, dubbed
>
>WINGS: Dark gray-poly yarn tied over top of muskrat
>
>HACKLE: Dark brown grouse hackle fibers

Baetis Shuck

>Dark brown Z-lon

Blue Quill

Copies most *Paraleptophlebia* species.

>HOOK: Mustad 94840 or 3906, size 18 or 20
>
>THREAD: Dark gray
>
>TAIL: Medium to dark gray hackle fibers

BODY: Eyed peacock herl, stripped or dark gray poly,
   dubbed

WINGS: Dark gray hackle tips

HACKLE: Light to medium blue dun

Dark Brown Spinner

HOOK: Same as above

THREAD: Dark brown

TAIL: Dark brown hackle fibers

BODY: Dark brown poly, dubbed

WINGS: Pale gray poly yarn, tied spent

Para Nymph

HOOK: 3906B, size 16 and 18

THREAD: Dark brown

TAIL: Mallard flank feather, dyed dark brown

BODY: Dark brown angora, dubbed

WINGS: One dark gray mallard quill tied down

HACKLE: Dark gray

Para Emerger

HOOK: 3906B, size 16 and 18

THREAD: Dark brown

TAIL: Dark brown hackle fibers

BODY: Dark grayish brown angora, dubbed and ribbed with
   fine gold wire

WINGS: Gray poly yarn pulled over top of dubbed brown
   angora

HACKLE: Dark brown hackle fibers

Para Shuck

Blackish brown Z-lon

Quill Gordon

Copies species like *Epeorus pleuralis.*

> HOOK: Mustad 94840 or 3906, size 14
>
> THREAD: Dark gray
>
> TAIL: Dark gray hackle fibers
>
> BODY: Eyed peacock herl, stripped and lacquered
>
> WINGS: Wood duck or imitation wood duck, divided; or dark gray hackle tips
>
> HACKLE: Dark gray hackle

Red Quill Spinner

Use same pattern as spinner listed under Hendrickson

Quill Gordon Nymph

> HOOK: 3906B, size 14
>
> THREAD: Dark brown
>
> TAIL: Fibers from a mallard flank feather, dyed dark amber
>
> BODY: Dark brown fur or angora, mixed with a bit of lighter brown or amber
>
> WINGS: Mottled brown turkey, tied down over thorax
>
> HACKLE: Cree or ginger variant hackle (dark and amber mixed)

Quill Gordon Emerger

> HOOK: Mustad 3906B, size 16 and 18
>
> THREAD: Tannish brown
>
> TAIL: Brown mallard flank
>
> BODY: Tannish brown angora
>
> WINGS: Dark gray turkey folded back over the body like a wet fly
>
> HACKLE: Grouse

Note: Since this dun emerges from its shuck at the bottom of the stream, you can tie the emerger like an ordinary wet fly and fish it near the bottom. Add a shuck to this wet fly.

Quill Gordon Shuck
> Dark brown Z-lon

Red Quill and Hendrickson
The Red Quill copies the male and the Hendrickson the female of
Ephemerella subvaria and several closely related subspecies. In
addition, the Red Quill effectively imitates many spinners like
Ephemerella subvaria, Epeorus pleuralis, and the male spinner of
Ephemerella invaria and *rotunda.*
> HOOK: Mustad 94840 or 3906, sizes 14 and 16
> THREAD: Brown
> TAIL: Medium gray hackle fibers
> BODY: Red Quill: reddish brown hackle fiber stripped of its
>   barbules and wound from the bend of the hook to the
>   wings. Hendrickson: tan poly, dubbed.
> WINGS: Wood duck, divided. Optional on Hendrickson
>   are gray hackle tips
> HACKLE: Medium gray hackle

Red Quill Spinner
> HOOK: Same as above
> THREAD: Brown
> TAIL: Bronze dun hackle fibers
> BODY: Dark tannish-brown poly, dubbed and ribbed finely
> with tan thread
> WINGS: Pale gray poly yarn, tied spent

Hendrickson Nymph
> HOOK: 3906B, size 12 and 14
> THREAD: Dark brown
> TAIL: Dark ginger hackle fibers

BODY: Black to dark brown angora, dubbed
WINGS: Mottled brown turkey, tied down over thorax
HACKLE: Ginger hackle

Hendrickson Emerger
    HOOK: Mustad 3906B or 9671, size 12 and 14
    THREAD: Tan
    TAIL: Tan grouse
    BODY: Grayish black angora
    WINGS: Dark gray turkey
    HACKLE: Tan grouse

Hendrickson Shuck
    Black Z-lon

Dark Quill Gordon
Copies species like *Rhithrogena jejuna*
    HOOK: Mustad 94840, size 14
    THREAD: Black
    TAIL: Very dark dun
    BODY: Very dark gray poly, ribbed with lighter gray thread
    WINGS: Dark gray hackle tips
    HACKLE: Dark dun

Dark Quill Gordon Spinner
    HOOK: Mustad 94840, size 14
    THREAD: Black
    TAIL: Dark gray
    BODY: Same as dun
    WINGS: Pale gray poly yarn tied spent

Black Quill
Copies *Leptophlebia cupida*
> HOOK: Mustad 94840, size 14
> THREAD: Dark brown
> TAIL: Dark bronze dun hackle fibers
> BODY: Eyed peacock herl, stripped
> WINGS: Dark gray hackle tips
> HACKLE: Dark brown hackle with a turn or two of tan
> hackle in the rear

Early Brown Spinner
> HOOK: Mustad 94833, size 14
> THREAD: Dark brown
> TAIL: Dark brown hackle fibers
> BODY: Dark reddish-brown polypropylene ribbed with pale
> yellow thread
> WING: Pale tan polypropylene
> HACKLE: Dark brown hackle

Black Quill Nymph
> HOOK: Mustad 3906B, size 12 or 14
> THREAD: Dark brown
> TAIL: Dark brown hackle fibers
> BODY: Chocolate brown angora, loosely dubbed
> WINGS: Dark mallard section
> HACKLE: Dark brown hackle

Black Quill Emerger
> HOOK: Mustad 3906B, size 14
> THREAD: Dark brown
> TAIL: Dark brown hackle fibers
> BODY: Dark brown rabbit

WINGS: Dark gray poly yarn
HACKLE: Dark grouse

Black Quill Shuck
Dark brown Z-lon

Sulphur Dun
Copies *Ephemerella rotunda, invaria, septentrionalis,* and to a lesser
degree, *dorothea.*
HOOK: Mustad 94840 or 3906, size 16 and 18
THREAD: Yellow
TAIL: Cream hackle fibers
BODY: Usually pale yellow poly with an orange (and some
times olive orange) cast
WINGS: Pale gray hackle tips
HACKLE: Cream hackle

Sulphur Spinner
HOOK: Same as above
THREAD: Tan
TAIL: Tan deer hair
BODY: Female with eggs: yellowish tan poly; female without
eggs: tan poly; male: bright red hackle stem, stripped
and wound around hook.
WINGS: Pale gray poly yarn, tied spent (also tie some
upright)

Sulphur Nymph
HOOK: Mustad 3906B, size 14, 16, and 18
THREAD: Grayish-brown
TAIL: Brown pheasant tail fibers
BODY: Brown (ground color) fur

WINGS: Dark gray mallard quill section, tied down over
thorax
HACKLE: Cree

Sulphur Emerger
HOOK: Mustad 3906B or 94840
THREAD: Tan
TAIL: Dark brown grouse hackle fibers
BODY: Pale tan angora, dubbed
WINGS: A short pale gray turkey feather or white poly yarn
HACKLE: Dark brown grouse fibers

Sulphur Shuck
Dark brown Z-lon
Copies many Baetis species like *little blue dun*
HOOK: Mustad 94840, size 22
THREAD: Gray
TAIL: Medium dun hackle fibers
BODY: Dark gray poly, dubbed
WINGS: Dark gray hackle tips
HACKLE: Dark gray hackle

Rusty Spinner
HOOK: Mustad 94833, size 20
THREAD: Dark Brown
TAIL: Dark brown hackle fibers
BODY: Dark brown poly, dubbed
WINGS: Pale gray poly yarn, tied spent

Pale Evening Dun
Copies species like *Leucrocuta aphrodite* and *Leucrocuta hebe*
HOOK: Mustad 94833, size 14 and 16

THREAD: Yellow

TAIL: Creamish-yellow hackle fibers

BODY: Creamish-yellow poly with olive cast (*L. hebe* has no
olive cast)

WINGS: Pale gray mallard flank

HACKLE: Yellowish-cream hackle

Pale Evening Spinner

HOOK: Mustad 98833, size 14 and 16

TAIL: Cream hackle fibers

BODY: Pale yellow poly

WINGS: White poly tied spent

HACKLE: Pale yellow hackle

Gray Fox

Copies *Stenonema fuscum*. Now considered by entomologists the
same as *Stenonema vicarium*.

HOOK: Mustad 94840 or 3906, size 12 or 14

THREAD: Cream

TAIL: Tan deer hair

BODY: Cream poly, dubbed

WINGS: Mallard flank feather, dyed pale yellowish-tan,
divided

HACKLE: Cree or one brown and one cream mixed

Ginger Quill Spinner

HOOK: Same as above

THREAD: Brown

TAIL: Dark brown hackle fibers

BODY: Eyed peacock herl, dyed tan and stripped, or grayish
brown poly, ribbed with brown thread

WINGS: Gray hackle tips (conventional); or pale gray poly

yarn, tied spent.

HACKLE: Dark ginger (conventional); or none with poly yarn wings.

Gray Fox Nymph

HOOK: Mustad 3906B, size 12

THREAD: Brown

TAIL: Fibers from a mallard flank feather, dyed brown

BODY: Brown angora yarn, tied on top over cream. Tie in brown at tail, and dub in cream so that top of body is brown and the belly is cream.

WINGS: Dark brown turkey, tied down over thorax

HACKLE: Dark cree

Gray Fox Emerger

HOOK: Mustad 3906B or 94840, size 12 and 14

THREAD: Brown

TAIL: Dark grouse

BODY: Tan angora

WING: Pale gray turkey

HACKLE: Dark grouse

Gray Fox Shuck

Medium to dark brown Z-lon shuck

March Brown

Copies *Stenonema vicarium.*

HOOK: Mustad 94840, 3906, size 12

THREAD: Yellow

TAIL: Dark Brown hackle fibers

BODY: Tan poly, dubbed and ribbed with dark brown thread

WINGS: Mallard flank feather, dyed yellowish brown and

divided

HACKLE: One cream and one dark brown, mixed

Great Red Spinner

HOOK: Same as above

THREAD: Dark brown

TAIL: Dark brown hackle fibers

BODY: Dark reddish brown poly, dubbed

WINGS: Pale gray poly yarn, tied spent

HACKLE: Dark brown with a turn or two of pale ginger
mixed

March Brown Nymph

HOOK: 3906B, size 12

THREAD: Brown

TAIL: Fibers from a mallard flank feather, dyed brown

BODY: Same as Gray Fox (above)

WINGS: Dark brown turkey, tied down over thorax

HACKLE: Dark cree

March Brown Emerger

HOOK: 3906B or 94840, size 12

THREAD: Brown

TAIL: Grouse

BODY: Cream angora

WINGS: Brown

HACKLE: Brown grouse

March Brown Shuck

Dark brown Z-lon shuck

Light Cahill

Copies *Stenacron interpunctatum* subspecies, which is sometimes found on small streams.

>HOOK: Mustad 94840 or 3906, size 14
>THREAD: Cream or tan
>TAIL: Cream hackle fibers
>BODY: Cream poly, fox fur, or angora, dubbed
>WINGS: Mallard flank feather dyed pale yellow, divided
>HACKLE: Cream

Light Cahill Spinner

>Same as dun except omit the hackle and add pale yellow poly yarn for wings. Tie them spent.

Light Cahill Nymph

>HOOK: Mustad 3906B, size 12
>THREAD: Brown
>TAIL: Fibers from a mallard flank feather, dyed brown
>BODY: Dark brown angora yarn on top and pale amber belly, dubbed
>WINGS: Dark brown turkey
>HACKLE: Dark cree

Light Cahill Emerger

>HOOK: Mustad 3906B, size 14
>THREAD: Tan
>TAIL: Dark grouse
>BODY: Tan angora
>WINGS: Pale gray turkey
>HACKLE: Light grouse

Light Cahill Shuck
> Dark brown Z-lon

Slate Drake
Copies many *Isonychia* species.
> HOOK: Mustad 94840 or 3906, size 12 or 14
> THREAD: Black
> TAIL: Dark gray hackle fibers
> BODY: Peacock herl (not from eye), stripped; or dark gray poly or muskrat, dubbed
> WINGS: Dark gray hackle tips
> HACKLE: One cream hackle tied in behind and one dark brown hackle tied in front

White-gloved Howdy
> HOOK: Same as above
> THREAD: Dark brown or maroon
> TAIL: Medium gray hackle fibers
> BODY: Dark mahogany poly, dubbed
> WINGS: Pale gray poly yarn

Isonychia Nymph
> HOOK: Mustad 3906B, size 10 or 12
> THREAD: Dark brown
> TAIL: Three dark brown hackle with one side cut off
> BODY: Very dark brown angora or opossum
> WINGS: Dark gray mallard quill section, tied down over thorax
> HACKLE: Cree, dyed pale olive

Isonychia Emerger
> HOOK: Mustad 3906B, size 14

THREAD: Black
TAIL: Black
BODY: Brownish black angora
WINGS: Black turkey
HACKLE: Dark gray hackle fibers

Isonychia Shuck
Black Z-lon

Brown Drake
Copies mayflies like *Ephemera simulans.*
HOOK: Mustad 94831, size 14
THREAD: Brown
TAIL: Dark brown deer hair
BODY: Grayish-tan poly
WINGS: Grayish-tan flank feather
HACKLE: Dark brown hackle with a few turns of ginger

Brown Drake Spinner
HOOK: Mustad 94831, size 10
THREAD: Brown
TAIL: Same as dun
BODY: Dark tannish yellow poly dark brown markings
WINGS: Pale tan poly yarn with a dark brown fibers tied
    upright or spent
HACKLE: Same as dun

Brown Drake Nymph
HOOK: Mustad 3906B or 9672, size 10 or 12
THREAD: Brown
TAIL: Three light brown hackle fibers
BODY: Pale tan angora or opossum

WINGS: Brown turkey, tied down and over thorax
HACKLE: Dark cree

Brown Drake Emerger
HOOK: Mustad 3906B or 94840
THREAD: Brown
TAIL: Light brown
BODY: Tan angora
WINGS: Tan turkey
HACKLE: Grouse

Brown Drake Shuck
Tan Z-lon

Pink Lady or Pink Cahill
Copies the female of *Epeorus vitreus.*
HOOK: Mustad 94840, size 14
THREAD: Cream
TAIL: Dark blue dun hackle fibers
BODY: Male: pale yellow; female: pinkish-cream poly
WINGS: Pale yellow mallard flank
HACKLE: Creamish-yellow hackle

Salmon Spinner
HOOK: Mustad 94840, 3906, size 16
THREAD: Pink
TAIL: Cream ginger hackle fibers
BODY: Coral polypropylene
WINGS: Pale gray polypropylene
HACKLE: Cream ginger hackle

Vitreus Nymph
> HOOK: Mustad 3906B, size 14
> THREAD: Tan
> TAIL: Dark brown fibers from a pheasant tail
> BODY: Dub amber on the entire body, bring butts of the pheasant tail up and over the body and tie in where you tie in the wings.
> WINGS: Brown turkey section
> HACKLE: Several turns of a ginger hackle

Vitreus Emerger
> HOOK: Mustad 3906B, size 14
> THREAD: Tan
> TAIL: Grouse
> BODY: Amber angora
> WINGS: Gray turkey
> HACKLE: Light grouse
> See note for Quill Gordon Emerger

Vitreus Shuck
> Dark brown Z-lon

Blue-Winged Olive Dun
Copies many *Drunella* species and *Dannella*-like *cornuta*, *longicornus*, *cornutella*, and *lata*.
> HOOK: Mustad 94840, 3906, size 14 to 20
> THREAD: Olive
> TAIL: Grayish-olive hackle fibers
> BODY: Light to medium olive poly, dubbed
> WINGS: Dark gray hackle tips
> HACKLE: Medium creamish-olive

Dark Olive Spinner

    HOOK: Same as above

    THREAD: Dark olive or black

    TAIL: Moose mane (dark brown)

    BODY: Dark olive poly (almost black with an olive cast)

    WINGS: Pale gray poly yarn, tied spent

Drunella Nymph

    HOOK: Mustad 3906B, sizes 14 to 18

    THREAD: Olive

    TAIL: Wood duck

    BODY: Dark brown angora tied over dubbed olive
       opossum

    WINGS: Brown turkey

    HACKLE: Ginger variant, dyed olive

Drunella Emerger

    HOOK: Mustad 3906B, sizes 14 to 18

    THREAD: Olive

    TAIL: Olive wood duck

    BODY: Olive angora

    WINGS: Gray turkey

    HACKLE: Dark grouse

Drunella Shuck

    Dark brown Z-lon

Green Drake

Copies *Ephemera guttulata.*

    HOOK: Mustad 94831 or 3906B, sizes 8 and 10

    THREAD: Cream

    TAIL: Moose mane

BODY: Cream poly, dubbed
WINGS: Mallard flank dyed yellowish green, divided
HACKLE: Rear: Cream hackle; front: dark brown hackle

Coffin Fly

HOOK: Mustad 94831, sizes 8 and 10
THREAD: White
TAIL: Light tan deer hair
BODY: White poly, dubbed
WINGS: Grayish-yellow poly yarn, tied spent

Green Drake Nymph

HOOK: Mustad 3906B or 9672, size 8 to 12
THREAD: Tan
TAIL: Three medium-brown hackle fibers, trimmed and tied in
BODY: Pale tan angora
WINGS: Dark brown turkey, tied down and over thorax
HACKLE: Cree

Green Drake Emerger

HOOK: Mustad 3906B or 94840, size 8 to 12
THREAD: Tan
TAIL: Grouse
BODY: Tan angora
WINGS: Pale yellow poly yarn
HACKLE: Light grouse

Green Drake Shuck

Pale grayish-tan Z-lon

Chocolate Dun

Copies species like *Eurylophella bicolor* and *Ephemerella needhami.*

      HOOK: Mustad 94840, 3906, size 16

      THREAD: Brown

      TAIL: Medium gray

      BODY: Chocolate brown poly, finely ribbed with lighter brown thread

      WINGS: Dark gray hackle tips

      HACKLE: Tan hackle

Chocolate Spinner

      HOOK: Same as above

      THREAD: Dark brown

      TAIL: Tannish-gray hackle fibers

      BODY: Dark rusty brown poly, dubbed

      WINGS: Pale gray poly yarn, tied spent

Chocolate Dun Nymph

      HOOK: Mustad 3906B, size 16

      THREAD: Brown

      TAIL: Light brown mallard flank feather fibers

      BODY: Light brown poly nymph dubbing

      WINGS: Dark gray mallard quill

      HACKLE: Brown hackle

Chocolate Dun Emerger

      HOOK: Mustad 3906B or 94840

      THREAD: Brown

      TAIL: Light brown grouse

      BODY: Brown angora

      WINGS: Gray poly

      HACKLE: Brown grouse

Chocolate Dun Shuck
>Light brown Z-lon shuck

Dark Green Drake
Copies small-stream species like *Litobrancha recurvata*.
>HOOK: Mustad 94833, 3906B, size 8 or 10
>THREAD: Dark gray
>TAIL: Dark brown moose mane
>BODY: Very dark slate poly, dubbed and ribbed with yellow thread
>WINGS: Mallard flank, heavily barred and dyed dark green
>HACKLE: Rear: tannish brown hackle; front: dark brown hackle

Brown Drake Spinner
>HOOK: Same as above
>THREAD: Brown
>TAIL: Brown hackle fibers
>BODY: Reddish-brown poly, dubbed and ribbed with yellow thread
>WINGS: Pale gray poly yarn, tied spent
>HACKLE: Dark brown

Dark Green Drake Nymph
>HOOK: Mustad 9672, size 8 or 10
>THREAD: Light brown
>TAIL: Three dark bronze hackles fibers trimmed and tied in
>BODY: Tan angora with a grayish cast, or opossum
>WINGS: Dark brown turkey
>HACKLE: Dark cree

Dark Green Drake Emerger
> HOOK: Mustad 9672 or 94840
> THREAD: Tan
> TAIL: Brown grouse
> BODY: Medium tan angora
> WINGS: Poly
> HACKLE: Light grouse

Dark Green Drake Shuck
> Medium tan Z-lon

Blue-Winged Olive Dun
Copies species like *Attenella (Ephemerella) attenuata.*
> HOOK: Mustad 94840, size 14
> THREAD: Olive
> TAIL: Blue dun hackle fibers
> BODY: Medium olive hackle stem or muskrat, dyed olive
> WINGS: Dark bluish-gray
> HACKLE: Medium olive

Dark Olive Spinner
> HOOK: Mustad 94840, size 14
> THREAD: Dark olive or black
> TAIL: Blue dun hackle fibers
> BODY: Dark brown fur with an olive cast
> WINGS: Pale gray hackle tips
> HACKLE: Blue dun

Cream Cahill
Copies species like *Stenonema pulchellum, modestum,* and *Stenacron gildersleevei.*
> HOOK: Mustad 94840, size 14 or 16

THREAD: Cream
TAIL: Tan hackle fibers
BODY: White or pale cream polypropylene
WINGS: Very pale cream mallard flank feather
HACKLE: Cream

Cream Cahill Spinner
HOOK: Mustad 94840 or 3906, sizes 14 and 16
THREAD: White
TAIL: Pale tan hackle fibers
BODY: White poly
WINGS: Use dun imitation and substitute pale gray poly
yarn for the wings.
HACKLE: Pale cream

Cream Cahill Nymph
HOOK: Mustad 3906B, size 14 or 16
THREAD: Olive brown
TAIL: Light brown hackle fibers
BODY: Dub pale creamish-gray on hook, then tie pale
brownish-olive yarn in at bend and bring over top to wing
case and tie in.
WINGS: Dark brown turkey
HACKLE: Dark olive brown

Cream Cahill Emerger
HOOK: Mustad 3906B or 94840
THREAD: Cream
TAIL: Brown grouse
BODY: Creamish-tan angora
WINGS: White poly
HACKLE: Brown grouse

Cream Cahill Shuck
>   Medium brown Z-lon

Light Cahill
Copies species like *Leucrocuta marginalis*.
>   HOOK: Mustad 94840 or 3906, size 14
>   THREAD: Cream
>   TAIL: Dark brown hackle fibers
>   BODY: Yellowish cream polypropylene
>   WINGS: Yellow mallard flank
>   HACKLE: One cream and one blue dun hackle

Light Cahill Spinner
>   HOOK: Mustad 94833, 3906, size 14
>   THREAD: Cream
>   TAIL: Dark brown hackle fibers
>   WING: Pale gray hackle tips or cream poly yarn tied spent
>   BODY: Fox belly fur dubbed brown
>   HACKLE: Front: dark brown; rear: cream with darker
>   markings

Michigan Caddis
Copies mayfly species like *Hexagenia limbata limbata*.
>   HOOK: Mustad 94831, size 6X
>   THREAD: Brown
>   TAIL: Brown hackle fibers
>   BODY: Yellowish-brown polypropylene
>   WINGS: Teal flank feather, dyed smoky gray and with an
>   olive cast
>   HACKLE: Cream ginger and brown

Michigan Caddis Spinner
>   HOOK: Mustad 94831, size 6X
>   THREAD: Brown
>   TAIL: Cream ginger hackle fibers
>   BODY: Brownish-yellow polypropylene
>   WING: Mallard flank feather
>   HACKLE: One dark brown and two cream ginger hackles

Michigan Caddis Nymph
>   HOOK: Mustad 3906B or 94840
>   THREAD: Brown
>   TAIL: Gray hackle fibers
>   BODY: Pale tan angora, dubbed
>   WINGS: Dark gray goose quill section
>   HACKLE: Sandy dun

Michigan Caddis Emerger
>   HOOK: Mustad 3906B or 94840
>   THREAD: Brown
>   TAIL: Dark woodcock
>   BODY: Tan angora
>   WINGS: Dark gray poly yarn
>   HACKLE: Light grouse

Michigan Caddis Shuck
>   Tan Z-lon

Yellow Drake
Copies species like *Ephemera varia*.
>   HOOK: Mustad 94840, size 10 or 12
>   THREAD: Pale yellow
>   TAIL: Pale deer hair

BODY: Pale yellow polypropylene (primrose)
WINGS: Pale yellow mallard flank
HACKLE: Creamish-yellow, with a turn of grizzly in front

Yellow Drake Spinner
HOOK: Mustad 94840, size 10 or 12
THREAD: Pale yellow
TAIL: Dark deer hair
BODY: Pale creamish-yellow polypropylene
WINGS: Mallard flank or pale poly, tied spent
HACKLE: Dun variant

Yellow Drake Nymph
HOOK: Mustad 3906B, size 10 or 12
THREAD: Tan
TAIL: Pale gray, trimmed
BODY: Amber angora or opossum
WINGS: Medium to light brown turkey
HACKLE: Ginger

Yellow Drake Emerger
HOOK: Mustad 3906B or 94840
THREAD: Cream
TAIL: Light grouse
BODY: Pale tan angora
WINGS: Pale gray poly yarn
HACKLE: Light grouse

Yellow Drake Shuck
Tan Z-lon

Big Slate Drake

Copies large mayflies like *Hexagenia atrocaudata*.

> HOOK: Mustad 94831, size 8
> THREAD: Dark gray
> TAIL: Dark gray hackle fibers
> BODY: Peacock, stripped (use bottom of herl)
> WINGS: Dark gray calf tail
> HACKLE: Dark brown

Dark Rusty Spinner

> HOOK: Mustad 94840, size 6
> THREAD: Dark brown hackle fibers
> BODY: Tannish-yellow polypropylene ribbed with dark brown thread
> WINGS: Brown mallard flank feathers or tan poly; one dark brown hackle in front and a tannish yellow one in the rear

Big Slate Drake Nymph

> HOOK: Mustad 3906B, size 6
> THREAD: Amber
> TAIL: Olive brown hackle fibers
> BODY: Tan angora, dubbed
> WINGS: Dark mallard quill
> HACKLE: Grouse

Big Slate Drake Shuck

> Tan Z-lon

Trico

Copies all *Tricorythodes* species.

> HOOK: Mustad 94840, size 20 to 24
> THREAD: Pale olive

TAIL: Cream hackle fibers

BODY: Pale olive green poly, dubbed; male dun: dark brown poly

WINGS: Pale gray hackle tips

HACKLE: Cream

Trico Spinner

HOOK: Mustad 94840, size 20 to 24

THREAD: Dark brown

TAIL: Female: short cream hackle fibers; male: long dark brown moose mane

BODY: Female: rear third is cream dubbed poly and front two-thirds is dark brown poly dubbed; male: dark brown dubbed poly and ribbed with a fine light tan thread

WINGS: White poly yarn, tied spent

Trico Nymph

HOOK: Mustad 3906B, size 22

THREAD: Black

TAIL: Dark brown hackle fibers

BODY: Dark brownish-black fur

WINGS: Dark gray mallard quill section

HACKLE: Dark reddish-brown

Trico Emerger

HOOK: Mustad 3906B or 94840, size 22

THREAD: Dark brown

TAIL: Dark brown grouse

BODY: Pale olive angora

WINGS: Gray poly yarn

HACKLE: Brown grouse

Trico Shuck
> Dark brown Z-lon

White Fly
Copies mayflies like *Ephoron leukon* and *Ephoron album.*
> HOOK: Mustad 94840, 14 and 16
> THREAD: White or cream
> TAIL: Pale blue dun hackle fibers
> BODY: Pale cream or white poly
> WINGS: Pale gray hackle tips or pale gray poly, upright
> HACKLE: White, with a turn of dark brown in front

White Fly Spinner (male only)
> HOOK: Mustad 94840, size 14 and 16
> THREAD: White or cream
> TAIL: Pale gray
> BODY: White (rear two-wraps brown)
> WINGS: Clear
> HACKLE: Front: dark brown rear; white

White Fly Nymph
> HOOK: Mustad 3906B, size 12
> THREAD: Tan
> TAIL: Light brown hackle fibers
> BODY: Pale tan
> WINGS: Mottled brown turkey
> HACKLE: Ginger

White Fly Emerger
> HOOK: Mustad 3906B or 94840, sizes 12 and 14
> THREAD: Tan
> TAIL: Light brown hackle fibers

BODY: Creamish-tan angora
WINGS: Pale gray poly
HACKLE: Ginger

White Fly Shuck
Tan Z-lon

ORDER TRICHOPTERA: Caddis Flies

Green Caddis
Copies species like *Rhyacophila lobifera*.
HOOK: Mustad 94840, sizes 14 and 16
THREAD: Green
BODY: Green polypropylene
WINGS: Brown deer body hair
HACKLE: Tan (optional deer hair)

Black Caddis-Grannom
Copies species like *Brachycentrus fuliginosus*, *B. numerosus*, and *B. solomoni*.
HOOK: Mustad 94833, size 10 to 16
THREAD: Black
TAIL: Optional—add tan Z-lon shuck
BODY: Black poly, dubbed; (optional) wind a dark brown
    hackle in at the bend of the hook and palmer it to the
    eye. Clip off the barbules on top.
WINGS: Dark brown deer or elk hair
HACKLE: Optional—dark brown

Tying Notes: If you use a hackle on your caddis pattern, make it two sizes smaller than you would on a mayfly of the same size. For example, when tying a size 14 Black Caddis use a hackle you'd ordinarily use for a size 18 mayfly pattern. This allows the pattern to ride even lower on the water.

Charlie Meck's Black Caddis
>   HOOK: Mustad 94833, sizes 10 to 16
>   THREAD: Black
>   TAILS AND WINGS: Dark brown Antron
>   BODY: Black superfine poly, dubbed and ribbed with a dark
>   gray thread
>   HACKLE: Dark brown

Tying Notes: Take two pieces of dark brown Antron yarn and tie in with the yarn extending back over the bend of the hook. Extend the other end of the Antron out over the eye about the length of the shank of the hook. Take the other end, which is extending out over the eye of the hook, and make several turns with your dubbing in front of it so it bends backward at an angle. This will be your wing. Trim the end to approximate the wing length of the natural.

Spotted Sedge-Tan Caddis
Copies species like *Symphitopsyche slossanae.*
>   HOOK: Mustad 94841, size 14 to 18
>   THREAD: Tan
>   TAILS: Optional—a light tan Z-lon shuck as long as the
>   shank of the hook
>   BODY: Tan Poly dubbed
>   WINGS: Brown deer hair or elk hair
>   HACKLE: Optional—tan, cut off underneath

Tying Notes: On many of my caddis I cut some of the hackle off underneath to make the downwing float lower on the surface.

Cream Caddis
Copies caddis flies like many *Psilotreta* species.
>   HOOK: Mustad 94833, size 12 to 16
>   THREAD: Cream
>   BODY: Cream
>   WINGS: Light deer hair or elk
>   HACKLE: Pale ginger

Dark Blue Sedge
Copies species like *Psilotreta frontalis*.
>HOOK: Mustad 94833, size 12
>THREAD: Dark gray
>WINGS: Dark bluish-gray hackle tips or deer hair dyed gray
>BODY: Peacock herl (not eyed) or dark gray poly
>HACKLE: Dark brown

Little Black Caddis
Copies species like *Chimarra atterima*.
>HOOK: Mustad 94833, size 14
>THREAD: Black
>WINGS: Medium gray mallard quills or dark deer hair
>BODY: Black fur dubbed
>HACKLE: Dark brown

Green Caddis
Copies many *Rhyacophila* species.
>HOOK: Mustad 94833, sizes 12 to 20
>THREAD: Olive green
>TAIL: Tan Z-lon the length of the shank of the hook
>BODY: Green, grayish-green, or olive green poly
>WINGS: Medium to dark deer hair or elk hair
>HACKLE: Light brown

Caddis Larva
>HOOK: Mustad 37160, sizes 12 to 18
>THREAD: Appropriate color (most often dark brown or black)
>BODY: Olive, green, brown, yellow, black, or tan fur dubbed and ribbed with fine wire, or use a rubber band of the appropriate color and tie in at the bend of the hook and

spiral to the eye.

THORAX: Dark brown fur, dubbed; or an ostrich herl, dyed
dark brown, wound around the hook several times

Emerging Caddis Pupa

HOOK: Mustad 37160, sizes 12 to 18

THREAD: Same color as the body color you select

BODY: Olive, green, brown, yellow, black, or tan fur or poly
nymph dubbing material

WINGS: Optional — dark mallard quill sections
shorter than normal, and tied in on both sides of the fly,
not on top, or brown Antron yarn.

HACKLE: Dark brown grouse or woodcock neck feather
wound around the hook two or three times.

ORDER PLECOPTERA : Stoneflies

Early Brown Stonefly

Copies species like *Strophopteryx fasciata.*

HOOK: Mustad 94840, size 16

THREAD: Dark brown

TAIL: Dark brown hackle fibers

BODY: Peacock (not eyed) stripped or brownish gray poly

WINGS: Mallard flank feather, dyed brown

HACKLE: Dark brown

Early Brown Stonefly Nymph

HOOK: Mustad 3906B, size 12

THREAD: Brown

TAIL: Fibers from a brown pheasant tail

BODY: Reddish-brown ultra-translucent dubbing

WINGS: Brown turkey

HACKLE: Brown

The Light Stonefly
Copies stoneflies like *Isoperla signata.*
    HOOK: Mustad 94840, size 12 to 14
    THREAD: Pale yellow
    TAIL: Cream ginger hackle fibers
    BODY: Pale yellow floss ribbed with tannish-yellow
    WINGS: Mallard flank feather, dyed pale tannish-yellow
    HACKLE: Cream ginger

Light Stonefly Nymph
    HOOK: Mustad 3906B, size 12
    THREAD: Tan
    TAIL: Fibers from a mallard flank feather, dyed brown
    BODY: Tan fox fur or nymph dubbing
    WINGS: Light brown turkey
    HACKLE: Cree

The Yellow Stonefly
Copies stoneflies like *Isoperla bilineata.*
    HOOK: Mustad 94840, size 14 or 16
    THREAD: Yellow
    TAIL: Short yellow hackle fibers
    BODY: Primrose poly, dubbed
    WINGS: Pale deer hair, dyed yellow
    HACKLE: Pale yellow hackle

Little Green Stonefly
Copies species like *Alloperla imbecilla.*
    HOOK: Mustad 94840, size 16
    THREAD: Green

TAIL: Short pale cream hackle fibers
BODY: Medium green poly, dubbed
WINGS: Pale gray hackle tips, tied down wing
HACKLE: Pale creamish-green

Alloperla Nymph
HOOK: Mustad 3906B, size 16
THREAD: Yellow
TAIL: Pale yellow
BODY: Pale yellow poly with a hint of olive
WING CASE: Pale yellowish-olive mallard flank
HACKLE: Pale yellow

Great Brown Stonefly
Copies species similar to *Acroneuria lycorias*.
HOOK: Mustad 94840 or 3906, size 10 or 12
THREAD: Dark brown
TAIL: Short dark brown hackle fibers
BODY: Dark brownish-gray poly, dubbed and ribbed with
yellow thread
WINGS: Dark gray deer hair
HACKLE: Dark brown

Great Brown Stonefly Nymph
HOOK: Mustad 3906B, size 10
THREAD: Brown
TAIL: Light brown hackle fibers
BODY: Light brown fur or nymph dubbing
WINGS: Brown turkey
HACKLE: Light brown

Acroneuria Nymph

Copies many species like *Acroneuria arida, abnormis,* and *carolinensis.*

>   HOOK: Mustad 3906B, size 10 and 12
>   THREAD: Dark brown
>   TAIL: Light brown hackle fibers
>   BODY: Dark olive brown yarn, laid over top of pale yellow dubbing fur
>   WINGS: Dark brown turkey
>   HACKLE: Cree

Great Stonefly Nymph

Copies many species like the common *Phasganophora capitata.*

>   HOOK: Mustad 3906B, size 8 and 10
>   THREAD: Tan
>   TAIL: Soft ginger hackle fibers
>   BODY: Dark cream below with darker brown on top
>   WINGS: Mottled turkey quill
>   HACKLE: Cree

Western Patterns

ORDER EPHEMEROPTERA: Mayflies

Western March Brown

Copies some *Rhithrogena* like *Rhithrogena morrisoni* and *hageni.*

>   HOOK: Mustad 94840, 3906, size 14
>   THREAD: Brown
>   TAIL: Medium brown
>   BODY: Medium brown poly, dubbed
>   WINGS: Medium gray hackle wings
>   HACKLE: Dark brown

Dark Tan Spinner
> HOOK: Mustad 94840 or 3906, size 14
> THREAD: Tan
> TAIL: Dark brown hackle fibers
> BODY: Dark brown poly, dubbed
> WINGS: Pale gray poly yarn

Western March Brown Nymph
> HOOK: Mustad 3903B, size 14
> THREAD: Dark brown
> TAIL: Imitation wood duck fibers
> BODY: Dark reddish brown fur
> WINGS: Dark brown turkey
> HACKLE: Dark cree

Western March Brown Emerger
> HOOK: Mustad 3906B or 94840, size 14
> THREAD: Brown
> TAIL: Light grouse
> BODY: Tan angora
> WINGS: Brown poly yarn
> HACKLE: Brown grouse

Western March Brown Shuck
> Dark brown Z-lon

Blue Quill
Copies all *Paraleptophlebia* species including *debilis*, *heteronea*, *memorialis*, *gregalis*, and *bicornuta*.
> HOOK: Mustad 94840 or 3906, size 18
> THREAD: Dark gray
> TAIL: Medium gray hackle fibers

BODY: Eyed peacock herl, stripped
WINGS: Dark gray hackle tips
HACKLE: Medium gray or dun

Blue Quill Spinner
HOOK: Mustad 94840, 3906, size 18
THREAD: Dark brown
TAIL: Dark brown hackle fibers
BODY: Dark brown poly, dubbed
WINGS: Pale gray poly yarn, tied spent

Para Nymph
HOOK: Mustad 3906B, size 16 and 18
THREAD: Dark brown
TAIL: Mallard flank feather, dyed dark brown
BODY: Dark brown angora, dubbed
WINGS: One dark gray mallard quill
HACKLE: Dark gray

Para Emerger
HOOK: Mustad 3906B or 94840 size 16 and 18
THREAD: Dark brown
TAIL: Dark brown hackle fibers
BODY: Dark grayish-brown angora, dubbed
WING: Gray poly yarn pulled over top of dubbed brown
    angora
HACKLE: Dark brown hackle fibers

Para Shuck
Blackish brown Z-lon

Blue Dun or *Little Blue-Winged Olive Dun*
Copies *Baetis bicaudatus, tricaudatus, intermedius,* and others and
some *Pseudocloeon* species.

> HOOK: Mustad 94840, 3906, sizes 18 and 20
> THREAD: Dark gray
> TAIL: Medium to dark gray hackle fibers
> BODY: Gray muskrat or medium gray poly with a slight olive
> cast, dubbed (the body of *Baetis bicaudatus* is more olive
> than the others).
> WINGS: On smaller sizes (20) use dark gray mallard quills;
> on larger sizes use dark gray hackle tips
> HACKLE: Blue dun

Rusty Spinner

> HOOK: Mustad 94840, sizes 18 and 20
> THREAD: Dark brown
> TAIL: Dark grayish brown hackle fibers
> BODY: Grayish brown poly, dubbed and ribbed with fine tan
> thread
> WINGS: Pale gray poly yarn, tied spent

Baetis Nymph

> HOOK: Mustad 3906B, size 18
> THREAD: Dark olive
> TAIL: Wood duck fibers, dyed dark olive
> BODY: Dark olive brown opossum
> WINGS: Dark gray mallard quill section
> HACKLE: Cree, dyed dark olive

Baetis Emerger

> HOOK: Mustad 94840, size 18
> THREAD: Dark olive

TAIL: Wood duck fibers, dyed dark olive

BODY: Dark olive brown opossum

WINGS: Dark gray mallard quill section

Baetis Shuck

Dark brown Z-lon

Little Blue Dun

Copies many Baetis species (was *Pseudocloeon*).

HOOK: Mustad 94840, size 22

THREAD: Gray

TAIL: Medium dun hackle fibers

BODY: Dark gray poly, dubbed

WINGS: Dark gray hackle tips

HACKLE: Dark gray hackle

Rusty Spinner

HOOK: Mustad 94840 or 3906, sizes 18 and 20

THREAD: Dark brown

TAIL: Dark brown hackle fibers

BODY: Dark brown poly, dubbed

WINGS: Pale gray poly yarn, tied spent

Blue Dun Nymph

HOOK: Mustad 3906 B, size 18 and 20

THREAD: Dark olive

TAIL: Dark olive wood duck fibers

BODY: Dark olive brown angora

WINGS: Dark gray mallard quill

HACKLE: Dark olive

Blue Dun Emerger

>   HOOK: Mustad 3906B, size 18 and 20
>   THREAD: Dark gray
>   TAIL: Dark grouse
>   BODY: Dark grayish brown angora
>   WINGS: Dark gray turkey
>   HACKLE: Dark grouse

Blue Dun Shuck

>   Dark brown Z-lon

Trico

Copies all *Tricorythodes* species.

>   HOOK: Mustad 94840 or 3906, size 20 to 24
>   THREAD: Pale olive
>   TAIL: Cream hackle fibers
>   BODY: Pale olive poly, dubbed
>   WINGS: Pale gray hackle tips
>   HACKLE: Cream

Trico Spinner

>   HOOK: Mustad 94840, size 20 to 24
>   THREAD: Dark brown
>   TAIL: Female: short cream hackle fibers; male: long dark
>   brown moose mane
>   BODY: Female: rear third is cream poly dubbed, and
> front two-thirds is dark brown dubbed poly. Male: dark
> brown poly dubbed and ribbed with a fine light tan thread.
>   WINGS: White poly yarn, tied spent

Trico Nymph

>   HOOK: Mustad 3906B, size 22

THREAD: Black
TAIL: Dark brown hackle fibers
BODY: Dark brownish black fur
WINGS: Dark gray mallard quill section
HACKLE: Dark reddish brown

Trico Emerger and Shuck—see Eastern

Blue-Winged Olive Dun
Copies Western *Drunella* hatches like *Drunella flavilinea*.
HOOK: Mustad 94840 or 3906, size 14 to 20
THREAD: Olive
TAIL: Grayish-olive hackle fibers
BODY: Light to medium olive poly, dubbed
WINGS: Dark gray hackle tips
HACKLE: Medium creamish-olive

Dark Olive Spinner
HOOK: Same as above
THREAD: Dark olive or black
TAIL: Moose mane (dark brown)
BODY: Dark olive poly (almost black with an olive cast)
WINGS: Pale gray poly yarn, tied spent

Blue-Winged Olive Nymph
HOOK: 3906B, sizes 14 to 18
THREAD: Olive
TAIL: Wood duck
BODY: Dark brown angora tied over dubbed olive opossum
WINGS: Brown turkey
HACKLE: Cree, dyed olive

Blue-winged Olive Emerger
> HOOK: Mustad 3906B, sizes 14 to 18
> THREAD: Olive
> TAIL: Light grouse
> BODY: Olive angora
> WINGS: Medium gray turkey
> HACKLE: Light grouse

Blue-winged Olive Shuck
> Dark brown Z-lon

Pale Evening Dun
Copies species like *Heptagenia elegantula.*
> HOOK: Mustad 94840 or 3906, size 16 to 20
> THREAD: Pale yellow
> TAIL: Cream hackle fibers
> BODY: Pale yellowish-cream poly, dubbed
> WINGS: Pale yellow hackle tips
> HACKLE: Cream

Pale Evening Spinner
> HOOK: Same as dun
> THREAD: Cream
> TAIL: Cream hackle fibers
> BODY: Pale yellowish-cream poly, dubbed
> WINGS: Pale gray poly yarn, tied spent

Pale Evening Nymph
> HOOK: Mustad 3906B, size 14
> THREAD: Dark brown
> TAIL: Mallard flank fibers, dyed brown
> BODY: Dark brown angora, loosely dubbed

WINGS: Dark mallard section
HACKLE: Grouse

Pale Evening Emerger
> HOOK: Mustad 94840, size 14
> THREAD: Tan
> TAIL: Brown grouse
> BODY: Tan angora
> WINGS: Gray poly
> HACKLE: Grouse

Pale Evening Shuck
> Dark brown Z-lon

Pale Morning Dun
Copies species like *Ephemerella inermis, infrequens,* and *lacustris.*
> HOOK: Mustad 94840 or 3906, sizes 16 and 18
> THREAD: Cream
> TAIL: Cream hackle fibers
> BODY: Varies from a bright olive to a creamish-yellow.
> Use poly and dub.
> WINGS: Pale gray hackle tips
> HACKLE: Cream

Pale Morning Spinner
> HOOK: Mustad 94840, sizes 16 and 18
> THREAD: Orange
> TAIL: Tan
> BODY: Tan
> WINGS: Pale gray poly yarn

Pale Morning Nymph

> HOOK: Mustad 3906, size 16 or 18
> THREAD: Dark brown
> TAIL: Mallard flank fibers, dyed ginger
> BODY: Belly is amber angora or nymph dubbing with a
> darker brown back
> WINGS: Brown turkey
> HACKLE: Cree

Pale Morning Emerger

> HOOK: Mustad 94840
> THREAD: Tan
> TAIL: Grouse
> BODY: Tan angora*
> WINGS: White poly yarn
> HACKLE: Grouse

*Note: Dun body colors vary tremendously from river to river.

Pale Morning Shuck

> Dark brown Z-lon

Dark Red Quill

Copies species like *Cinygmula ramaleyi*.

> HOOK: Mustad 94840, size 16 or 18
> THREAD: Brown
> TAIL: Medium dun hackle fibers
> BODY: Dark reddish-brown hackle stem, stripped
> WINGS: Dark mallard quills, dark gray calf tail, or hackle
> tips
> HACKLE: Bronze dun

Red Quill Spinner

 HOOK: Mustad 94840, size 16 or 18

 THREAD: Brown

 TAIL: Pale dun hackle fibers

 BODY: Reddish-brown hackle stem

 WINGS: Pale tan polypropylene, tied spent

 HACKLE: Brown

Red Quill Nymph

 HOOK: Mustad 3906B, size 16

 THREAD: Dark brown

 TAIL: Mallard flank, dyed amber

 BODY: Dark grayish-brown furry foam over amber angora

 WINGS: Dark mallard quill

 HACKLE: Dark grouse or partridge

Dark Red Quill Emerger

 HOOK: Mustad 3906B or 94840, size 16

 THREAD: Brown

 TAIL: Light green

 BODY: Dark brown angora

 WINGS: Dark gray poly

 HACKLE: Brown grouse

Dark Red Quill Shuck

 Dark gray Z-lon

Quill Gordon

Copies western species like *Epeorus longimanus.*

 HOOK: Mustad 94840 size 12 or 14

 THREAD: Gray

 TAIL: Medium dun hackle

BODY: Pale to medium gray poly or muskrat fur, dubbed

WINGS: Dark mallard quills, dark gray calf tail, or dark gray hackle tips

HACKLE: Pale tannish-gray

Red Quill Spinner

HOOK: Mustad 94840, size 12 or 14

THREAD: Tan

TAIL: Moose mane

BODY: Pale yellowish-brown poly

WINGS: Pale tan polypropylene

HACKLE: Ginger with a turn of brown

Quill Gordon Nymph

HOOK: Mustad 3906B, size 14

THREAD: Dark brown

TAIL: Mallard flank dyed amber

BODY: Dark brown furry foam over top

WINGS: Dark mallard quill

HACKLE: Dark grouse or partridge

Quill Gordon Emerger

HOOK: Mustad 3906B or 94840, size 14

THREAD: Brown

TAIL: Medium grayish brown angora

BODY: Dark gray poly yarn

WINGS: Brown grouse

Quill Gordon Shuck

Dark brown Z-lon

Red Quill

Copies *Serratella tibialis.*

    HOOK: Mustad 94840, size 16 or 18

    THREAD: Brown

    TAIL: Pale gray hackle fibers

    BODY: Dark reddish-brown poly

    WINGS: Pale gray hackle tips

    HACKLE: Creamish-yellow

White-gloved Howdy

    HOOK: Mustad 94840, size 16 or 18

    THREAD: Dark brown

    TAIL: Gray hackle fibers

    BODY: Dark purplish-brown poly

    WINGS: Pale gray poly

    HACKLE: Pale yellow

Dark Brown Dun

Copies *Baetis hageni (parvus).*

    HOOK: Mustad 94840, size 20

    THREAD: Dark brown

    TAIL: Ginger cream hackle fibers

    BODY: Dark brown polypropylene

    WINGS: Gray mallard quills

    HACKLE: Ginger cream

Dark Brown Spinner

    HOOK: Mustad 94840, size 20

    THREAD: Brown

    TAIL: Pale dun hackle fibers

    BODY: Dark brown polypropylene

    WINGS: Pale gray polypropylene

HACKLE: Ginger cream

Dark Brown Nymph
    HOOK: Mustad 3906B, size 20
    THREAD: Dark olive
    TAIL: Dark olive mallard flank
    BODY: Dark olive angora
    WINGS: Dark mallard quill
    HACKLE: Dark olive fibers

Hexagenia limbata limbata
(See tying description in earlier Eastern and Midwestern section)
Speckle-Winged Dun
Copies *Callibaetis americanus.*
    HOOK: Mustad 94840, size 14 and 16
    THREAD: Tan
    TAIL: Cream ginger hackle fibers
    BODY: Medium gray polypropylene
    WINGS: Dark gray mallard flank
    HACKLE: Pale bronze dun

Speckle-winged Spinner
    HOOK: Mustad 94840, 14 and 16
    THREAD: Gray
    TAIL: Cream ginger hackle fibers
    BODY: Pale gray polypropylene
    WINGS: Mallard flank feather
    HACKLE: Pale bronze dun

Speckle-winged Nymph
    HOOK: Mustad 3906B, size 14
    THREAD: Brown

TAIL: Pheasant tail fibers
BODY: Medium brown angora
WINGS: Dark mallard quill
HACKLE: Dark brown grouse

Speckle-winged Emerger
HOOK: Mustad 3906B, size 14
THREAD: Brown
TAIL: Dark grouse
BODY: Tannish-gray angora
WINGS: Gray turkey
HACKLE: Dark grouse

Speckle-winged Shuck
Dark brown Z-lon

Western Green Drake
Copies species like *Drunella grandis.*

HOOK: Mustad 94840, size 10 or 12
THREAD: Dark olive
TAIL: Moose mane
BODY: Olive black polypropylene, ribbed with pale yellow
thread
WINGS: Impala, dyed dark gray
HACKLE: Grayish black

When the Western green drake appears at midday, it's time to match the hatch.

Great Red Spinner

     HOOK: Mustad 94840, size 10 or 12

     THREAD: Black

     TAIL: Moose mane

     BODY: Same as dun

     WINGS: White polypropylene, tied spent

     HACKLE: Brownish black

Green Drake Nymph

     HOOK: Mustad 3906B, size 12

     THREAD: Dark brown

     TAIL: Amber mallard flank feather

     BODY: Dark olive angora

     WINGS: Mottled brown turkey

     HACKLE: Olive brown

Green Drake Shuck
>   Dark olive brown Z-lon

Light Cahill
Copies species like *Cinygma dimicki.*
>   HOOK: Mustad 3906B, size 12
>   THREAD: Yellow
>   TAIL: Ginger hackle fibers
>   BODY: Pale creamish-yellow polypropylene
>   WINGS: Wood duck (or imitation) flank feather
>   HACKLE: Ginger cream

Light Cahill Spinner
>   HOOK: Mustad 94840, size 12
>   THREAD: Yellow
>   TAIL: Ginger hackle fibers
>   BODY: Yellowish cream polypropylene
>   WINGS: Pale gray polypropylene
>   HACKLE: Yellowish-cream

Pale Brown Dun
Copies species like *Cinygmula reticulata.*
>   HOOK: Mustad 94840, size 12 or 14
>   THREAD: Tan
>   TAIL: Ginger cream hackle fibers
>   BODY: Pale brown polypropylene
>   WINGS: Yellow mallard flank
>   HACKLE: Ginger cream

Dark Rusty Spinner
>   HOOK: Mustad 94840, size 12 or 14
>   THREAD: Brown

TAIL: Dark brown hackle fibers
BODY: Dark brown polypropylene
WINGS: Pale yellow polypropylene
HACKLE: Dark brown

Pink Lady

Copies species like *Epeorus albertae.*
HOOK: Mustad 94840, size 12
THREAD: Cream
TAIL: Cream ginger hackle fibers
BODY: Grayish cream polypropylene
WINGS: Gray mallard quills or dark gray hackle tips
HACKLE: Cream or badger

Salmon Spinner
HOOK: Mustad 94840, size 12
THREAD: Cream
TAIL: Dark brown moose mane
BODY: Female: pinkish-red poly; male: cream gray
  polypropylene
WINGS: Pale gray polypropylene
HACKLE: Pale blue dun

Pink Lady Nymph
HOOK: Mustad 3906B, size 12
THREAD: Brown
TAIL: Brown mallard flank
BODY: Medium brown furry foam over tan angora
WINGS: Light mottled turkey
HACKLE: Sandy dun

Pink Lady Emerger
>   HOOK: 3906B or 94840, size 12
>   THREAD: Brown
>   TAIL: Brown grouse
>   BODY: Tan poly yarn
>   WINGS: Light grouse

Pink Lady Shuck
>   Medium brown Z-lon

Gray Drake
Copies species like *Siphlonurus occidentalis*.
>   HOOK: Mustad 94840, size 12
>   THREAD: Dark brown
>   TAIL: Medium dun hackle fibers
>   BODY: Brownish-black polypropylene with tan thread for
>   ribbing
>   WINGS: Dark gray mallard flank
>   HACKLE: Pale bronze dun

Brown Quill Spinner
>   HOOK: Mustad 94840, size 12
>   THREAD: Dark brown
>   TAIL: Dark brown moose mane
>   BODY: Dark reddish-brown polypropylene ribbed with tan
>   thread
>   WINGS: Pale gray polypropylene
>   HACKLE: Dark brown hackle

Gray Drake Nymph
>   HOOK: 3906B, size 10
>   THREAD: Dark brown

TAIL: Light dun fibers
BODY: Medium gray angora
WINGS: Mallard quill
HACKLE: Sandy dun

Gray Drake Emerger
HOOK: 3906B, size 10
THREAD: Dark brown
TAIL: Pale gray hackle fibers
BODY: Gray angora
WINGS: Medium turkey
HACKLE: Light grouse

Gray Drake Shuck
Gray Z-lon

Gray Fox
Copies many species like *Heptagenia solitaria.*
HOOK: 94840, size 12
THREAD: Tan
TAIL: Bronze dun hackle fibers
BODY: Yellowish-tan polypropylene
WINGS: Pale gray hackle tips
HACKLE: Bronze dun

Ginger Quill Spinner
HOOK: Mustad 94840, size 12
THREAD: Tan
TAIL: Ginger hackle fibers
BODY: Eyed peacock herl, dyed tan and stripped
WINGS: Pale gray polypropylene
HACKLE: Ginger

Gray Fox Nymph
>HOOK: Mustad 3906B, size 14
>THREAD: Brown
>TAIL: Brown mallard flank
>BODY: Dark brown furry foam over pale yellow
>WINGS: Dark mottled turkey
>HACKLE: Grouse or partridge

Gray Fox Emerger
>HOOK: Mustad 3906B or 94840 size 14
>THREAD: Tan
>TAIL: Brown grouse
>BODY: Tan angora
>WINGS: Brown poly
>HACKLE: Brown grouse

Gray Fox Shuck
>Dark brown Z-lon

Pale Brown Dun
Copies *Rhithrogena hageni.*
>HOOK: Mustad 94840, size 12
>THREAD: Olive
>TAIL: Cream hackle fibers
>BODY: Tannish-olive polypropylene
>WINGS: Gray mallard quills or dark gray hackle tips
>HACKLE: Cream ginger

Dark Tan Spinner
>HOOK: Mustad 94840, size 12
>THREAD: Tan
>TAIL: Gray hackle fibers

BODY: Pale olive tan polypropylene
WINGS: Pale gray polypropylene
HACKLE: Cream mixed with dark tan

Pale Brown Nymph
HOOK: Mustad 3906B, size 12
THREAD: Dark brown
TAIL: Wood duck (few fibers)
BODY: Greenish brown rabbit with claret hackle
WINGS: Dark brown turkey
HACKLE: Dark brown

Pale Brown Dun Emerger
HOOK: Mustad 3906B or 94840
THREAD: Tan
TAIL: Light grouse
BODY: Light grayish olive angora
WINGS: Brown poly yarn
HACKLE: Brown grouse

Pale Brown Shuck
Light olive brown Z-lon

Dark Brown Dun
Copies species like *Ameletus cooki.*
HOOK: Mustad 94840, size 12 or 14
THREAD: Dark brown
TAIL: Dark brown hackle fibers
BODY: Dark brown polypropylene
WINGS: Teal flank feather
HACKLE: Dark brown

Dark Brown Spinner
> HOOK: Mustad 94840, 12 or 14
> THREAD: Dark brown
> TAIL: Dark brown hackle fibers
> BODY: Dark brown polypropylene
> WINGS: Teal flank feather, dyed yellow
> HACKLE: Dark brown

Quill Gordon
Copies Western species like *Rhithrogena futilis.*
> HOOK: Mustad 94840, size 12
> THREAD: Gray
> TAIL: Rusty dun hackle fibers
> BODY: Tannish gray polypropylene
> WINGS: Gray mallard quills or dark gray hackle tips
> HACKLE: Rusty dun

Quill Gordon Spinner
> HOOK: Mustad 94840, size 12
> THREAD: Black
> TAIL: Dark dun hackle fibers
> BODY: Peacock herl, eyed, stripped
> WINGS: Pale gray polypropylene
> HACKLE: Dark dun

Dark Red Quill
Copies many species like *Rhithrogena undulata.*
> HOOK: Mustad 94840, size 12
> THREAD: Dark brown
> TAIL: Dark blue dun hackle fibers
> BODY: Dark brown hackle stem
> WINGS: Gray mallard quills or dark gray hackle tips

HACKLE: Dark brown

Red Quill Spinner
>HOOK: Mustad 94840, size 12
>THREAD: Dark brown
>TAIL: Ginger to dark brown hackle fiber
>BODY: Red to dark brown hackle stems
>WINGS: White or pale gray poly yarn
>HACKLE: Ginger to dark brown

Great Red Quill
Copies Western species like *Timpanoga (Ephemerella) hecuba.*
>HOOK: Mustad 94840, size 10 or 12
>THREAD: Brown
>TAIL: Moose mane
>BODY: Large reddish-brown hackle stem, stripped
>WINGS: Dark gray impala
>HACKLE: Dark brown

Great Red Spinner
>HOOK: Mustad 94833, size 10 or 12
>THREAD: Dark brown
>TAIL: Moose mane
>BODY: Dark brown hackle stems, stripped
>WINGS: Pale gray hackle tips
>HACKLE: Dark brown

Dark Olive Dun
Copies Western species like *Drunella coloradensis.*
>HOOK: Mustad 94840, size 12
>THREAD: Dark brown
>TAIL: Gray hackle fibers

BODY: Olive brown polypropylene

WINGS: Gray mallard quills or dark gray hackle tips

HACKLE: Ginger

Dark Brown Spinner

HOOK: Mustad 94840, size 12

THREAD: Dark brown

TAIL: Dark brown moose mane

BODY: Dark brown polypropylene

WINGS: Pale tan polypropylene

HACKLE: Dark brown

ORDER PRECOPTERAS: Stoneflies

Salmon Fly

Copies *Pteronarcys californica.*

Simple Salmon

HOOK: Mustad 94831, size 8

THREAD: Orange

BODY: Burnt orange poly, dubbed

WINGS: Dark elk hair

Tying Notes: Tie the pattern just as you would a size 14 caddis pattern. Dub in poly for a size 14 pattern, then tie in a wing. In front of the first wing, dub in some more poly, then another wing, until you've finished at the eye. The final product gives the impression of a continuous wing—not five or six separate segments.

Jay Kapolka fishes during a salmon fly hatch on the Deschutes River in Oregon.

Willow Stonefly

Copies *Hesperoperla pacifica.*

> HOOK: Mustad 94720, size 6 to 8XL
> THREAD: Tan
> TAIL: Short brown hackle fibers
> BODY: Creamish brown polypropylene
> WINGS: Creamish mallard flank
> HACKLE: Brown

Golden Stonefly

Copies stoneflies like *Calineuria californica.*

> HOOK: Mustad 94720, size 8
> THREAD: Yellow
> TAIL: Moose mane
> BODY: Pale yellow poly, ribbed with brown poly
> WINGS: Pale tan deer hair
> HACKLE: Cream and brown, mixed

ORDER TRICOPTERA: Caddis Flies

October Caddis
Copies several Dicosmoecus species.
        HOOK: Mustad 94840, size 6
        THREAD: Orange
        BODY: Orange poly, dubbed
        WINGS: Brown deer hair
        HACKLE: Brown

Black Caddis (See Eastern patterns)
Tan Caddis (See Eastern patterns)

Chapter 11
A Final Cast

I've kept detailed records of every fly-fishing trip I've been on for the past thirty-five years. In those records I list the stream, weather, flies used, which ones caught trout, what hatches I saw, and water and air temperatures. I know exactly how many trout I caught on each trip with this record. Since I've used the tandem rig I've caught many more trout on hatchless days than just using a dry fly. In fact, I catch three to four times as many trout on the rig when there's no hatch. I've also found that using the setup allows me to fish throughout the day rather than waiting for rising trout and a hatch or spinner fall. In the summer that means I can fish from noon to evening and catch many more fish than just prospecting with a dry fly or waiting for a hatch.

If you try the tandem method, I feel certain you too will increase your catch considerably. Along with this increase in your catch you have added responsibilities.

First and foremost, if this sport is to continue to thrive in the United States you've got an obligation to return every fish to the stream with as little harm as possible. I've seen many do-gooders who plan to return a trout after they show the fish to everybody and take plenty of photos. If at all possible, try not to touch the trout. And to make releasing trout easier never, and I say never, use barbed hooks. If you must handle a trout, handle it as little as possible.

I'm most interested in tricking the trout into taking my pattern; that's the ultimate to me. Bringing in the fish and releasing is just ancillary. I have one favorite stream where I've never seen another fly-fisher in five years. I've caught hundreds of trout on this stream, some up to twenty inches long. Often after catching a couple of trout here I don't even bother setting the hook on others. I just want to see if I can get them to strike the imitation. I remember one late-September when this stream held a good slate drake hatch. Trout rose widely and took a Slate Drake pattern readily. I didn't even lift the rod and set the hook on more than a dozen trout that day. Just to know that these trout struck and I didn't hurt them was pleasure enough for me.

You too must use consideration when you fish. With the increased interest in fly-fishing in the past decade there's a frightening possibility that our streams and rivers will become too crowded. It's already happening. I've already seen busloads of fly-fishers at some of the more popular streams and rivers. Can you imagine the pressure this puts on the water, the trout, and the landowner?

Recently Paul Kurincak, owner of the Upstream Angler in Morgantown, West Virginia, and I fly-fished central Pennsylvania's Spring Creek one late-summer morning. Paul brought a friend along, Gordon Moon, from London, England. Gordon had never fly-fished in the United States. He fished only infrequently on England's many private trout waters. Gordon kept asking me for assurance that it was lawful to fish the water. It seems that in England most of the land is posted against public fishing. Gordon continuously commented on the lack of public trout fishing in England and how lucky we were in the States with our many open streams. If we don't mend our ways, the same thing will happen here within a decade or two.

In the past two decades I've already seen an number of streams go private. Much of this stems from profit motive. One landowner sees how much another makes from leasing fishing rights and his land becomes private. States and organizations must do more to keep streams open so all can enjoy this rewarding sport for years to come.

In the past decade fly-fishing has grown exponentially to become an avocation of choice for many men and women. As you fly-fish you'll find that there's much more to fly-fishing than catching trout. It's the total experience—using the correct pattern, getting the right float, hooking the trout, landing it, and safely releasing it to fight again—and, of course, fishing with friends. As Craig Josephson wrote recently after he and I returned from a trip to some of Arizona's best rivers: "...it's not the number or size of the fish that you catch, but the total experience that you always remember... memories of the fish soon fade. Oh, I'll remember a few of the really memorable ones, but they will pale in comparison to the times we had, the people we met, and the beautiful country we saw."

Index

G

H

Lost Stream Map Found and Restored

The "Stream Map of Pennsylvania" was completed in 1965 after a thirty-year effort by Howard Higbee, a former Penn State Professor.

Professor Higbee succeeded in creating a map of the highest detail possible...a map that shows every stream and lake. He painstakingly plotted the location of 45,000 miles of streams onto a 3 x 5 foot map.

The map sold extremely well—until it was lost several years later. Incredibly, the printer entrusted with the original drawing and printing plates declared bankruptcy, then carelessly hauled Higbee's 30 years of work to the landfill.

The few remaining dog-eared copies became a prized fisherman's possession. Professor Higbee was offered $400 for one of his last maps. And state agencies were forced to keep their few remaining copies under lock and key.

The experts had always told Professor Higbee that reprints were impossible, because the maps were printed in non-photographic blue. Then, in 1991, at the age of 91, Howard Higbee's dream came true. Computers made it possible to reprint the map. Holding an updated map, Howard said, "I never thought I'd live to see this day."

Then, by combining Professor Higbee's knowledge with new technology it was possible to create stream maps of other states.

"If your're looking for the most definitive maps ever created, then Professor Higbee's Stream Maps are without question the finest."
-- Howard Brandt, NEWARK STAR LEDGER

"It's an angler's dream, a masterpiece, a map that contains streams you won't find on other maps." "The possibilities for exploring new waters are endless when you fathom the scope of the map."
-- George Smith, THE TIMES LEADER, Wilkes-Barre, Pa.

"It is in showing where to find out-of-the-way trout streams that makes the map such a treasure to the fisherman."
-- Joe Gorden, TRIBUNE-DEMOCRAT, Johnstown, Pa.

Free Guide Book *Included with each map. Use this guide to pinpoint the best fishing in the state. Easily locate productive trout streams, lakes, dams, reservoirs, ponds, and select waters.*

Professor Higbee's Stream Maps are available in some bookstores, sporting goods stores, and fishing tackel stores. They may be ordered directly from Vivid Publishing, Inc., P. O. Box 1572, Williamsport, PA 17703, Phone orders: **1-800-STREAMS.**
State maps currently available:

Pennsylvania, 3 by 5 foot
New York, 3 1/2 by 4 1/2 foot
Michigan, 4 by 4 foot
New England (5 states), 3 by 4 foot

Coming soon: Montana and more state stream maps.

$19.95 for either rolled or folded paper. $39.95 for glass-like lamination, lifetime guarantee, write-on-wipe-off surface, and brass eyelettes for easy hanging. Add $3.50 shipping per order, Pennsylvania residents add 6% sales tax.